100 HIKES in

WASHINGTON'S
SOUTH CASCADES
AND OLYMPICS

100 HIKES in

WASHINGTON'S
SOUTH CASCADES AND OLYMPICS

Chinook Pass • White Pass • Goat Rocks • Mount St. Helens • Mount Adams

THIRD EDITION

**Ira Spring &
Harvey Manning**

THE
MOUNTAINEERS

Published by
The Mountaineers
1001 SW Klickitat Way, Suite 201
Seattle, WA 98134

© 1985, 1992 by Ira Spring and Harvey Manning
© 1998 by The Mountaineers

Published simultaneously in Great Britain by Cordee, 3a DeMontfort Street, Leicester, England, LE1 7HD

Manufactured in the United States of America

Edited by Christine Clifton-Thornton
Maps by Gray Mouse Graphics
All photographs by Bob and Ira Spring unless otherwise noted
Cover and book design by Jennifer Shontz
Layout by Gray Mouse Graphics

Cover photograph: *Beargrass along the Sunrise Trail, Gifford Pinchot National Forest*
Frontispiece: *Hoh Lake (Hike 87)*

Library of Congress Cataloging-in-Publication Data
Spring, Ira.
    100 hikes in Washington's South Cascades and Olympics: Chinook Pass, White Pass, Goat Rocks, Mount St. Helens, Mount Adams / Ira Spring & Harvey Manning. — 3rd ed.
        p.   cm.
        Includes index.
        ISBN 0-89886-594-8
        1. Hiking—Washington (State)—Guidebooks. 2. Hiking—Cascade Range—Guidebooks. 3. Hiking—Washington (State)—Olympic Mountains—Guidebooks. 4. Washington (State)—Guidebooks. 5. Cascade Range—Guidebooks. 6. Olympic Mountains (Wash.)—Guidebooks. I. Manning, Harvey. II. Title.
GV199.42.W2S66   1998
917.97'0943—dc21   98-20117
                                                                    CIP

♻ Printed on recycled paper

CONTENTS

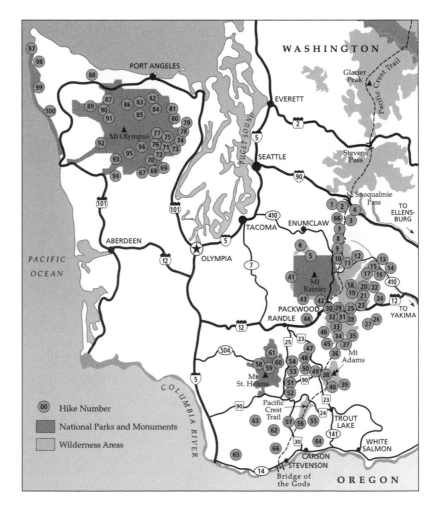

MAP SYMBOLS

(90)	interstate highway
(2)	U.S. highway
(530)	state route
[26]	National Forest primary road
[FH7]	forest highway
[689]	logging road (3 digits)
[2040]	secondary road (4 digits or more)
/790/	trail number
▲	campground
⌂	backcountry campsite
⌂	backcountry shelter
♦	ranger station or guard station
⌂	building
♖	fire lookout
✕	mine
)(	pass

═══	freeway or divided highway
▬▬▬	paved road
▬ ▬ ▬	gravel road
═══	improved road (coarse gravel or dirt)
– – ═══	primitive road (jeep road)
—+—	gated road
- - - - -	trail
··········	cross-country route
+++++++	railroad
– · – · –	power line
	boundary (national forest, national park, wilderness area, or recreation area)
	lake, stream
	waterfall
	glacier
✺ ✺ ✺	marsh
🌲🌲	trees

Whalehead Ridge from the Purcell Mountain trail (Hike 44)

INTRODUCTION

The country sampled by these 100 hikes has many characteristics in common throughout, and in common, too, with companion volumes on the region north of Snoqualmie Pass. There are, however, significant differences from place to place caused by variations in climate, geology, elevation, and the amount and sort of human use. The Olympic Mountains have an "ocean side"—the west side and south slopes where storms from the Pacific wash ashore like so many giant waves on a beach—and a "rainshadow side"—the relatively arid north and east where the clouds tend to be empties. The two merge in the middle of the range, a spacious wilderness of glaciers and crags and flower fields, rainforests and subalpine parklands and alpine tundras, and one of the largest wildlife populations in America.

The Cascade Range south from Snoqualmie Pass to Norse Peak Wilderness is a checkerboard of private and public tree farms more densely inhabited by logging trucks than hikers, who find few attractions except the Pacific Crest National Scenic Trail, which goes from one scenic clearcut to another.

As Rainier, set off west of the crest (with its attendant Clearwater, Glacier View, and Tatoosh Wildernesses), rises higher and sprawls wider in the eye of the south-walking traveler, the main line of the range rears up in the craggy peaks of the Norse Peak Wilderness, for every crag a bright meadow. Chinook Pass divides that preserve from the William O. Douglas Wilderness, which extends south to White Pass; the hiker's view extends west to storm-wet, rain-green, ice-white Mount Rainier National Park and east to steppes of Central Washington, where sunshine-country and snow-country plants blossom side by side.

From White Pass south the story is all volcanoes: the deep-dissected ruins of a fire mountain, once perhaps on the scale of Adams, in the Goat Rocks Wilderness; Adams, outbulked only by Rainier, in the Mount Adams Wilderness; a landscape spattered with cinder cones and covered by lava flows, some eroded and forested, as in the Trapper Creek Wilderness; others high and meadowed, as in the Indian Heaven Wilderness; and never to be ignored, not even before 1980, the centerpiece of the Mount St. Helens National Volcanic Monument.

The hiking season in low-elevation valleys of the Olympics—and on the zero-elevation beaches—encompasses the whole year; higher up, the flowers may not poke through snowbanks until late July, a mere several weeks before their frozen seeds are blanketed by the new winter's white; higher still, there are no flowers ever, and no real hiking season either, only a climbing season. There are places on the east of the Cascades where on any day of the year a person has an 85 percent chance of getting a sunburn, and others, on the west slope of the Olympics, where on any day of the year a person has an 85 percent chance of getting soaking wet right through his rubber boots and rainproof parka, and others, as on the Cascade Crest, where hikers within a mile of each other are at one and the same time gasping from thirst (east) and sputtering like a whale (west).

JURISDICTION

Mount Rainier and Olympic National Parks have been set aside, in the words of the National Park Act of 1916, "to conserve the scenery and the natural and historic objects and wildlife. . . ." Each visitor must therefore enjoy the parks "in such manner and by such means as will leave them unimpaired for the enjoyment of future generations." A good motto for park users is: "Take only a picture, leave only a footprint." Motorized (and mechanized, including "mountain bikes") travel on park trails is forbidden and horse travel closely regulated. Hunting is banned—but not fishing. Pets are not allowed on trails because their presence would disturb wildlife.

Backcountry permits are required for all overnight hikers in national parks and may be obtained at ranger stations on the entry roads.

Under U.S. Forest Service jurisdiction in the South Cascades are the Goat Rocks, Mount Adams, Clearwater, Glacier View, Tatoosh, Trapper Creek, Indian Heaven, William O. Douglas, and Norse Peak Wildernesses, and in the Olympics, Wonder Mountain, Mount Skokomish, The Brothers, Buckhorn, and Colonel Bob Wildernesses, where "the earth and its community of life are untrammeled by man, where man himself is a visitor who does not remain." Motorized (and mechanized) travel is forbidden absolutely and horse travel is beginning to be regulated or, at some places, even eliminated; foot travel and camping are currently less restricted, though the backcountry population explosion will require increasing controls to protect fragile ecosystems.

Also under the jurisdiction of the Forest Service is the Mount St. Helens National Volcanic Monument, where management plans are still evolving, one wary ear always cocked to hear what more the volcano may have to say on the subject.

MAPS

The sketch maps in this book are intended to give only a general idea of the terrain and trails. Once out of the city and off the highways, the navigation demands precision.

The U.S. Forest Service system of road numbers gives main roads two numerals. For example, the Randle-to-Trout Lake road is No. 23 and is shown on Forest Service maps as 23 and described in the guidebook as road No. 23. Secondary roads have the first two numerals of the main road plus two additional numerals. For example, from road No. 23 the secondary road to the Killen Creek trailhead is numbered 2329 and shown on the forest map as 2329. Three more numerals are added for a spur road, so a spur from road No. 2329 to Takhlakh Lake becomes road No. 2329026. It is shown as 026 on road signs and on Forest Service road maps. In this guidebook the road is identified as (2329)026.

A veteran traveler of the South Cascades, relying on his faithful file of well-worn Forest Service maps, had best never leave civilization without a full tank of gas, survival rations, and instructions to family or friends on when to call out the Logging Road Search and Rescue Team. A party would do better to obtain the current National Forest recreation maps, which are cumbersome for the trail but essential to get about on the renumbered roads. These maps may be obtained for a small fee at ranger stations or by writing Forest Supervisors at:

> Mt. Baker–Snoqualmie National Forest
> 21905 64th Ave. West
> Mountlake Terrace, WA 98043
> Wenatchee National Forest
> P.O. Box 811
> Wenatchee, WA 98801
> Gifford Pinchot National Forest
> 10600 N.E. 51st Circle
> Vancouver, WA 98682
> Olympic National Forest
> 1835 Black Lake Boulevard
> Olympia, WA 98502

The best maps in the history of the world are the topographic sheets produced by the U.S. Geological Survey (USGS), sold by map shops and sporting goods stores. However, revision is so occasional that information on roads and trails is always largely obsolete. Essential as they are for off-trail, cross-country explorers, in this book we have recommended them only when there is no alternative.

Among the merits of the USGS is that it sells the data "separations" (from which its sheets are published) on a nonprofit, cost-only, public-service basis. This has enabled commercial publishers to buy the separations, add and delete information, and issue maps that are designed specifically for hikers and are kept up to date. Though the USGS base map is always available, for areas where they exist we recommend the maps in the Green Trails series, which covers virtually all hiking areas in the Cascades and Olympics, and the Custom Correct series for the Olympics.

Also available from ranger stations, as well as from map shops and sporting goods stores, are the Forest Service maps for the Goat Rocks, Mount Adams, William O. Douglas, Tatoosh–Glacier View, and Indian Heaven–Trapper Creek Wildernesses, excellent for hikers.

CLOTHING AND EQUIPMENT

Many trails described in this book can be walked easily and safely, at least along the lower portions, by any person capable of getting out of a car and onto his feet, and without any special equipment whatever.

To such people we can only say, "Welcome to walking—but beware!" Northwest mountain weather, especially on the ocean side of the ranges, is notoriously undependable. Cloudless morning skies can be followed by afternoon deluges of rain or fierce squalls of snow. Even without a storm a person can get mighty chilly on high ridges when—as often happens—a cold wind blows under a bright sun and pure blue sky.

No one should set out on a Cascade or Olympic trail, unless for a brief stroll, lacking warm long pants, a wool (or the equivalent) shirt or sweater, and a windproof and rain-repellent parka, coat, or poncho; on feet, sturdy shoes or boots plus two pairs of wool socks and an extra pair in the rucksack.

As for that rucksack, it should also contain the Ten Essentials, found so by generations of members of The Mountaineers, often from sad experience:

1. Extra clothing—more than needed in good weather.
2. Extra food—enough so something is left over at the end of the trip.
3. Sunglasses—necessary for most alpine travel and indispensable on snow.
4. Knife—for first aid and emergency firebuilding (making kindling).
5. Firestarter—a candle or chemical fuel for starting a fire with wet wood.
6. First aid kit.
7. Matches—in a waterproof container.
8. Flashlight—with extra bulb and batteries.
9. Map—be sure it's the right one for the trip.
10. Compass—be sure to know the declination, east or west.

CURRENT INFORMATION

We live in an age of crisis unprecedented in human history. Two hundred years ago our planet was peopled by 1,000,000,000 souls; 80 years ago, the number had doubled; by the turn of the millennium, the prediction is 6,000,000,000, and if we are not then Called Home (as some expect), double that by midcentury. Nothing in our past has prepared us to deal with what threatens to be more catastrophic than any war, genocide, pandemic, drought, flood, plague of locusts, or Ice Age that we as a species have known. With the situation already verging on the dire (families disintegrating, institutions collapsing, bridges sinking, freeways and skyways a mess), what will it be when children now being born come to maturity? There is dark talk that since our superintelligent (that is, idiot) computers can't cope with 2000, the jig is up.

All that is civilization's problem. The problems of our cozy little Shangri La (the wilderness) are, by comparison, petty. But they don't seem so when we're there. Where once was the Big Lonesome, now there is that gollydang population explosion. Where once the "freedom of the hills" meant unconstrained philosophical anarchism, now there is giviment, black helicopters just over the horizon.

Well, to quote the old saying, "Daddy told us never to argue about politics or religion unless you're fixin' to put up your fists." A certain number of wildland travelers are so irritated, so enraged, so defiant that the only real pleasure they get is plotting to overthrow the government, and we won't argue ("Daddy told us . . .") that's a bad idea. However, most of us appreciate that the giviment officials in immediate (which is to say, *not* based in Washington City) management of our trails are truly excellent public servants doing the very best they can in a period of sudden use overloads, conflicting demands, mixed signals from Washington City, and too little financial support from there or anywhere.

All this is a prelude to give warning that in time of swift transition, a guidebook cannot be revised often enough to keep up to date on the conditions of roads and trails, rules and regulations governing the backcountry, the need (or not) for permits, the requirement (or not) for fees. Following paragraphs outline the general considerations affecting your behavior. However, the times they are a-changin' fast, land managers are engaged in

The Silver Star trail (Hike 65)

constant experimentation, striving to preserve the natural ecosystems while minimizing restrictions. Nature, too, is ever busy. When in doubt, seek current information by telephone about roads, trails, permits. The Forest Service-Park Service Information Center in Seattle—(206) 470-4060—is worth a try when it's not a toll call. The staffers do their best but they are so few and the roads and trails and ranger districts so many that whatever they say may be out of date. Far more reliable are the offices close to the scenes; toll calls though they usually will be, those are the numbers given in our data blocks at the head of trip descriptions. Call well ahead; the offices usually are open only during business hours on weekdays.

FEES AND PERMITS AND RESERVATIONS

A system of parking fees at trailheads has been instituted as a source of funds for trail maintenance, which Congress is loath to supply, what with the urgent need to do something about Mars. Kinks are being worked out. The only sure thing is the wisdom of knowing what the system is before arriving at the trailhead.

Entry fees are charged at some trailheads into national parks, Indian Nations, and the Mount St. Helens National Volcanic Monument.

Permits for backcountry travel and camping are usual at national parks and some wilderness areas, doubtless at more locations in the future.

The y'all come, camp-anywhere, laissez faire freedom of the past is yielding, at popular sites, to limits on the number of designated sites, beaten-to-death barrens being closed for revegetation. Reservations perhaps must be obtained in advance. Call ahead.

PARTY SIZE

In popular areas the party size may be limited to a dozen or fewer. Very large families and club outing groups should rethink their plans. Until recent years The Mountaineers regularly dispatched into the wilds masses of humanity resembling barbarian hordes out on invasion; small parties once were condemned as outlaws. "The past is a foreign country. They do things differently there."

PETS

Some 12,000 years ago a partnership was struck between humans and canines; there persists among many of us (both people and best friends) the conviction that it ain't natural for man to go walking without a dog.

But the handwriting is on the wall. Pets always have been forbidden on national park trails and the ban is spreading to over-peopled National Forest wildernesses. Owners who keep their animals under tight control—on a leash—and prevent them from barking at strangers, attacking them, stealing their bacon, and committing nuisances, can help slow expansion of the exclusion policy. Otherwise, try to find trails still empty or leave the best friend home.

CAMPING

Most backcountry campsites do not require permits and are not designated. However, measures are being taken to cope with blight. High-use spots may be classified and signed, "Day Use Only." Others have a blanket rule against camps within 100 feet of the lakeshore or streambank. In others the existence of barrens is accepted but to prevent the sprawl of slums the policy is "Use Established Sites."

Careful monitoring of backcountry camping has been in progress only a few years. Much remains to be learned. And unlearned? The conventional wisdom is to avoid meadows because they are fragile, camp instead in the woods because they are tough. However, a contrary thesis is emerging that though meadows quickly become mudbowls they easily regreen. While a forest may appear healthy, the trees may be slowly dying from soil compaction. There is, however, general agreement that spreading a sleeping bag on a large granite boulder or on a snowfield doesn't bother anything, except maybe the lichen or iceworms.

A sleeping pad keeps the bag dry and bones comfortable. Tent or tarp must never be ditched unless the ground has no vegetation to be disturbed.

Try always to camp invisibly, well away from the trail, to avoid intruding on the wildland isolation of others. When this isn't feasible, camp quietly. No yelling, no yodeling, learn to whisper and hum. Tell little children how Mohican mothers used to smother their babes lest their squalling be heard by the Iroquois; better a kid or two die rather than the whole tribe. Convey the suspicion that this is Iroquois country.

FIRE

Recollecting those long millennia our ancestors huddled in the cave, are we not ungrateful wretches to accuse the campfire of being antisocial? No doubt. But year by year the wood fire is coming down the mountain, already banned absolutely in most meadowlands, elsewhere not allowed above a certain elevation. No longer is even sealevel a free-fire zone; on the Olympic National Park Coastal Strip, fires must be no closer than 10 feet to driftwood logs and may not exceed 3 feet in diameter.

Today's novices will not take many backpacks before they learn never to count on a wood fire to keep warm (that's what clothes are for) or to cook meals (that's why you carry a stove). Of course, minimalists (cheapskates) don't encumber themselves with stoves; there is no nutritional value to the warmth in food; as our ancestors knew long before they climbed down out of the trees into the caves, "Though the food is cold, the inner man is hot."

The pleasures of a roaring blaze on a cold mountain night are indisputable, but a single party on a single night may use up ingredients of the scenery that were long decades in growing, dying, and silvering. In forests, fires perhaps may still be built with a clear conscience. Impact should be minimized by using only established fire pits and using only dead and downed wood. When finished, be certain the fire is absolutely out—drown the coals and stir them with a stick and then drown the ashes until the smoking and steaming have stopped completely and a finger stuck in the slurry feels no heat. Embers can smoulder underground in dry duff for days, spreading gradually and days later starting a forest fire.

If you decide to build a fire, do not make a new fire ring—use an existing one. In popular areas patrolled by rangers, its existence means this is an approved, established, or designated campsite. If a fire ring has been heaped over with rocks, it means the site has been disestablished.

LITTER AND GARBAGE

"If you can carry it in full, you can carry it out empty." Pack it out—*Pack it all out!*

If a wood fire is built, paper can be burned; all unburnables, including cans, metal foil, plastic, glass, and the "paper" that has so much plastic in the mix that it won't burn, must be carried out.

Never bury garbage. If fresh, animals will dig it up and scatter the remnants. Burning before burying doesn't help; tin cans don't disintegrate in less than 40 years, aluminum and glass last centuries.

Leave no leftover food for the next travelers; by the time they arrive the local inhabitants will have done their dirty in it. Especially don't cache plastic tarps; weathering and critter-nibbling soon make a useless, miserable mess.

SANITATION

Where privies are provided, use them.

Where not, eliminate body wastes well removed from campsites and watercourses. First scratch a shallow hole in the "biological disposer layer." If toilet paper is used (leaves are better), touch with a match and when the flames are dead cover the evidence.

WATER

In the late 1970s began a great epidemic of giardiasis, caused by a parasite that spends part of its life cycle swimming free in water and part in the intestinal tract of wildlife, dogs, and people. Actually, the "epidemic" was solely in the press; *Giardia* were first identified in the eighteenth century and are present in the public water systems of many cities of the world and many towns in America—including some in the foothills of the Cascades. Long before the "outbreak" of "beaver fever," there was the well-known malady, the "Boy Scout trots." This is not to make light of the disease; though most humans feel no ill effects (but may become carriers), a few have noticeable or even severe symptoms, such as devastating diarrhea. The reason giardiasis has become "epidemic" is that there are more people in the backcountry—more people drinking water contaminated by animals—and more people contaminating the water.

Whenever in doubt, boil the water 10 minutes. Keep in mind that *Giardia* can survive in water at or near freezing for weeks or months—a snow pond is not necessarily safe. Boiling is 100 percent effective against not only *Giardia* but the myriad of other filthy little blighters that may upset your digestion or—as with some forms of hepatitis—destroy your liver.

If you cannot boil, use one of the several iodine treatments available (chlorine compounds have been found untrustworthy in wildland circumstances), such as Potable Aqua or the more complicated method that employs iodine crystals. Rumors to the contrary, iodine treatments pose no threat to the health.

High-tech filters sold in backpacking shops carry certifications and guarantees and hefty price tags and have an impressively tekky, very nifty look. As is true of many another advance of technology, a filter is one more thing to go wrong. Murphy's Law applies. *Caveat emptor.* Iodine is cheap and light and never fails.

While protecting against invisible contaminants, also take care to guard the visible purity of the public water supply. Don't wash dishes in streams or lakes, loosing food particles and detergent. Haul buckets of water to the

Fording the Queets River (Hike 92)

woods or rocks, and wash and rinse there. Don't wash bodies in streams or lakes. Don't swim in waters being taken internally by others.

Carry a collapsible water container to minimize the trips to the water supply that beat down a path through delicate vegetation. A water-carrier has a serendipity. Hikers, especially beginners and fishermen, like to camp near water. Thus, the near-water camps are the mob scenes. By pausing at a stream or lake to fill a container and continuing on the trail a half-hour to the top of a dry ridge, a hiker gets away from the madding crowd, finds solitude, and peacefully enjoys the big views.

HORSES

Most horse riders (and llama leaders) do their best to be good neighbors on the trail and know how to go about it. The typical hiker, though, is ignorant of the difficulties in maneuvering a huge mass of flesh (containing a very small brain) along narrow paths on steep mountains.

The first rule is the horse has the right of way. For his own safety as well as that of the rider, the hiker must get off the trail—preferably on the downhill side, giving the clumsy animal and its perilously perched rider the inside of the tread. If necessary—as, say, on the Goat Rocks Crest—retreat some distance to a safe passing point.

The second rule is, when you see a horse approaching, do not keep silent or stand still in a mistaken attempt to avoid frightening the beast. Continue normal motions and speak to it, so the creature will recognize you as just another human and not think you a silent and doubtless dangerous monster.

Finally, if you have a dog along, get a tight grip on its throat to stop the nipping and yapping, which may endanger the rider and, in the case of a surly horse, the dog as well.

THEFT

A quarter-century ago theft from a car left at a trailhead was rare. Not now. Equipment has become so fancy and expensive and hikers so numerous that stealing is a high-profit industry. Not even wilderness camps are entirely safe, but the professionals mainly concentrate on cars. First and foremost, don't make crime profitable for the pros. If they break into a hundred cars and get nothing but moldy boots and tattered T-shirts they'll give up. Don't think locks help—pros can open your car door and trunk as fast with a picklock as you can with your key. Don't imagine you can hide anything from them—they know all the hiding spots. If the hike is part of an extended car trip, arrange to store your extra equipment, perhaps at a nearby motel.

Be suspicious of anyone waiting at a trailhead. One of the tricks of the trade is to sit there with a pack as if waiting for a ride, watching new arrivals unpack—and hide the valuables—and maybe even striking up a conversation to determine how long the marks will be away.

The ultimate solution, of course, is for hikers to become as poor as they were in the olden days. No criminal would consider trailheads profitable if the loot consisted solely of shabby khaki war surplus.

Among such dark thoughts, not to be omitted is the awareness of the swelling social discontent in a time when the rich get ever richer and the poor ever poorer. As common, perhaps, as theft is vandalism for the sake of—well, for the same satisfaction, maybe, as a drive-by shooting. Many a fortune-favored hiker keeps his Beemer locked in a garage at home, and at the trailhead parks a beater.

SAFETY

Why the "Ten Essentials?" To keep your safety margin from thinning out to nothing. Inclusion of a trail in this book does not mean it will be safe for you. The route may have changed since the description herein was written. Creeks flood. Gravity pulls down trees and rocks. Brush grows up. The weather changes from season to season, day to day, hour to hour. Wind blows, rain soaks, lightning strikes, the sun sets, temperature drops, snow falls, avalanches happen.

A guidebook cannot guarantee that you are safe for the trail. Strength and agility vary from person to person. You vary from decade to decade, year to year, day to day, morning to afternoon to dark and stormy night.

You can reduce backcountry risks by being informed, equipped, and alert, by recognizing hazards and knowing and respecting your limits. However, you cannot eliminate risk, and neither can the attorney hired by your next of kin. An old saying from the Alps is that when a climber is injured, he apologizes to his friends, and when a climber is killed, his friends apologize for him. It's a dangerous world out there. Perhaps you'd be happier as an armchair adventurer. But you may want to strap yourself in as a precaution against earthquakes

---

A NOTE ABOUT SAFETY

Safety is an important concern in all outdoor activities. No guidebook can alert you to every hazard or anticipate the limitations of every reader. Therefore, the descriptions of roads, trails, routes, and natural features in this book are not representations that a particular place or excursion will be safe for your party. When you follow any of the routes described in this book, you assume responsibility for your own safety. Under normal conditions, such excursions require the usual attention to traffic, road and trail conditions, weather, terrain, the capabilities of your party, and other factors. Keeping informed on current conditions and exercising common sense are the keys to a safe, enjoyable outing.

—*The Mountaineers*

SAVING OUR TRAILS

PRESERVATION GOALS FOR THE 1990s AND BEYOND

In the early 1960s, The Mountaineers began publishing trail guides as another means of working "to preserve the natural beauty of Northwest America," through putting more feet on certain trails, in certain wildlands. We suffered no delusion that large numbers of boots improve trails or enhance wildness. However, we had learned to our rue that "you use it or lose it," that threatened areas could only be saved if they were more widely known and treasured. We were criticized in certain quarters for contributing to the deterioration of wilderness by publicizing it, and confessed the fault, but could only respond, "Which would you prefer: A hundred boots in a virgin forest? Or that many snarling wheels in a clearcut?"

As the numbers of wilderness lovers have grown so large as to endanger the qualities they love, the rules of "walking light" and "camping no trace" must be more faithfully observed. Yet the ultimate menace to natural beauty is not hikers, no matter how destructive their great vicious boots may be, nor even how polluting their millions of *Giardia* cysts are, but doomsday, arriving on two or three or four or six or eight wheels, or on tractor treads, or on whirling wings—the total conquest of the land and water and sky by machinery.

VICTORIES PAST

Conceived in campfire conversation of the 1880s, Olympic National Park was established in 1938, the grandest accomplishment of our most conservation-minded president, Franklin D. Roosevelt. (Confined to a wheelchair and never himself able to know the trails with his own feet, FDR nevertheless saw the fallacy in the sneering definition of wilderness as "preserves for the aristocracy of the physically fit" and knew the value of dreams that never could be personally attained.)

A renewal of the campaigns after World War II brought—regionally, in 1960—the Glacier Peak Wilderness and—nationally, in 1964—the Wilderness Act, whereby existing and future wildernesses were placed beyond the fickleness of bureaucracies.

The year 1968 saw the North Cascades Act, achieving another vision of the nineteenth century, the North Cascades National Park, plus the Lake Chelan and Ross Lake National Recreation Areas, Pasayten Wilderness, and additions to the Glacier Peak Wilderness.

In 1976 the legions of citizens laboring at the grass roots, aided by the matching dedication of certain of their congressmen and senators, obtained

Forest along the Greenwater trail (Hike 7)   **21**

There was no limit on party size in 1959 when U.S. Supreme Court Justice William O. Douglas led seventy people on a march protesting a proposed road that would have destroyed the character of the nationally famous wilderness beach of Olympic National Park (Hike 99). In addition to the justice, there were newspaper, radio, and TV reporters and a support party of well-known environmentalists. The march put an end to the tourist industry's demand for a coastal highway.

the Alpine Lakes Wilderness. In 1984 the same alliance, working at the top and at the bottom and all through the middle, all across the state, won the Washington Wilderness Act encompassing more than 1,000,000 acres, including in the purview of this volume these new wildernesses: Clearwater, Norse Peak, William O. Douglas, Glacier View, Tatoosh, Indian Heaven, Trapper Creek, Wonder Mountain, Mount Skokomish, The Brothers, Buckhorn, and Colonel Bob, plus additions to Goat Rocks and Mount Adams.

Is, therefore, the job done?

GOALS AHEAD
Absolutely not.

To examine more closely the above series of dates, note the recurring interval of 8 years. Then ask, where was the bounty of 1992? The Washington Wilderness Act gave protection to 1,000,000 acres. But the measure drawn up by the thirty-eight organizations of the Washington Wilderness Coalition encompassed 2,500,000 acres—and that was itself

drastically reduced from the want-lists of the member groups. Is the glass one-third full? Or two-thirds still empty?

What should have happened in 1992? Washington Wilderness Act II. We are, at this writing, 6 years overdue. Granted, the affairs of Washington City have been in turmoil, and the Congressional delegation of Washington State mirrors the fugue of Foggy Bottom, but nevertheless. . . .

This wildland is your land, and it is your obligation to be its steward, in the ways discussed earlier in these pages, and its advocate, working for Washington Wilderness Act II.

Letters. Well-informed letters about the wildland. Your feet, taking one step at a time at a studiously slow pace, know the land better than the heads of any elected officials. Insert into those heads what your feet know. Your feet bones are connected to your leg bones, leg bones to the hip bones, hip bones to the backbone, backbone to the head bone, head bone to the letter-writing finger bones.

Your feet have *information*, direct boot-on-trail knowledge of the earth. Really-truly information, not showtime sound-bites. Your fingers—by typewriter, ballpoint pen, pencil, goose quill—produce *personal* letters, *human* letters, the postage stamp on the envelope promising authenticity, which indeed lies within, guaranteed by the words that conjure up the pain of blisters and the reek of sweaty socks. Our friends in government often tell us that the torrent of robot communications vomited into the etheric roar is conscientiously tabulated, by robot, but that *human letters are read.* They further tell of hot debates in staff meetings when one or two really-truly human letters were passed around and turned the tide in our favor.

Warning: Informants also tell us of occasions when their office wires were clogged by electronic yap, but no human letters having been received, the decision-makers concluded that hikers didn't care.

So write.

THE WILDERNESS VISION

With 90 percent of the original forest cover of the state already logged, it should be self-evident that sacrificing the remaining 10 percent could not put off more than several years the necessity to shore up the creaky forest industry for the long-run future.

The ancient forests and all the life systems co-existing there, from dung beetles and slime to cougar and bear and people, are what wilderness preservation is about. But wilderness ain't what it used to be when it was best known as the habitat of the Enemy of Mankind, or when Thoreau preached that "in wildness is the preservation of the world," or even when Congress adopted Zahniser's eloquent definition, a place "where earth and its community of life are untrammeled by man, where man himself is a visitor who does not remain."

The argument now is heard that a good idea thought up when our species was only just taking aim on its second billion and hadn't yet learned to fly can't handle our current sixth billion, much less the twelfth billion on its way down the birth canal. We are reminded, though, that in the 1960s there were pundits of academia who argued that the national park idea was moribund—and so it indeed was until the North Cascades Act of 1968 stirred the ashes from which rose the phoenix of the most massive additions to the park system in its history. It's not good ideas that turn dumb, it's pundits.

Every attempt to revise the Wilderness Act of 1964 must be repulsed, because to open the door a crack for perhaps reasonable and useful adjustments would let in a horde howling that the wilderness be "opened up to the people"—defined as people in helicopters, on bicycles, carrying portable spas and electricity generators and Coke machines.

WILDERNESS DEEPS AND WILDERNESS EDGES: SOLITUDE

The language of the Wilderness Act might be strictly interpreted as requiring limits on the number of people allowed in any given spot at any given time. Surely, finding the privacy in the out-of-doors to pick your nose is highly valued in a world of six billions, and will be more so at twelve billions. Yet where a trail presently attracts 100 walkers a day, if the limit is set to preserve solitude for 5, what's to be done about the other 95? The physical resource—the plant and animal life—and certainly the quality of the experience deriving from solitude may benefit from fewer humans, but it may well be that if wilderness use shrinks, so will wilderness support—those human letters emanating from those educated foot bones. The wilderness idea cannot well afford the loss of such support when at least 2,000,000 acres of Washington earth subject to multiple-abuse cry out for shelter under the Wilderness Act.

Solitude certainly should be a very high priority in the wilderness cores, the "deep wilderness" demanding a good many miles of hauling a pack, a number of nights of backcountry camping. The supply of deep wilderness in Washington has been sadly diminished by logging roads and highways. Of the sixty-five Cascade trips described in this book, only several could by any stretch be called "deep"; the Olympics do better, with a half-dozen,

Mount Rainier from the Norse Peak trail (Hike 9)

and some of the range's deepest are not treated at all but left to the tanta-lized imagination.

One method of creating more "deep" is to add those 2,000,000 orphan acres. Another is to put to bed roads which have outlived their usefulness or whose cost of maintenance has become too heavy.

Rationing the "edge wilderness"—that which is accessible on short and easy day hikes and overnights by short legs, gimpy legs, and inexperienced legs—would endanger the popularity of wilderness and in the long run its very survival. Many—perhaps nearly all—adult wilderness walkers were introduced to the mysteries beyond reach of the automobile at an early age, were "green-bonded" there in the same way a baby is bonded to a mother. To make such green-bonding difficult for the young is to risk the loss of adult defenders of wilderness.

It may be that heavy traffic on close-to-city "edges" should be accepted as complacently as the masses of pilgrims ascending Fujiyama in lockstep, as the unbroken procession of rope teams from Camp Muir to the crater of Mt. Rainier, as the sociability of Swiss trails where on rainy days hundreds of colorful umbrellas line the way from tramway tops to the glacier edges, the larger umbrellas sheltering whole families, nobody in a rush, everybody smiling. Strategic design and tread placement to keep feet from straying can be supplemented by friendly little signs warning that each man kills the thing he loves if he insists on putting his boots on it.

When more "edge" is called for by population growth, again the opportunities abound in the 2,000,000 acres. Additionally, outside the dedicated parks and wildernesses there are highlands skinned by "timber miners" at elevations where a second crop of commercial trees will not grow for 500 years or more, far too long for credible tree farming. Within decades, however, the land of "reconstituted roadless areas," of "wilderness-edge backcountry" will green up in scrub and shrubs, streams will restabilize, and wildlife populations will settle into balance. Old logging roads can be allowed to dwindle to footpaths, campsites established where backpackers can look out at night to the lights of farms and cities—and by turning, look inward to starlit wilderness cores.

The regional wilderness under state and local auspices can supplement the national wilderness. As an example, the Mountains-to-Sound Greenway along Interstate 90 from Seattle to the Cascade Crest, a corridor mostly outside the Alpine Lakes Wilderness yet within a half-hour's drive or less from the homes of millions of people, contains the wildland trails of the Mount Si Natural Resources Conservation Area and the West Tiger Mountain NRCA, managed by the state Department of Natural Resources (DNR); the Squak Mountain State Park, managed by Washington State Parks; the Cougar Mountain Regional Wildland Park, managed by King County Parks; the Rattlesnake Mountain Scenic Area, jointly managed by the DNR and King County; and the Middle Fork Snoqualmie River Corridor, managed by a state-county-federal consortium.

WHEELS

A defining feature of wilderness is freedom from the wheel—from its speed and, worse than that, its fretful hastiness and, still worse, its inevitable homocentric tendency to arrogantly dominate, to ruthlessly brutalize. Interestingly, in the late nineteenth century, when the bicycle first achieved practicality and popularity, European armies employed it for "commando" units, replacement for cavalry squadrons. In World War I the motorcycle was an important weapon, and in World War II, the "jeep." All three are alive and well today, in peace and in war—the enemy they now attack being slowness.

In his novel, *Slowness*, Milan Kundera asks, "Why has the pleasure of slowness disappeared? Ah, where have they gone, the amblers of yesteryear? Have they vanished along with footpaths . . . with nature? There is a Czech proverb that describes their easy indolence. 'They are gazing at God's windows.' "

To eyes riding wheels, the views out the windows are blurred, if not too homogenized by speed to be seen. However, it is very late in history to disinvent any of the several species of wheeled vehicles.

Wheels on vehicles with four apiece and motors attached. Were it not for the automobile, few of us would have much wilderness experience of any kind; if Seattle were our trailhead, Snoqualmie Pass would be next thing to an expedition. Lacking roads, children could not begin their green-bonding so young, and any wilderness newcomer does well to dip toes in the edges before braving the deeps. A review of our guidebooks abundantly testifies to our appreciation of the recreational value of roads. It also can be seen in our pages that there is no shortage of non-wilderness edges.

The shortage is of deep wilderness. The Olympics have remained nearly as well endowed as in the 1930s. The South Cascades were, then, perhaps the equal or superior in depth, but there, in the National Forest that bears his name, Gifford Pinchot's "greatest good of the greatest number in the long run" has been interpreted as—to pungently mix metaphors—a spiderweb of roads through motheaten forests. When the trees are logged the justification for retaining the logging roads disappears. Unfortunately, forest engineers now defend their constructions (destructions) for their recreational value. Some do indeed have that. But a great many provide recreation purely for wheels, effectively banning feet.

Incongruously, there are pedestrians—even members of organizations dedicated to wilderness preservation—who so love "edge" hikes enabled by the logging roads that they want all deeps made into edges and no edges ever restored to pristine deepness. One is torn between pity and contempt.

Wheels on vehicles with two apiece and motors attached. The motorcycle is two-wheels-less and some-tons-less than a car, consumes far less fossil fuel, takes up less space, and what with the wind in your ears and bugs in your teeth is splendid on roads. However, upon leaving a road, it transforms a footpath not to another species of trail but to a totally different genus—a *trail* becomes a *motorway*, which is to say, *road*.

In the summer of 1997, a district ranger in the Cascades addressed a letter to "Dear Trail Users." He expressed his fondness for machinery in the wilds, then sadly announced cancellation of plans for a new system of wheelways, saying "The primary reasons for this are the noise, disturbance, and refuse associated with concentrated motorized activity."

Thus the horns of the Forest Service dilemma, its Scylla and Charybdis. Rangers with both feet on the ground know the distinction between a trail and a motorway and know that "multiple use" by feet and wheels is an impossibility, a fraud. But above the real earth the song of the cloud cuckoos is, "Vroom vroom."

Among the National Forests of Washington, Gifford Pinchot vies for ranking as number one on the list of worst offenders; for a few representative crimes against the peace of God's windows, see Hikes 47-54. The proposal for a Dark Divide Wilderness, which failed to make the cut for the Washington Wilderness Act of 1984, is high on the priority list for an Act II. In addition, however, closures are sought of selected roads to create roadless areas with wheelfree trail corridors.

In this past quarter-century, the concerted efforts of tens of thousands of conservationists have protected large expanses of wildland from invasion by machines—but during the same period, a comparative handful of off-road vehicle (ORV) users have taken away more miles of trail, converting them to de facto roads, than the conservationists have saved. As the score stood in 1985, 45 percent of Washington trails were machinefree by being in national parks and wildernesses; of the other 55 percent, half were open to motorcycles—and thus were not truly trails at all. The situation in 1998

Mount Adams and beargrass from Juniper Ridge (Hike 48)

is very little better—and, in large part due to the abrupt invasion of the "mountain bike," far worse.

Wheels on vehicles with two apiece and no motors. The bicycle, though probably not, as we are encouraged to believe, second only to wings as the transportation of choice in Heaven, is easy on our ears, our air, and our fossil fuel; it grants freedom from a five-figure, three-ton incubus; in cities it is part of a solution to ossification by gridlock; and in open country it is fun. However, in the brand-new off-road manifestation, the fat-tire ("mountain") bike, it is to trails as the Tatars were to Cathay.

Wheels of bicycles, just as of motorcycles, expel feet. The bicycle transforms a footway not to another species of trail but to a totally different genus—footway becomes *bikeway*. We hikers are not sniffy puritans who banish bikers from trails. Say we, park your wheels and come walk with us.

There is such a thing as a *multi-use, non-motorized travelway*, amicably usable by walkers, joggers, runners, wheelchair users, bikers, and rollerskaters. The way must, of course, segregate them by speed, walkers and wheelchair users in one lane, runners and bikers in another, and whenever space is available for another, a third for horses. Dumping all the cats in the same gunnysack and instructing them to purr does not work.

Many fat-tire bikers are also hikers, were such before the new vehicle arrived here from Mt. Tamalpais in the middle-late 1980s, and still are. They know and value and respect the differences between a museum and a gymnasium, a cathedral and a circus. These hiker-bikers are in major part members of "green" organizations and vigorously support wilderness protection. But a great many bikers do not belong to such groups, never open their mouths on the subjects, and thereby permit their wheels to be "spoken for" in public discourse by a small group of crusaders, some on the payrolls of the wheel industry (when did a bootmaker ever hire prophets to evangelize for walking?). They spout, as is common on streetcorner soap boxes, ecstatic silliness. Behind the babblers, though, are gray eminences who adroitly employ the technique of "newspeak," described in Orwell's *1984*, the replacement of old words by new in order to expunge from social memory—and thereby from existence—what the old words denoted. For "trail," newspeak substitutes "singletrack," implying (and convincing mind-free bikers) that the route was meant for wheels even before there were any.

This too shall pass. Bicycles, skinny-tire and fat-tire both, must have more room, and in large part it must be new room.

Hikers fully support bikers' efforts to obtain suitable bikeways. But they never will accept wheels piggybacking on footways as presently is being attempted by the Forest Service, Washington State Parks, and most municipal parks departments.

The Laws of Thermodynamics state that energy is more diffuse at the conclusion of an action than at the start—the "entropy" has been increased. The measurement of entropy is the means by which physicists determine whether we are living forward or backward in time. The Laws tell us that time will (so to speak) end when all the energy in creation has been fully diffused in a universe-wide still gray silence. That's Progress.

We live in a period of social confusion, political anarchy, and turmoil on our travelways unprecedented in history. The growth in world population from 1,000,000,000 humans to 6,000,000,000 in just 2 of the 120 centuries since sheep were domesticated in the Tigris Valley might be Progress for the real estate industry but certainly not for the hermit business. The growth in the number of Americans from 120,000,000 in 1920 to 203,000,000 in 1970 to 249,000,000 in 1990 brings to mind the expression (predating even the automobile) "going to Hell on wheels."

The Golden Rule of humane civilization is tolerance—don't knock the other guy's national origin, sexual orientation, religion, politics, music, haircut, or sport. Moral relativism has perils, yet surely is superior to intolerant absolutism. Nevertheless, though it certainly was very bad of the Church to burn Joan of Arc at the stake, the only good thing that could be done with a Dracula is drive a stake through his heart.

Though the arrogance of the swift mocks the thoughtfulness of the slow, a material-moral absolutism grounded on the Laws of Thermodynamics judges the wilderness surely and purely *good* and the destruction of trails by wheels surely and purely *bad*.

THE POLITICS OF WHEELS VS. LETTERS

In his farewell address, President Eisenhower warned against the dangers to the nation of the military-industrial complex which, during his term in office, had through its conquest of Congress gained effective control of the federal government. In these past few years we have witnessed the ripening of a similar conspiracy to tyrannize, a machinery-bureaucrat complex which will not rest content until it has gained full control of the nation's wildlands.

The U.S. Forest Service has outlived—by over-cutting—its primary old mission of providing the nation a sustained yield of forest products. To win a new base of support, the Forest Service has shifted its highest priority from logging to recreation.

The 380,000 miles of National Forest logging roads—eight times the size of the entire United States interstate highway system—are now bragged up by the rangers for their recreation value. Having pledged its troth to machines, the Forest Service feels compelled to love two wheels as passionately as four. Which means the word "trail" is preserved for traditional footways-hoofways even as they are being converted to wheelways.

Two figures dramatically—shockingly—illustrate the solidity of the machinery-bureaucracy marriage.

In the five National Forests of the Washington Cascades, trail miles total 6,646. To separate out the trails appealing to day-hikers (ranging from an easy 3-mile round trip to a strenuous 16-miler), the machinefree trail miles in that category total 1,197. *Only 15 percent of day-hiker trails—the wilder-ness-edge trails of chief interest to the hiking population, short and tall, young and old—are machinefree.*

A statewide survey has counted approximately 1,000,000 hikers. The Washington State Department of Licensing has issued ORV registrations to 41,300 machines. *The ratio of hikers to riders is approximately 25 to 1; yet the ratio of motorcycle miles to machinefree miles on these wilderness-edge day-trip trails is 22 to 1!* Exactly the reverse of justice! The world turned upside-down!

A final monstrous unfairness. By action of the Legislature, 1 percent of revenues from the state gas tax was dedicated to enhancing recreation on roads not funded by the Department of Transportation. Fair enough. However, because "Travel Off State Highways" was deemed inconveniently cumbersome, the shorthand adopted was "Off Road Use." This was misinterpreted by a muddle-headed Legislature (its head expertly muddled by the high-paid machinery lobbyists) to mean off-road vehicles, and the revenues (the NOVA Fund) were dedicated entirely to ORV recreation. Later the split was amended to 80 percent ORV and 20 percent non-motorized, a step toward justice yet still grossly preferential to the motorized minority. As Congress decreased its trail budget, Forest Service nostrils began twitching; the ORV money became virtually its sole source of trail funds.

The ORV share of NOVA funds over the years has come to $35,000,000. Much of that has gone to the Forest Service to convert hiking trails to ORV roads. As one example of such conversion in the area covered by this book, though the Dark Divide is a proposed National Wilderness (awaiting Washington Wilderness Act II), the Randle Ranger District of Gifford Pinchot National Forest has expanded ORV opportunities to 90 percent of its trails.

Environmentalists urge three courses of action:

1. The Legislature to adjust the 80-20 distribution formula to 30 percent ORV, 70 percent non-motorized.
2. Washington City—Congress and the White House—to require the Forest Service to cease flagrantly disobeying the federal law that stipulates that where motorized use is in conflict with non-motorized, the motorized must yield.
3. *Write those letters!*

1 | McClellan Butte

Round trip: 9 miles
Hiking time: 7 hours (day hike)
High point: 5162 feet
Elevation gain: 3700 feet

Hikable: July through October
Map: Green Trails Bandera (No. 206)
Information: North Bend Ranger
District, phone (360) 888-1421

The sharp little peak has a challenging look from Interstate 90 and avalanche snows at one point can be truly dangerous through the spring. However, a trail safe enough in high summer climbs steep and strenuously to panoramas west over lowlands to Seattle, Puget Sound, and the Olympics, south over uncountable clearcuts to Mt. Rainier, and east to Snoqualmie Pass peaks. The lower part of the route displays numerous scars and artifacts of man's present and past activities; the recorded history of the area dates from 1853, when Captain George B. McClellan journeyed approximately this far up the Cedar River valley seeking a pass through the Cascades suitable for the U.S. Army and a railroad. The trail is badly eroded and tough walking, but is nevertheless very popular. The peak calls.

Drive Interstate 90 to Exit 42, signed "West Tinkham Road," and go off on road No. 55. Cross the Snoqualmie River bridge, pass the highway workshop, and in a scant 0.5 mile turn right to the trailhead and parking lot, elevation 1500 feet.

Trail No. 1015 enters forest to a bridge over Alice Creek, climbs a bit, crosses a powerline swath and reenters woods again, reaches a long-abandoned,

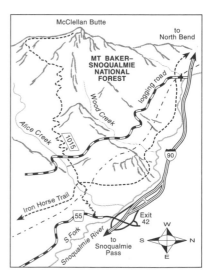

Thimbleberry

I-90 corridor from McClellan Butte

overgrown railroad grade, and at ½ mile crosses the Iron Horse Trail, the former Milwaukee Railroad grade. An old clearcut leads into the woods again; at 1 mile, 2200 feet, is a private logging road.

The grade steepens, going by a sometime spring in a cool grove of big old trees, and switchbacks up the north side of the butte. At about 2½ miles the trail rounds to the east side and crosses an avalanche gully whose treacherous snowbank usually lasts into July. Numerous switchbacks sidehill below cliffs, with occasional views, to the south ridge of the peak at 4 miles, 4500 feet. The route follows the crest a short bit, edging clearcuts in Seattle's Cedar River Watershed, rounds the east side of the mountain, drops 100 feet to a small pond, and climbs again to the ridge crest a short way from the summit.

For most, the magnificent panoramas here are far enough. The last bit to the tiptop adds few new views and a lot of beneath-the-feet air. A person inexperienced in three-point suspension and subject to vertigo does best not to go and say he did.

2 | ANNETTE LAKE

Round trip: 7½ miles
Hiking time: 4 hours (day hike or backpack)
High point: 3500 feet
Elevation gain: 1500 feet

Hikable: June through November
Map: Green Trails Snoqualmie Pass (No. 207)
Information: North Bend Ranger District, phone (360) 888-1421

A very popular and often crowded subalpine lakelet ringed by open forest, cliffs, and talus of Abiel Peak rising above. For lonesome walking try early summer or late fall in the middle of the week in terrible weather.

Drive Interstate 90 toward Snoqualmie Pass to Exit 47, signed "Denny Creek/Asahel Curtis Picnic Area." Go off the freeway, turn right 0.1 mile, then left on road No. 55 for 0.4 mile to the parking lot, elevation 2000 feet.

The way starts in an old clearcut, crosses Humpback Creek, and in 1 mile passes under a powerline and enters forest. At 1½ miles, 2400 feet, cross the Iron Horse Trail, the abandoned Milwaukee Railroad grade.

Now comes the hard part, switchbacking steeply upward in old forest on the slopes of Silver Peak. At one point an uprooted tree provides a broad walkway. Occasional talus openings give looks over the valley to Humpback Mountain. After gaining 1200 feet in 2½ miles, at the 3600-foot level a small creek is crossed and a final mile of minor ups and downs culminates in the lake outlet, 3¾ miles, 3500 feet.

Wander the east shore for picnic spots. Study the architecture of the little cliffs. Listen to the waterfall splashing into the lake.

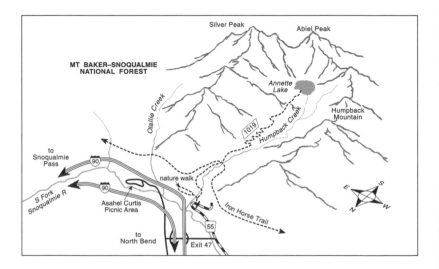

Camping may or may not be attractive—or possible. Call the Forest Service beforehand to learn where and how and if; the lake is so mobbed that great care is being taken to prevent it from becoming a muddy/dusty slum.

Annette Lake

3 | COLD CREEK LOOP—SILVER PEAK

Loop trip: 6 miles, with peak 8 miles
Hiking time: 3½ hours, with peak 6
hours (day hike)
High point: loop 4400 feet, with peak
5603 feet
Elevation gain: loop 1400 feet, with
peak 2600 feet

Hikable: July through October
Map: Green Trails Snoqualmie Pass
(No. 207)
Information: Cle Elum Ranger
District, phone (509) 674-4411

Considerable forest survives, and lovely are the trees. The lakes mirror them, and the sky. Summit views are straight down from your toes to Annette Lake, north to Snoqualmie Pass peaks, west to the Olympics, south over motheaten ridges rolling mournfully to Rainier, and east across valley-drowning Lake Keechelus reservoir to Mt. Margaret, patched by clearcuts as if suffering from terminal mange.

Long gone are the pristinity and remoteness that ranked this among the most popular hikes near Snoqualmie Pass. Much of the old beauty remains to justify inclusion in this book—the Beauty that has survived four decades of romping and chomping by the Beast. Here is a central scene of the Checkerboard Crime, the Northern Pacific Land Grant. Blame not the timber companies; though they are receivers of stolen goods, the statute of limitations permits them to do as they please with the privatized loot, and their pleasure is to expeditiously "liquidate the inventory." Those logging roads were built not by foresters but by bottom-line accountants. ("The bigger the dividends to stockholders, m'dear.") Custodian of the intervening squares of the checkerboard which remain in ownership of the United States, the Forest Service sincerely tries to follow the precepts of "multiple-use"; thus there

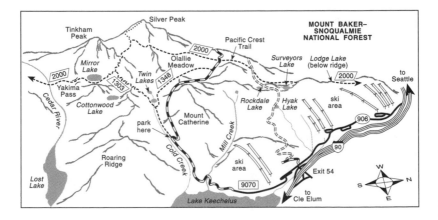

still are trails. Enjoy the sky, much bigger in cheerful stumplands of "thrifty young forest" than in gloomy cloisters of decadent old giants in an ancient-forest cathedral.

Drive Interstate 90 east from Snoqualmie Pass 2 miles and go off on Hyak Exit 54. Turn right and then left into the large Pacific West-Hyak ski area parking lot. Halfway through the lot, go left on a road obscurely signed "Hyak Estates Division 3 and 4." Pass houses and go to the right of the Wastewater Treatment Plant; here the way becomes Forest Service road No. 9070. At 3.3 miles from I-90 is the Cold Creek trailhead, signed "Twin Lakes," elevation 3000 feet. (If your sole interest is the ascent of Silver, stay on No. 9070 another 2 miles to the Pacific Crest Trail at Olallie Meadow, 4200 feet. Walk the Crest Trail south 1½ miles to the Gardiner Ridge trail, as noted below.)

Alternating between clearcuts and forest, Silver Peak standing 2300 feet above it all, Cold Creek trail No. 1303 attains Lower Twin Lake at about ¾ mile. Here is a junction.

Mount Rainier from near the top of Silver Peak

Go either direction; the loop has as much uphill one way as the other. We describe it clockwise because that's how we happened to do it.

Cross the outlet stream and grind out 1300 feet in 1¾ miles to the Pacific Crest Trail and the 4400-foot high point, 2½ miles from the road (sign says "2 miles"). Turn right (north). For the sidetrip ascent of Silver Peak, in an up-and-down ½ mile watch carefully for the sign marking Gardiner Ridge trail, an old route to Hanson Creek that was abandoned because it is partly in the Cedar River Watershed. Easy to miss, the sidetrail gains 600 feet in a scant ½ mile (that seems a long 1 mile) to heather-and-shrub parkland. The mountainside is broken by a large talus; some hikers go straight up the rocks but skirting them left or right is easier. Above the talus follow the flowery ridge crest, then 200 feet of steep felsenmeer to the 5603-foot summit.

Returned from the sidetrip ascent to the Pacific Crest Trail, continue northward to road No. 9070 at Olallie Meadow, turn right on it and in about 400 feet find trail No. 1348 and follow it 1 mile back to Twin Lakes and so home.

4 | MOUNT CATHERINE

Round trip: 3 miles
Hiking time: 3 hours (day hike)
High point: 5052 feet
Elevation gain: 1300 feet

Hikable: Late June through October
Map: Not shown on any map
Information: Cle Elum Ranger District,
   phone (509) 674-4411

A better name for Mt. Catherine would be Mount False Hope. Three times a hiker is positive the top is at hand, only to see a high point ahead.

Though the trail is occasionally maintained, and is listed in the Cle Elum District Trail Guide, it is not on the USGS, Green Trails, or Forest Service recreation maps. Its existence is explained by an ancient map that shows a 1930s airway beacon on the summit, leading intrepid birdmen of Lucky Lindy's generation into the Cascade Crest and more often through it. The beacon is one of a line of beacons across the country that included others atop McClellan Butte, Rattlesnake Mountain, and West Tiger Mountain. The line has been gone since the late 1940s or so.

The views south to Mt. Rainier and north into the Alpine Lakes Wilderness make Mt. Catherine an attractive alternative to boot-busy paths along

Tinkham Peak from Mount Catherine

the Mountains-to-Sound Green Freeway. However, hikers must deal with two serious obstacles. In early summer, a treacherously steep snowfield may put the final summit off-limits except to ice-axe–equipped climbers. In late summer a summit attempt may be foiled by lush blue masses of delicious huckleberries thrusting themselves into the hiker's mouth.

Drive Interstate 90 east of Snoqualmie Pass 2 miles and go off on Hyak exit 54 to the large Pacific West-Hyak ski area parking lot. Halfway through the lot, go left on a road obscurely signed "Hyak Estates Division 3 and 4." Pass houses and go to the right of the Wastewater Treatment Plant. At the end of the pavement the way becomes Forest Service road No. 9070. At 1 mile is a junction; keep left on road No. 9070. At 3 miles, at the first switchback, pass the Twin Lakes trailhead, and just over 5 miles from I-90 reach the Mt. Catherine trailhead on the right side of the road across from a small, poor parking space, elevation 3700 feet. Don't be confused by an abandoned road 0.5 mile short of the trailhead.

Trail No. 1348 starts up a rocky, abandoned logging spur to a landing. Cross the landing to true trail and in two long switchbacks up a 1970s clearcut, enter the forest. A dozen more switchbacks in ¾ mile gain 800 feet to—the top? No, a top, but merely of the wooded ridge. With little downs, lots of ups, and a few peek-a-boo views, the ridge crest continues over more tops, until the trees grow smaller, the views bigger, and the way ascends heather clumps past an old cabin site, with a cable for a final scramble to the genuine rocky top.

Gaze north up Gold Creek to the sharp fang of Mt. Thompson and the hump of Chickamin Ridge, down to Tonka toys on I-90 and the Lilliput of Snoqualmie Pass 2000 feet lower. Don't waste much time on the south; from close-by Silver and Tinkham Peaks to the distant vastness of Mount Rainier, the route of the Pacific Crest National Scenic Trail is the clearcut checkerboard of the Northern Pacific Land Grant, bringing to mind the famous exhortation of Horace Greeley, "Go West, young logger, and *steal*."

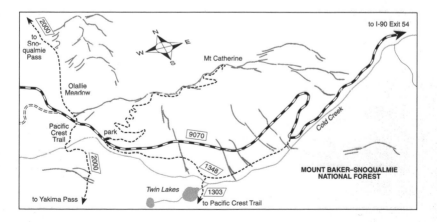

5 | BEARHEAD MOUNTAIN

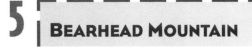

Round trip: 6 miles
Hiking time: 4 hours (day hike)
High point: 6089 feet
Elevation gain: 1800 feet

Hikable: July through October
Map: Green Trails Enumclaw (No. 237)
Information: White River District,
   phone (360) 825-6585

The highest point in the Clearwater Wilderness is an old lookout site standing above meadows that in late July and early August are a riot of color—the brilliant blue of lupine, the red of paintbrush, and a rainbow of half a hundred (or a hundred?) other species. Give this a 10 on the aesthetics scale; for an equally stunning 0, look west over miles upon miles of clearcuts; north and east are bits of virgin forest that were scheduled for the chainsaw and at the last minute saved by the 1984 Washington Wilderness Act. Yet the eye is hard-pressed to focus on either the 10 or the 0, what with the proximity of the Great North Wall of Mt. Rainier. Even from this distance the avalanches on the Willis Wall are awesome, the more so because few of the monstrous masses of tumbling ice can be heard.

Drive SR 410 to a complicated intersection at the southwest corner of Buckley, turn south on SR 165, drive for 1½ miles, and turn left, staying on SR 165, following signs to "Carbon River Entrance, Mount Rainier National Park," passing Wilkeson, Carbonado, and crossing the one-lane bridge over the Carbon River. At the far side of the bridge, SR 165 goes uphill toward Mowich Lake; stay left on what is now Carbon

Beargrass along the Bearhead Mountain trail

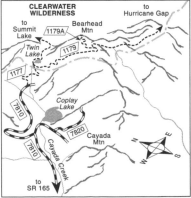

Mount Rainier and an old lookout site on Bearhead Mountain

River Road. Just before the entrance to Mount Rainier National Park, turn left on road No. 7810, cross the Carbon River on wooden bridges, and climb 5.3 miles from the river to a junction with road No. 7820. Keep left, staying on No. 7810, and at 6.7 miles reach the road-end and Bearhead Mountain and Summit Lake trail No. 1177, elevation 4300 feet. (Note: The Carbon River bridge frequently washes out. Also, recurring slides may require the trailhead to be moved back. Check with the ranger.)

Trail No. 1177 ascends a clearcut, makes a big switchback, and enters dense forest. At 1 long mile is the boundary of the Clearwater Wilderness, and a bit farther is tiny Twin Lake (single, the twin missing) and a junction, 4800 feet. The left fork is to Summit Lake; go right on Carbon trail No. 1179, which contours and climbs another long mile around steep slopes to the ridge top and a second junction at 5400 feet. Go left ¾ mile on trail No. 1179A to the summit. Settle down and spread out your lunch. Your eyes, too, will feast.

6 | SUMMIT LAKE

Round trip: 5 miles
Hiking time: 3 hours (day hike or backpack)
High point: 5400 feet
Elevation gain: 1200 feet

Hikable: July through October
Map: Green Trails Enumclaw (No. 237)
Information: White River District, phone (360) 825-6585

It's not on the summit of anything, but surely is a little pretty of a subalpine lake amid fields of flowers, foreground for a classic photo of Mt. Rainier.

Drive to the Summit Lake–Bearhead trailhead (Hike 4), elevation 4300 feet.

Hike trail No. 1177 (Hike 4) to the 4800-foot junction with Carbon trail No. 1179; keep left on No. 1177.

The path crosses the outlet and heads uphill, passing subalpine ponds or marshes, depending on the season. Nearly at the top of the ridge, the way traverses the slopes on a fairly level grade, at one point emerging from timber into a small meadow with a view of Rainier. At 2½ miles, 5400 feet, is Summit Lake. Bordering the shores are fields of beargrass and, in season, a brilliant garden of flowers. Campsites are scattered in the trees. To preserve the vegetation, hikers must camp 100 feet from the shore.

No campfires are allowed in the Summit Lake basin. Backpackers who need a hot supper and lack a stove can stay on the righthand shore, fill water jugs before leaving the lake, and find campsites ¼ mile beyond, toward the Rooster Comb.

For the first and most essential sidetrip, follow the trail around the lake to a steep path up a 5737-foot hill. Look down to Coplay Lake. Look up to Mt. Rainier. Look out to the boggling panorama of clearcutting.

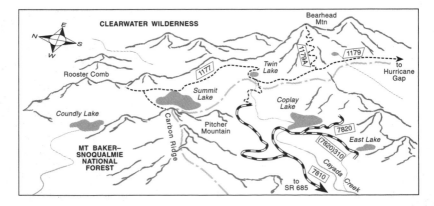

Summit Lake and Mount Rainier (John Spring photo)

7 | GREENWATER RIVER—ECHO LAKE

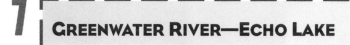

Round trip: 14 miles
Hiking time: 7 hours (day hike or backpack)
High point: 4100 feet
Elevation gain: 1640 feet

Hikable: May through mid-November at lower elevations
Map: Green Trails Lester (No. 239)
Information: White River Ranger District, phone (360) 825-6585

Once as awesome a cathedral of ancient Douglas fir as any protected in a national park or dedicated wilderness, among the grandest valley forests in the nation, the Greenwater greenery has been whacked down and shipped overseas by loggers—though they knew full well as they were whacking ("Hurry! Hurry! Whack faster!") that the valley would soon be purchased and installed in the gallery of American treasures. The callous haste is not forgotten. The Norse Peak Wilderness, which came just too late, has saved a sample, a jewel the more precious for the butcher-shop setting of bottom-line "free enterprise." Amid the surviving big old trees are sparkling forest lakes and a lovely subalpine lake.

Drive SR 410 east of Enumclaw past Federation Forest State Park to the hamlet of Greenwater. Continue 2 miles and turn left on road No. 70. About 9 miles from the highway cross the Greenwater River and in another 0.4 mile turn right on road No. 7033 to the trailhead, elevation 2600 feet.

Follow Greenwater trail No. 1176 across the clearcut to a magnificence of trees thrusting high above devil's club, vanilla leaf, trillium, and moss—much, much moss. (Yet just a short way up the steep valley walls on either side is loggers' "daylight," and from it the storm waters formerly held back by forest are carrying gravel and boulders and logging slash down to the river.)

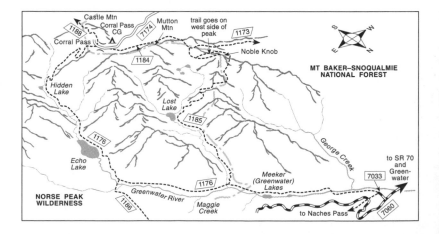

The Greenwater River trail

At ¾ mile the trail crosses the Greenwater and at 1½ miles recrosses at the first of the two little Meeker (Greenwater) Lakes. The second is at 2 miles. At 3½ miles the trail reaches a junction with Lost Creek trail No. 1185, a 3-mile sidetrip to Lost Lake. So far the trail has gained only 200 feet a mile, but near the 5-mile mark it leaves the valley bottom and starts seriously up. At 5½ miles pass a junction with trail No. 1186. At 6½ miles cross a 4100-foot high point and drop 300 feet to 3819-foot Echo Lake, ringed by wooded ridges, with a glimpse of meadows and crags of Castle Mountain.

The trail continues 6 miles to Corral Pass. The entire route, near lakes and along river, offers numerous campsites. At Echo Lake campers must keep 100 feet from the water; the west shore is closed.

8 | NOBLE KNOB

Round trip: 7 miles
Hiking time: 5 hours (day hike or backpack)
High point: 6011 feet
Elevation gain: 500 feet in, 300 feet out

Hikable: July through October
Map: Green Trails Lester (No.239)
Information: White River Ranger District, phone (360) 825-6585

If you want flowers, burn the trees. As the result of a fire set by lightning (or somebody) in the 1920s, the fields of color here rival those of Paradise. In stark contrast to the yellows and blues and reds close at hand is the whiteness of the north side of Mt. Rainier, not far away across the valley, close enough to see crevasses in the Emmons Glacier and cinders of the crater rim.

The trail lies along the edge of Norse Peak Wilderness. Note the extensive rehabilitation work done by the Forest Service in meadows ravaged by jeepers and motorcyclists—destroyers that never should have been allowed in the first place, but were blithely permitted by the Forest Service to run riot until Congress cried "Stop" with the 1984 Washington Wilderness Act.

Drive SR 410 east of Enumclaw some 31 miles to an obscure street sign pointing to Corral Pass. At 55 mph one could easily miss the small sign on the right and the road on the left. It is best to check the mileage starting at the well-signed Buck Creek forest road. In 1.3 miles from Buck Creek, pass Alta Lodge, and 0.5 mile farther turn left on Corral Pass road No. 7174. Drive 6 steep miles to Corral Pass and a junction. To the left is the Noble Knob trail, 1184, elevation 5651 feet.

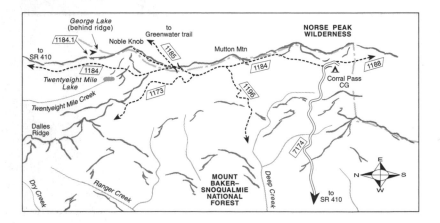

The trail contours a hillside, alternating for ¾ mile between flowers and groves of subalpine trees, and then follows the now-abandoned jeep road another ¾ mile. A short, abrupt bit concludes with a resumption of trail. At 2 miles pass Deep Creek trail No. 1196 and at 2½ miles reach a 5900-foot saddle. From here the trail drops steadily. At 3 miles, directly above Twentyeight Mile Lake, pass Dalles Ridge trail No. 1173. Shortly beyond, at 5600 feet, is a three-way junction.

The left fork, trail No. 1184, descends past George Lake (1 mile from the junction a sidepath contours right to the lake, 5500 feet, and campsites) to road No. 72. The right fork goes down past Lost Lake to the Greenwater trail (Hike 6). Take the middle trail, cross a large, treadless meadow, and with one switchback in a path overgrown in blossoms, traverse completely around the mountain to the old lookout site atop 6011-foot Noble Knob.

The Noble Knob trail

9 | NORSE PEAK LOOP— BIG CROW BASIN

Round trip: to Norse Peak 11½ miles
Hiking time: 7 hours (day hike or backpack)
High point: 6856 feet
Elevation gain: 3000 feet

Hikable: late June through early November
Maps: Green Trails Bumping Lake (No. 271), Lester (No. 239)
Information: White River Ranger District, phone (360) 825-6585

Here's a surefire recipe for happy wandering: big meadows and little lakes, flowers here and flowers there and flowers all around, panoramas from Snoqualmie Pass peaks to Mt. Adams and from golden hills of Central Washington to green plains of Puget Sound, and the yodeling purely optional. Actually, you may not feel like yodeling if a big heavy lump is

Crystal Mountain ski area from the Norse Peak trail

disfiguring your back, up and relentlessly up to the 6856-foot top of Norse Peak, onetime lookout site, and that's why day-tripping is a popular choice. Some pedestrians will find the fragrance of the trail a bit much, horse traffic having been drastically increased by the establishment of a trailhead rent-a-steed service and two horse camps.

Drive SR 410 east some 33 miles from Enumclaw to Silver Springs summer homes. A bit beyond, just before the Mount Rainier National Park boundary, turn left toward the Crystal Mountain ski area. At 3.3 miles go left to the first horse camp and official trailhead, elevation 3850 feet. Trail No. 1191 parallels the highway for ¾ mile before tilting upward. (Room for two cars to park beside the highway here.) Soon the tip of Rainier appears over the ridge and by 2¾ miles the entire summit is in view. At 4¼ miles is a junction, 6160 feet. For a loop adding 2½ miles to the round trip, go left on trail No. 1161, contouring above delightful Goat Lake Basin (look for goats across the valley on Castle Mountain), cross Barnard Saddle, go right on the Pacific Crest Trail, passing Big Crow Basin, and climb to the summit of Norse Peak.

If ignoring the loop, at the junction keep right on trail No. 1191, climbing to the 6600-foot ridge a short distance from the summit. Look northeast into Big Crow Basin and east to Lake Basin and appealing Basin Lake. Look down to the Crystal Mountain ski area, a favorite of locals who can't afford to weekend in Alta; unfortunately, the pretty snow melts and the summer hiker is treated to a mish-mashed hodgepodge of bulldozer gouges.

For Basin Lake, from Norse Peak drop down to the Pacific Crest Trail and hike south a short ½ mile and go left on trail 907. Cross over a low green ridge to the lake, 6200 feet.

An alternate route to Norse Peak is via the Bullion Basin trail, to Blue Bell Pass, there intersecting the Pacific Crest Trail.

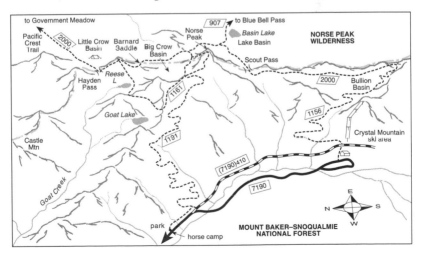

10 | CRYSTAL MOUNTAIN LOOP

Round trip: to viewpoint 6 miles
Hiking time: 3½ hours (day hike)
High point: 5500 feet
Elevation gain: 1300 feet

Loop trip: 8 miles
Hiking time: 5 hours (day hike)
High point: 6552 feet
Elevation gain: 2450 feet

Hikable: July through September
Map: Green Trails Bumping Lake
(No. 271)

Information: White River Ranger
District, phone (360) 825-6585

A Forest Service trail wanders along the boundary of Mount Rainier National Park through striking views of Rainier and the White River. Flowers in one season, huckleberries in another. Hikers who get up early enough in the morning have a good chance of seeing elk; those starting late must dodge bicycles and horses, National Park regulations being absent and thus all the cats sharing the same Forest Service gunnysack.

The trip comes in two versions: one afoot uphill and downhill, the other uphill on the Crystal Mountain chairlift, downhill on a trail-road combination. Both will be described here, the "natural" version first.

Drive SR 410 from Enumclaw (Hike 8) and turn left on Crystal Mountain Highway. In 4.3 miles turn right on road No. (7190)510 for 0.4 mile to the trailhead, elevation 4100 feet.

Trail No. 1163 begins as a service road under a powerline but soon becomes legitimate, climbing gently through clearcuts, then an old burn, in loose, dusty pumice soil. Shade is scarce and water nonexistent. (Did you remember to fill the canteen?) Heat and thirst are forgotten when, in 3 miles, at 5500 feet, the crest of Crystal Mountain is attained and Mt. Rainier overpowers the horizon. This is a great place to soak up the view and go home.

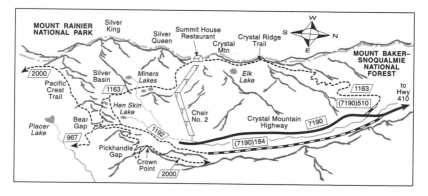

White River valley and Mount Rainier from the Crystal Mountain trail

However, if impelled by the bearish urge to see the other side of the next rise, carry on. The ridge varies from narrow (a cliff on the park side) to broad and rounded. Below the meadow crest are vast fields of huckleberries. And the views! Chances are a party will find ample rewards long before completing the 3 steady-climbing ridge-crest miles to the top terminal of Chair No. 2, 6 miles from the road.

For the loop trip's olio of lakes, meadows, and huckleberries, descend a service road that starts near the terminal. In ⅓ mile find legitimate trail No. 1163, switchbacking down through Silver Basin, past Hen Skin Lake, to a junction with Silver Creek trail No. 1192. Follow it 1 mile to an old mining road, No. (7190)184; descend this 2 miles to Crystal Mountain Highway, cross the pavement, and return to the starting point.

Now for the non-natural all-downhill tour. (Let it be noted this version is no good for elk-watching; by the time of day the chairlifts start running, the animals have finished eating and retired to the forest to chew their cuds.) Drive to the ski area parking lot, elevation 4200 feet, ride Chair No. 2 to the top, elevation 6776 feet, find the Crystal Ridge Trail, and hike either way. Both are so interesting and different that you may want to go back a second time for the other direction or, as we did, start early in the morning so you can see the elk and hike the whole loop at one go.

11 | SOURDOUGH GAP

Round trip: 6 miles
Hiking time: 4 hours (day hike or backpack)
High point: 6400 feet
Elevation gain: 1100 feet in, 200 feet out

Hikable: July through October
Maps: Green Trails Mt. Rainier (No. 270), Bumping Lake (No. 271)
Information: Naches Ranger District, phone (509) 653-2205

A delightful bit of the Pacific Crest Trail (probably the easiest meadow walk in this entire book) through flower gardens and grassy fields to a high pass. A good overnight hike for beginners, except that camping space is limited and very crowded on weekends—and cars left overnight at the trailhead may be vandalized. Do the trip in early August when flowers are at climax.

Drive SR 410 east from Enumclaw or west from Yakima to the summit of Chinook Pass, 5432 feet. East 0.2 mile of Mount Rainier National Park's boundary, find the Pacific Crest trailhead parking lot.

Follow the Pacific Crest Trail northward, paralleling the highway, at times on cliffs almost directly above the road. At about 1½ miles the way rounds a ridge, leaves the highway, and starts a gentle climb to Sheep Lake, 2½ miles, 5700 feet—a great place to camp if it's not crowded. But it almost always is, and the meadows have been badly damaged. Find better camping on benches a few hundred feet away.

The moderate ascent continues through flowers, a final long switchback leading to Sourdough Gap, 3 miles, 6400 feet. (At about 500 feet below the

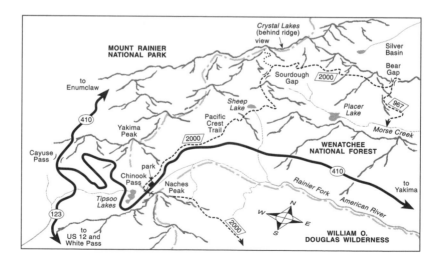

Sheep Lake with Chinook Pass in the distance

gap, the summit of Mt. Rainier can be seen briefly between two peaks to the west.)

Views from the gap are limited. For broader vistas, continue on the trail another ½ mile, descending a little to a small pass with looks down Morse Creek to Placer Lake, an artificial reservoir dammed up by miners years ago.

12 | UNION CREEK

Round trip: 8 miles
Hiking time: 4 hours (day hike or backpack)
High point: 4500 feet
Elevation gain: 1300 feet in, 400 feet out

Hikable: late June through October
Map: Green Trails Bumping Lake (No. 271)
Information: Naches Ranger District, phone (509) 653-2205

A pleasant valley walk through forests by a mountain stream, highlighted by superb falls. The woodland camps beside the waters are joyful spots to watch the dippers dip-dip-dip.

From Chinook Pass drive SR 410 east 9.2 miles. Between mileposts 78 and 79, just before the highway crosses Union Creek, turn left to the start of trail No. 956, elevation 3500 feet. (From Yakima drive SR 410 west about 10 miles from the Bumping River junction to Union Creek.)

In ½ mile look up Union Creek to a large waterfall. After the trail crosses the creek and commences switchbacks, two spurs drop to the falls, both worth investigating, the second the more exciting. The trail climbs 600 feet in the first mile, often steeply, and then goes up and down to another fine falls on North Fork Union Creek, crossed on a bridge at the falls' top. Downhill some and uphill more, the way ascends to 4500 feet and then drops to campsites at the creek level, 4 miles, 4250 feet.

The trail follows the creek closely almost ½ mile before beginning a long, steep uphill to Cement Basin trail No. 987 at 6½ miles and the Pacific Crest Trail at 7 miles, near Blue Bell Pass and remains of the old Blue Bell Mine.

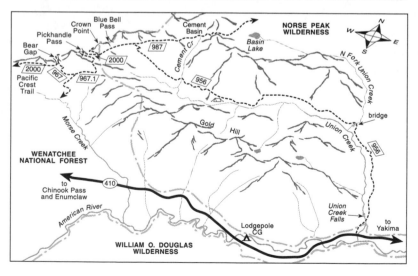

The Union Creek trail

13 | CROW LAKE WAY

Round trip: to Grassy Saddle 10 miles
Hiking time: 8 hours (day hike or backpack)
High point: 5900 feet
Elevation gain: 2700 feet in, 500 feet out

Hikable: early June to hunting season
Map: Green Trails Bumping Lake (No. 271)
Information: Naches Ranger District, phone (509) 653-2205

A steep trail, waterless except for that in canteens, climbs from valley forests to high meadows, compensating for the sweat and struggle by offering exciting views of the needlelike spires of Fifes Peaks and the meanders of the American River. The route can be continued past pretty little Grassy Saddle to the large, boggy meadows surrounding Crow Creek Lake, a favorite haunt of elk and deer, fun to watch in the summer but best shunned in the season when hunters outnumber huntees.

Drive SR 410 east of Chinook Pass some 12.5 miles (1.5 miles east of Pleasant Valley Campground) and between mileposts 81 and 82 find the trailhead on the left side of the road, elevation 3400 feet.

Crow Lake Way trail No. 953 enters Norse Peak Wilderness several hundred feet from the highway and commences a long, steady uphill haul, gaining 2200 feet in 3½ miles. Switchbacks climbing through forest to a hogback are followed (with glimpses of Fifes Peaks) by dramatic drop-offs overlooking American Ridge. The views grow step by step to a 5800-foot high point at 4 miles, a good turnaround for day-trippers.

The trail swings into Survey Creek drainage and at 4½ miles crosses a broad divide, 5900 feet, to Crow Creek drainage. West are rolling green meadows inviting a tour. At about 5 miles, 5600 feet, are Grassy Saddle, a small creek, and, half-hidden in trees, a tiny lake. Campsites nearby are great bases for explorations.

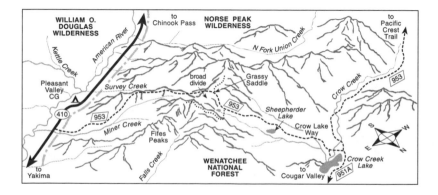

For the first, roam the basin at the head of Falls Creek. The unmarked trail starts at the far end of the lake, skirts a rockslide, and climbs to the basin edge at 6400 feet. The basin rim can be followed like the lip of a cup in a semicircle to cliffs of Fifes Peaks. Other explorations are the 6400-foot hill to the west and, longer, the 3 miles along Crow Lake Way, in green meadows, to Crow Creek Lake.

Fifes Peaks

14 | FIFES RIDGE

Round trip: to first viewpoint 6 miles
Hiking time: 8 hours (day hike or backpack)
High point: 5400 feet
Elevation gain: 1100 feet

Hikable: May through October
Map: Green Trails Bumping Lake (No. 271)
Information: Naches Ranger District, phone (509) 653-2205

Overlook the spectacular cliffs and pinnacles of Fifes Peaks. Gaze around the horizon to Rainier, Stuart, Adams, and Goat Rocks. Direct your eyes past the tips of your toes, down to silvery wanderings of the American River, where you came from. Lift your eyes to American Ridge, across the valley in the companion William O. Douglas Wilderness.

From Chinook Pass drive SR 410 east 13.5 miles, 2.6 miles beyond Pleasant Valley Campground, and between mileposts 82 and 83 find the trailhead parking area on the uphill side of the highway near Wash Creek, elevation 3320 feet. (From Yakima drive SR 410 west to 2.5 miles beyond the Bumping Lake junction.)

Fifes Ridge trail No. 954 climbs moderately along the west bank of Wash Creek about 1 mile, takes a deep breath, and tilts the angle to gain 1800 feet in the next 2 miles—fortunately, in forest shade. At 1½ miles Wash Creek is crossed and at 2 miles recrossed.

At 2¾ miles the trail tops Fifes Ridge at an unmarked junction. If your trip is an overnight backpack, go straight ahead, descending 300 feet and contouring to camps along Falls Creek. For the high views, turn right and

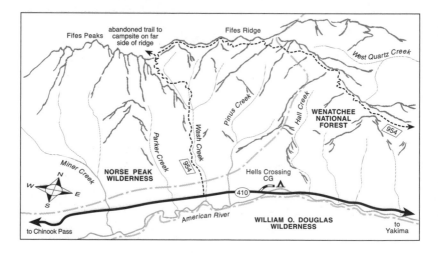

Fifes Ridge

continue up, at 3 miles gaining a 5400-foot bare knoll and first viewpoint of the dramatic south face of Fifes Peaks. Fill your eyes but continue 2 miles, up and down Fifes Ridge, to a 6315-foot knoll and the climax panoramas. While views don't get any better, there are a couple more miles of them and camping along the ridge.

Old maps show a trail completely around Fifes Peaks. Don't believe it. Whatever path may have existed earlier in the century has long since vanished.

15 MESATCHEE CREEK— COUGAR LAKES

Round trip: to American Ridge 11 miles
Hiking time: 7 hours (day hike)
High point: 5850 feet
Elevation gain: 1350 feet

Round trip: to Cougar Lakes 22 miles
Hiking time: allow 2 to 3 days
High point: 6000 feet
Elevation gain: 2900 feet in, 1400 feet out

Hikable: mid-July through September
Maps: USFS William O. Douglas Wilderness, Green Trails Bumping Lake (No. 271)

Information: Naches Ranger District, phone (509) 653-2205

The hiking distance to Cougar Lakes is longer by this approach than from the Bumping River (Hike 19). However, the ascent up the creek valley is a proper joy, and the ramble along American Ridge (Hike 16) is the most fun of the whole trip.

Drive SR 410 east from Chinook Pass 6.6 miles and near milepost 76 turn right and go 0.4 mile on road No.(1700)460 to Mesatchee Creek trail No. 969, elevation 3600 feet.

The first 1¼ level miles lie along an old road, perhaps partly the original miners' road to Morse Creek. Cross the American River on a log, enter William O. Douglas Wilderness, and in 1½ miles intersect Dewey Lake trail No. 968. Go left, staying on No. 969, which gets down to business, switchbacking upward. Mesatchee Creek now can be heard, the sound soon followed by sight of a waterfall and then, at last, the creek. At 2½ miles the way moderates and at 3¾ miles, 4900 feet, crosses the creek to an excellent camp.

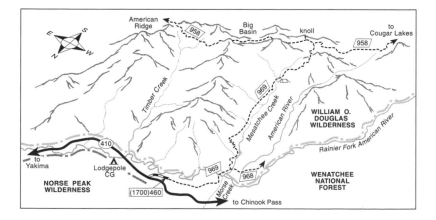

Mesatchee Creek Falls

The trail traverses a 1929 burn, now a miniaturized Christmas-tree forest of little subalpine fir and western larch. At 4½ miles cross a small stream (limited camping) and at 5½ miles join American Ridge trail No. 958, 5850 feet.

It is not compulsory to head for Cougar Lakes—the ridge itself is an excellent destination. Go east a few hundred yards to a knoll with views of Bumping Lake, Mt. Adams, the rugged summits of House Rock, Crag Mountain, Mt. Aix, Bismark Peak, the more rounded Nelson Ridge, and the volcanic cone of Tumac Mountain.

For Cougar Lakes turn west, losing 300 feet, switchbacking up 500 feet over a green meadow to a 6000-foot high point, and descending again, at 9½ miles intersecting Swamp Creek trail No. 970, 5000 feet. Keep straight ahead, shortly passing the American Lake trail, climbing to a 5400-foot high point and dropping to Cougar Lakes, 11 miles, 5015 feet.

16 | AMERICAN RIDGE

Round trip: from Goose Prairie to viewpoint 12 miles
Hiking time: 7 hours (day hike or backpack)
High point: 6310 feet
Elevation gain: 2950 feet
Hikable: June through November

Maps: USFS William O. Douglas Wilderness, Green Trails Bumping Lake (No 271), Old Scab Mountain (No. 272)

One-way trip: from Goose Prairie to Pacific Crest Trail 19 miles
Hiking time: allow 3 days
High point: 6946 feet
Elevation gain: 5500 feet
Hikable: late July through October

Information: Naches Ranger District, phone (509) 653-2205.

As the crow flies, American Ridge is 19 miles long, but with twists, turns, and switchbacks, the trail takes 27 miles to complete the traverse. The way is mostly rough and sometimes steep, but the meadowlands are

Nelson Ridge from American Ridge

Elk band

beautiful and lonesome. Flowers are in full bloom at the east end of the ridge about Memorial Day (the usual time that Chinook Pass opens) and at the west end in early August. The east end makes an excellent early season trip when other high trails are still snowed in. Look for avalanche and glacier lilies and a rare pink-and-purple flower called steer's head, because that's exactly what it looks like.

The entire ridge is worth hiking, but in June only the east end is free of snow, and by August this stretch is dry and hot. Therefore the recommendation is to hike from Goose Prairie to an intersection with the American Ridge trail and turn east (in June) or west (in August) along the crest.

Drive SR 410 east from Chinook Pass 19 miles (or west from Yakima) and turn right on the Bumping River road. In 0.6 mile is the eastern trailhead, signed "American Ridge trail No. 958"; if you plan a complete traverse of American Ridge, start here, elevation 2800 feet.

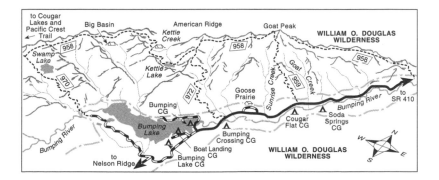

At 5.7 miles pass the Goat Creek trailhead (Hike 17), pass Goose Prairie, and 9.3 miles from SR 410 find Goose Prairie trail No. 972 on the right side of the road, elevation 3360 feet. Park in a small camp on the left.

The Goose Prairie trail is in woods all the way, climbing steadily but never steeply, beginning in fir and pine forest typical of the Cascades' east slopes and ascending into Alaska cedars, subalpine firs, and wind-bent pines. At 1½ miles the path crosses several small streams and ascends a series of nine switchbacks, at 2 miles recrossing the same streams. At 4¾ miles a spring runs most of the summer—possible camping here. At 5 miles the ridge top is attained and so is the intersection with American Ridge trail No. 958, elevation 6200 feet.

Day-hikers (any season) should follow the ridge west, climbing ½ mile to a point where the trail starts down into Kettle Creek drainage. Leave the trail and continue ½ mile more up the ridge to a 6310-foot knoll with fine views of Mt. Rainier, Mt. Aix, and miles of ridges north and south.

Early-season overnight hikers should turn east, following the ridge through forest and meadows to Goat Peak (Hike 17) at 11 miles, site of the former American Ridge Lookout, elevation 6473 feet, and a view of the spectacular cliffs of Fifes Peaks. If transportation has been arranged, a party can continue 7½ miles down to the Bumping River road and the previously mentioned American Ridge trailhead, completing a one-way trip of 18½ miles, an elevation gain of about 3600 feet.

Midsummer and fall overnight hikers should turn west, climbing near the top of the 6310-foot knoll and then descending to campsites at shallow Kettle Lake, 6 miles, 5650 feet. (Below the lake is a small spring.) The trail contours around the head of Kettle Creek, climbing to the ridge crest at 10 miles, 6946 feet, and dropping again to Big Basin at 11 miles, 6300 feet, a

Bumping Lake from Goat Peak

cirque with good campsites, bands of elk, and glorious scenery.

With some ups and more downs, the trail follows the ridge top from meadows back into subalpine forest at a low point of 5500 feet, then up to meadowland at 6000 feet and a campsite at 13½ miles. At 16½ miles is a junction with Swamp Lake trail No. 970, a popular route leading to Cougar Lakes in 1 mile and a steep way trail that joins the Pacific Crest Trail; No. 958 goes right, reaching American Lake at 18 miles and the Crest Trail at 19½ miles.

If transportation can be arranged, a one-way trip can be made via the Crest Trail to Chinook Pass, a total distance of 26½ miles, or via the Swamp Lake trail to Upper Bumping Road, a total of 21 miles.

17 | GOAT PEAK

Round trip: 10 miles
Hiking time: 6 hours (day hike)
High point: 6473 feet
Elevation gain: 3400 feet
Hikable: late June through October

Maps: USFS William O. Douglas Wilderness, Green Trails Bumping Lake (No. 271), Old Scab Mountain (No.272)
Information: Naches Ranger District, phone (509) 653-2205

A former lookout site on the highest summit of 17-mile-long American Ridge gives views down to the American River, north across the valley to impressive cliffs of Fifes Peaks, south over Bumping Reservoir to Aix and

Adams, and west over Chinook Pass to Rainier. Four trails converge near the top of Goat Peak. Two are reached from SR 410: trail No. 968B from Pleasant Valley Campground and very steep trail No. 968C from Hells Crossing Campground. The peak is a quick sidetrip for hikers on the American Ridge trail (Hike 16), but that's a journey of a number of days; trail No. 959, the easiest but not necessarily the shortest approach from the road, is described here. The trail is dry so carry water; for camping go early in summer when snowmelt rills are running.

Mountain daisy

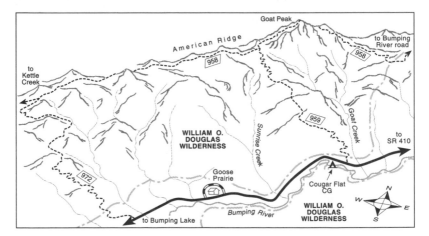

Mount Rainier from Goat Peak

Drive SR 410 east 19 miles from Chinook Pass (or west from Yakima), turn right on Bumping River road, and go 5.7 miles to Goat Creek trail No. 959, elevation 3100 feet.

The trail, never near the creek for which it is named, briskly climbs steep forest slopes in long and short switchbacks, in 4 strenuous miles intersecting American Ridge trail No. 958. A short distance from the ridge top the views begin.

Go north on the crest 1 mile to a short spur that climbs 300 feet to the summit, 6473 feet. With a second car the return to Bumping River road can be made by either trail No. 958 or No. 972 (Hike 16).

18 | COUGAR LAKES

Round trip: 12 miles
Hiking time: 8 hours (day hike or backpack)
High point: 5300 feet
Elevation gain: 1700 feet in, 300 feet out

Hikable: mid-July through October
Maps: USFS William O. Douglas Wilderness, Green Trails Bumping Lake (No. 271)
Information: Naches Ranger District, phone (509) 653-2205

Two alpine lakes, a big one and a little one, surrounded by generous flower fields in late July and early August, blueberries in early September, and fall colors in October. From ridges above, wide views of Mt. Rainier and the Cascade Crest country. Bumping River must be forded on this approach, not too difficult in the low water of midsummer and early fall, but when spring snows are melted and after the fall monsoons begin, start on either the Bumping Lake trail No. 971 on the north side of the lake, adding an extra 4 miles each way, or the Mesatchee Creek trail (Hike 15), perhaps a better alternative.

Drive SR 410 east from Chinook Pass 19 miles (or west from Yakima), turn right on the Bumping River road, and follow it 11 miles to the end of

Little Cougar Lake and House Rock

pavement at Bumping Lake, at which point the road becomes No. 1800. At 2.5 miles stay on road No. 1800 as it makes a sharp right; turn and go another 3.6 miles to the road-end and Swamp Lake trailhead No. 970, elevation 3600 feet.

The flat forest path leads in ½ mile to a ford of the broad and shallow Bumping River; the water is cold and the rocks sharp, so wear wool socks or tennis shoes—or boots without socks, which thus are kept dry for redonning. A bit farther is a junction with the Bumping Lake trail No. 971. Go straight ahead, climbing moderately and steadily, in woods and occasional openings, to the outlet of Swamp Lake, 3¾ miles, 4800 feet; campsites at and near the trail shelter.

The trail ascends several hundred feet in ¾ mile to an indistinct divide and a junction with the American Ridge trail No. 958 (Hike 16). Go left ¼ mile to another junction. The right-hand trail climbs past American Lake to the Pacific Crest Trail. Take the left trail, No. 958A, rounding a ridge spur at 5300 feet and dropping into the lake basin; at 6 miles, 5015 feet, is the isthmus between the Cougar Lakes.

To the right is Little Cougar Lake, at the foot of the basalt cliffs of House Rock. To the left is Big Cougar Lake. The shores offer numerous legal camps (100 feet from water), but rockfall may menace west-side sites.

For extended horizons, climb a steep and perhaps very muddy mile on the boulder-strewn path leading from the inlet of Big Cougar to the Pacific Crest Trail at 6000 feet. Look for mountain goats, marmots, and rock conies (pikas). For maximum scenery and gardens, wander north on the Pacific Crest Trail and in about 1½ miles turn right on the trail down to American Lake (No. 958) and back to Cougar Lakes, completing a 5-mile loop.

To preserve the vegetation, camp at least 100 feet from the lakeshores and—whenever possible—200 feet from the Pacific Crest Trail.

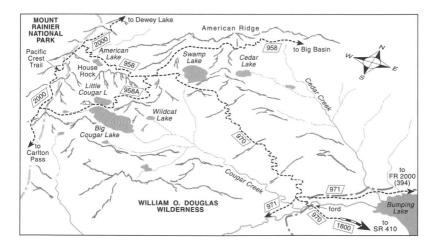

19 | BUMPING RIVER

Round trip: 16 miles

Hiking time: allow 2 days

High point: 4200 feet

Elevation gain: 500 feet, plus many ups and downs

Hikable: August through September

Maps: USFS William O. Douglas Wilderness, Green Trails Bumping Lake (No. 271)

Information: Naches Ranger District, phone (509) 653-2205

A very easy (except for one bit) forest trail ascends the meandering Bumping River, through a valley that is a year-round home of deer and a band of elk, often seen by quiet hikers, and finally rises to the river's source on the Cascade Crest. The walk is magnificent in late June and early July when wildflowers are blooming in the woods; however, that non-easy bit—the ford of the Bumping River—is then downright dangerous, so the recommendation is to wait for the snowmelt to run low.

Drive SR 410 east from Chinook Pass 19 miles (or west from Yakima), turn right on the Bumping River road, and follow it 11 miles to the end of pavement, at which point the road becomes road No. 1800. In another 2.5 miles stay on road No. 1800 as it makes a sharp right turn and drive 2.5 miles to Fish Lake Way, trail No. 971A, elevation 3800 feet.

The first 1¾ miles climb a bit and drop some 360 feet to the Bumping River. This much can be hiked in the season of forest flowering without difficulty. However, the horse ford never is absolutely a breeze for pedestrians and until a certain time in summer is a horror. If a person dislikes the look of it, he can bushwhack upstream to see if, by chance, a footlog is available. The final alternative is to drive back to Bumping Lake, drive across the dam to the end of road No. (1800)394, and hike Bumping Lake trail No. 971 the 4½ miles to the junction of trail No 971A.

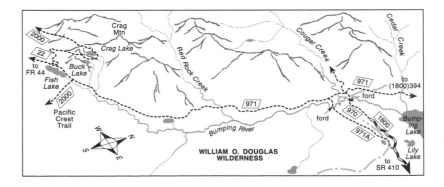

Fish Lake

Once across the river the trail is a pussycat. At 2 miles go left on Bump-ing Lake trail No. 971. At 4½ miles from the road cross Red Rock Creek on a log to a pair of nice camps. At 5½ miles pass a small nameless lake on the left. The Pacific Crest Trail is attained at 7¾ miles and, in a final ¼ mile, Fish Lake, 4200 feet, shallow and swampy, but with possible campsites.

Before starting home, be sure to sidetrip north on the Crest Trail, climb-ing 1200 feet to steep and luscious alpine meadows with broad views of volcanoes, active and dormant.

20 | NELSON RIDGE—MOUNT AIX

Round trip: to Mt. Aix 12 miles
Hiking time: 10 hours (day hike)
High point: 7766 feet
Elevation gain: 4200 feet
Hikable: mid-June to October

Maps: USFS William O. Douglas Wilderness, Green Trails Bumping Lake (No. 271)
Information: Naches Ranger District, phone (509) 653-2205

High gardens in the blue sky of the rainshadow, amid views east to the brown vastness of the heat-hazy Columbia Plateau, west to the shimmering white hugeness of Mt. Rainier, and south along the Cascade Crest to the Goat Rocks and Mt. Adams. Plus closer looks over meadows and forests of the William O. Douglas Wilderness. This is not a beginner's trail— the way is steep, hot, and dry. Carry plenty of liquid.

Because of their position on the east slope of the Cascades, and the mostly southwest exposures of the trail route, Nelson Ridge and Mt. Aix are free of snow weeks earlier than country a few miles distant. And if the tread at the hanging valley of Copper Creek is all white, as it may be through June, a short and simple detour up through trees leads back to clear ground. Actually, the maximum flower display comes when patches of snow still linger. The locals consider this trail—whether to the promontory at 4 miles, to Nelson Ridge at 5 miles, or to Mt. Aix at 6 miles—the best early-summer hike in the entire Bumping River area.

Drive SR 410 east from Chinook Pass 19 miles (or west from Yakima), turn right on the Bumping Lake road, and follow it 11 miles to the end of pavement, at which point it becomes road No. 1800. Continue 2.5 miles to a junction. Go straight ahead on road No. 1808 (shown on some maps as No. 395) another 1.5 miles. Just before the Copper Creek bridge, turn left

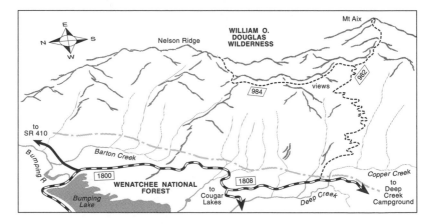

Looking south along Nelson Ridge

up a steep road signed "Mt. Aix Trail No. 982." In a few yards park, elevation 3600 feet.

The merciless trail attains highlands with minimum delay. For openers, the path ascends deep forest nearly to a branch of Copper Creek but never gets to the water, instead switchbacking up a steep hillside. (Across the Copper Creek valley, above Miners Ridge, Rainier appears, and grows with every step.) At 2¼ miles the trail swings into open subalpine forest at the lip of a hanging valley but again never gets to the water. Switchbacks now trend out from the valley into open forest distinguished by superb specimens of whitebark pine.

At 3½ miles are an all-summer spring and a small but cozy campsite excavated from the hillside, more than acceptable when the way beyond is under snow. At nearly 4 miles, 6400 feet, a grassy promontory with views of Rainier, Adams, and the Goat Rocks is a dandy campsite in early summer, after snowbanks have melted partly away, while snowmelt is still available. This far makes a satisfying destination for a day hike, especially when slopes above are snowy or the party is pooped.

From the promontory the trail traverses shrubby forest and scree southward and upward to the 7100-foot wide open, up-and-down crest of Nelson Ridge and a junction with the Nelson Ridge trail No. 984, crying out for rambling in either or both directions on trail or not, no matter. From Nelson Ridge the way contours and climb another 1 final rocky mile to the summit of 7766-foot Mt. Aix, onetime site of the first fire lookout in the district.

21 | TUMAC MOUNTAIN— TWIN SISTERS LAKES

Round trip: to Twin Sisters Lakes 4 miles
Hiking time: 2½ hours (day hike or backpack)
High point: 5100 feet
Elevation gain: 800 feet

Hikable: July through October
Maps: USFS William O. Douglas Wilderness, Green Trails Bumping Lake (No. 271), White Pass (No. 303)

Round trip: to Tumac Mountain 10½ miles
Hiking time: 5 hours (day hike or backpack)
High point: 6340 feet
Elevation gain: 2050 feet

Information: Naches Ranger District, phone (509) 653-2205

Hike through alpine meadows by myriad lakes and ponds to the most varied view of volcanism in the Washington Cascades. Tumac itself—postglacial, and probably younger than 10,000 years—is no simple cone but, rather, built of both cinders and lava. The summit presents a panorama of volcanism of other ages: Spiral Butte, another infant, at the south end of the lava plateau; youthful St. Helens, expected by geologists to continue to grow and violently blow again and again; bulky, mature, deeply dissected Rainier and Adams; and the old, old Goat Rocks, remnant of a once-mighty Adams-size volcano now reduced to mere roots. Do the climb in mid-July when upper slopes are covered with red and white heather plus a peppering of bright red paintbrush. The trip can be 1 day or overnight, camping at one of the lovely Twin Sisters Lakes.

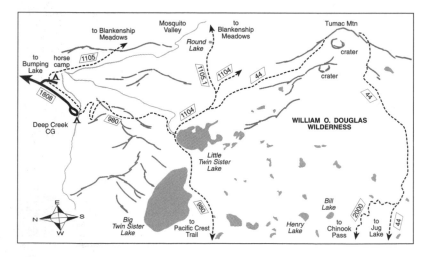

Drive SR 410 east from Chinook Pass 19 miles (or 30 miles from Naches), turn right on the Bumping River road, and follow it 11 miles to the end of pavement, at which point it becomes road No. 1800. Continue 2.5 miles to a junction. Go straight ahead on road No. 1808 (shown on some maps as No. 395) another 7 miles, passing the horse camp at 6.5 miles, to the road-end at Deep Creek Campground, elevation 4300 feet.

Find Twin Sisters trail No. 980 on the north side of the campground. The way gains 800 feet in 2 miles (all in woods) to the smaller of the Twin Sisters Lakes, 5100 feet. The "little" lake (only a comparison, both are quite large) has numerous bays and rocky points. To reach the "larger"

Beargrass and Mount Aix from Tumac Mountain

Twin Sisters Lake, follow trail No. 980 westward a scant ½ mile. Both lakes are outstandingly scenic and have beautiful campsites. They have many delightful sand beaches, the more so since the replenishment of May 18, 1980.

From "little" Twin Sister Lake, turn left on trail No. 1104 and cross the outlet stream. In ½ mile the trail turns left toward Blankenship Meadows. Keep straight ahead on Tumac Mountain trail No. 44, which aims at the peak. The way climbs steadily in open meadows 1 mile. Note how small trees are taking over the meadowland, a phenomenon that only recently has received attention. Are the trees just now growing after the Little Ice Age, or are they returning after catastrophic forest fires, insect invasion, or uncontrolled stock-grazing of years ago? Whatever the reason, meadows all over this portion of the Cascades are rapidly changing to forest, especially here and at Mt. Rainier.

The final mile is steep and the soft soil badly chewed up by horses, but the views get steadily better and become downright exciting on the 6340-foot summit, at the 1920s site of a fire lookout. The most striking is northeast, down to Blankenship Meadows and the three Blankenship Lakes (Hike 24). To the west are many tree-ringed lakes, a few of which can be seen, including Dumbbell Lake (Hike 25). Mt. Aix and neighbors dominate the northeast horizon. In other directions are the volcanoes.

To protect the vegetation, campers must use sites at least 100 feet from the lakeshores. At the "larger" Twin Sister, most of the permitted camps are on the south side, one on the north.

Incidentally, don't try to puzzle out an Indian source for "Tumac." Two "Macs," probably McAllister and McCall, grazed sheep in the area.

22 | RATTLESNAKE MEADOWS

Round trip: 20 miles
Hiking time: allow 2 to 3 days
High point: 3800 feet
Elevation gain: 600 feet, plus many ups and downs
Hikable: August and September

Maps: USFS William O. Douglas Wilderness, Green Trails Old Scab Mountain (No. 272)
Information: Naches Ranger District, phone (509) 653-2205

The William O. Douglas Wilderness has a split personality: The ocean-side west, misty-lush all the way up to the Pacific Crest, and the rainshadow east, where "desert" plants mingle with subalpine, the sun shines (almost) all the time, and (yes) there are (a few) rattlesnakes. The quintessence of the east is the Rattlesnake (Creek), and a person easily could spend a week ascending the stream to its source, exploring sidetrails to 7000-foot peaks. For a hiker the objections to the trail are two: The first

Rattlesnake Creek

2-odd miles are on a jeepers' "trail" (their exclusion must be arranged); even so, this stretch would be a delightful early-summer walk except that at 3 miles is the first of 14 fords, ruling out the trip for the average pedestrian until the low water of August. Put on smelly old tennis shoes at the fords and maybe they will be clean by the end of the series.

Drive SR 410 some 39 miles east of Chinook Pass, and between mileposts 108 and 109 go right on the second of the two Niles Roads; or, drive west from Naches about 12 miles and go left on the first Niles Road. In 1.4 miles (just before a cement bridge), turn left on road No. 1500. Stay on it, and beware of misleading sideroads. At 11 miles from the highway pass the dramatic Mt. Aix viewpoint and in exactly 1 more mile turn right on road No. (1500)620 and drive 0.7 mile to the road-end and trail No. 981, elevation 3100 feet.

Hike about ¼ mile and join a jeep track at the crossing of Three Creek. Go steeply up and then down. At 1 mile the way comes to Rattlesnake Creek, where camping would be bliss were it not for the jockeys on two, three, four, and six wheels.

A last mile of jeep road leads to the wilderness boundary (which must be extended down the valley) and the start of true, quiet trail. But then, shortly beyond, at 2¼ miles, is that fearsome first ford, knee-deep even in low water. By late August or so, however, the wading is stimulating yet not perilous. As for the rest of the fords, none is quite as menacing; some years they can be avoided by following game traces along the streambed.

At 4½ miles is a junction. The right fork is an arduous climb to Justice Douglas' favorite, Hindoo Valley, a trip on its own. To complete the Rattlesnake, however, go left on trail No. 1114, up and down steeply. At 7½ miles pass trail No. 1101, an alternate route from road No. 1500. At 9½ miles cross the Rattlesnake the fourteenth time near Strawberry Meadows. At 10 miles ramble into Rattlesnake Meadows, 3900 feet.

The trail continues 7 more miles to Indian Creek Meadows, well worth doing. If that is the destination, however, there are quicker routes (Hike 24).

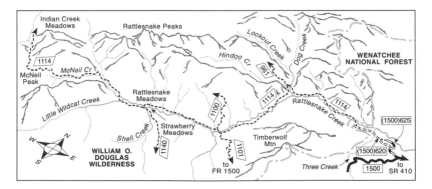

23 | FRYINGPAN LOOP

Loop trip: 15 miles
Hiking time: 8 hours (day hike or backpack)
High point: 5200 feet
Elevation gain: 2000 feet

Hikable: mid-July through October
Maps: USFS William O. Douglas Wilderness, Green Trails White Pass (No. 303)
Information: Packwood Ranger District, phone (360) 494-0600

The low-top forests of subalpine trees, intimate green meadows interspersed, the wildflowers and lakes and lakes, the birds and the bees and the chipmunks, are enough to fill a day. Overnight is better. The counterclockwise loop is recommended to avoid hauling a pack steeply to Jug Lake. Day-hikers can shorten the loop to 9½ miles.

Candidly, the trip has four problems: one natural, three human. *Mosquitoes:* Walk fast and bathe in repellent, or don't go until the frosts of September. *Signs:* Some junctions have no signs, and at some that do, the signs give only numbers. *Maps:* Some Forest Service maps do not show all the trails, and many trails are missing from the USGS maps, so a hiker must carry a weighty mass of paper. *Horses:* The cavalry rides this region in numbers approaching the squadrons of Phil Sheridan, Jeb Stuart, and the Cossacks, and where trails are wet, horses churn the soil to mud and a hiker may simply sink out of sight in black muck and nevermore be seen.

Drive US 12 east of Packwood. At the junction with SR 123 to Mt. Rainier, stay on US 12 another 1.3 miles and turn left on road No. 45. In 0.3 mile turn left on road No. 4510. At 4.5 miles from the highway turn right on the Soda Springs Campground road to its end in 5 miles, elevation 3200 feet.

At the far end of the campground set out on Cowlitz trail No. 44. In 2½ miles intersect Jug Lake trail No. 43. Go straight ahead, staying on No. 44, to a junction at 4 miles of trails No. 41, 44, and 45. For the shorter day hike,

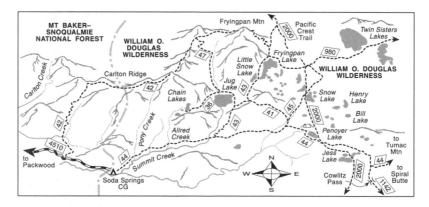

saving about 3 miles, take No. 45. Mosquito-undaunted backpackers proceed on No. 44 to Penoyer Lake, 5000 feet, 4¾ miles, and splendid camping (when the frost is in the huckleberries).

For the next stage of the loop, continue 1 mile on No. 44 to the Pacific Crest Trail, 5191 feet, 5¾ miles from the road. Turn north on the Crest Trail, gently up and down, passing numerous lakes and ponds and marshes, 2 miles to a junction on the left with trail No. 45, the shorter route. A short distance farther is a second junction. The right, trail No. 980, goes a near-level 1½ miles to Twin Sisters Lakes (Hike 21); the left, an abandoned trail, goes directly to Fryingpan Lake. Continue on the Crest Trail 1 more mile and turn left on Jug Lake trail No. 43.

In ½ mile pass Fryingpan Lake amid large meadows, continue on past long and narrow Little Snow Lake, and lose 400 feet to a ¼-mile spur path to ever-popular Jug Lake, 4416 feet, 2 miles from the Crest Trail.

Beyond the spur, No. 43 levels briefly and plunges 400 feet to the Cowlitz trail (No. 44), which returns the looper in 2 miles to the start, completing the 15 miles.

Jug Lake

24 | INDIAN CREEK— BLANKENSHIP LAKES

Round trip: to Blankenship Lakes 12 miles
Hiking time: 6 hours (day hike or backpack)
High point: 5200 feet
Elevation gain: 2000 feet in, 200 feet out

Hikable: mid-July through October
Maps: USFS William O. Douglas Wilderness, Green Trails White Pass (No. 303)
Information: Naches Ranger District, phone (509) 653-2205

Pocket meadows, vast grasslands, and mountain lakes combine in a beauty unique for the Cascades. The map calls the area "Mosquito Valley," and rightly so. Though the meadows are magnificent when bright green, the bugs are then numbered in the billions; the hike is much more enjoyable in late summer and fall.

To encourage hikers to advance their education by learning to know where they are, trails are signed only by their numbers and not their destinations. It's a thrifty system, excellent for upper-division students, but guaranteed to confuse and lose the freshmen lacking a Green Trails or Forest Service map.

Drive US 12 east from White Pass 8.3 miles. A few hundred feet before Indian Creek Campground, turn left on road No. 1308. Drive past summer homes and at a junction in 0.8 mile keep left, still on road No. 1308; at 2.8 miles from the highway is the parking lot by the trailhead signed "Indian Creek trail, No. 1105," elevation 3400 feet.

The first 2 miles of trail are an old

Indian Creek Falls

mining road, now closed because ¼ mile from the start it enters the William O. Douglas Wilderness. Just before the end of the road, find the start of true trail, which drops steeply 200 feet into a canyon, crosses Indian Creek, and climbs very steeply out of the canyon. At about 2½ miles listen for a waterfall to the right; step to the canyon edge to see the lovely falls. They are just a few feet off the path, but a couple of tries may be needed to find the only really good vantage.

The trail crosses Indian Creek again at about 3 miles, recrosses at 4 miles, and at 4½ miles enters the large (½-mile-long) Indian Creek Meadows. Good camping. Stay on trail No. 1105, passing trail No. 1148 to Pear and Apple Lakes. The tread is faint as it traverses the meadow and heads west but becomes distinct again beyond the grass. At 5 miles pass the other end of trail No. 1148, to Apple Lake, and at just under 6 miles take a short sidetrail to the first of the three Blankenship Lakes, 5200 feet, a fair spot for a basecamp. To preserve the vegetation, camp at least 100 feet from shores.

The first thing to do is explore the other two lakes, a stone's throw from each other below 6340-foot Tumac Mountain, a small volcano (Hike 21), which is perhaps the second thing to do.

Another ½ mile along trail No. 1105 are Blankenship Meadows—many little clearings and one huge expanse. The lushness of the meadow grass overpowers and excludes most flowers, but beargrass and lupine grow in the woods, and bog orchid and elephanthead in boggy spots. (Blankenship Meadows can also be reached by a 4-mile hike from road No. 1808 starting at the Deep Creek horse camp [Hike 21].)

A 3-mile side trip to Pear and Apple Lakes is mandatory, done as a one-way walk, first to shallow Apple Lake on trail No. 1148, then on the same trail to deep Pear Lake (more good camping), and returning to the main route on trail No. 1148.

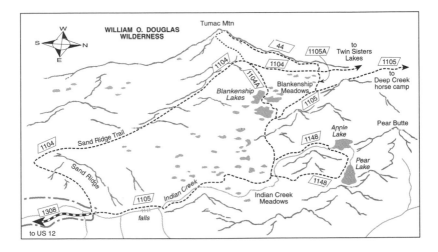

25 | SAND AND DUMBBELL LAKES

Round trip: to Sand Lake 6 miles
Hiking time: 4 hours (day hike)
High point: 5295 feet
Elevation gain: 900 feet
Hikable: mid-July through November

Maps: USFS William O. Douglas Wilderness, Green Trails White Pass (No. 303)
Information: Naches Ranger District, phone (509) 653-2205

Round trip: to Dumbbell Lake 13 miles
Hiking time: 7 hours (day hike or backpack)
High point: 5600 feet
Elevation gain: 1200 feet in, 500 feet out
Hikable: mid-July through November

If you like serene subalpine lakes, this is certainly the trail—there are dozens of them, large and small. If you like tall, photoworthy subalpine trees, this is the trail—there are thousands of lovely specimens. And if you like autumn walking through the bright red leaves of huckleberry bushes, this is the trail—there are miles of color. The hike along a delightful section of the Pacific Crest Trail can be done as a day trip to Sand Lake or an overnight to Dumbbell Lake. But don't expect solitude. Even on a rainy day these trails are busy.

Drive US 12 east from White Pass 0.7 mile, turn left into White Pass Campground, and continue about 0.25 mile to the trailhead near Leech Lake, elevation 4412 feet. This is Pacific Crest Trail No. 2000. The signing system gives trail numbers rather than destinations, confusing the authors—and saints preserve the tenderfeet. Any straying from the Crest (2000) Trail requires a Green Trails or Forest Service map to avoid getting hopelessly lost.

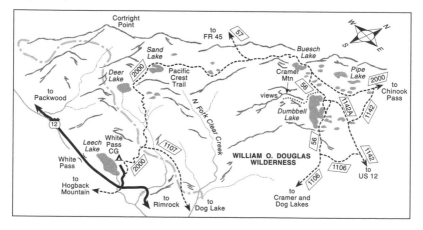

Fog blowing over Sand Lake

The trail starts in forest, climbing 800 feet in 2¾ miles to Deer Lake, 5206 feet, still in woods. At 3½ miles is Sand Lake, 5295 feet, numerous arms reaching into meadows and forest. Though the water is very clear, the shallow lake seems to have neither inlet nor outlet. Sand Lake is an excellent turnaround for day-hikers. (Many a person who long had wondered why the lakes hereabouts are so sandy understood after Mount St. Helens lost its head.)

Now the trail wanders past numerous small lakes, climbing to 5600 feet at 4 miles. Several places offer glimpses southward of Mt. Adams and the Goat Rocks; Spiral Butte can be seen through the trees to the east.

At about 5 miles the trail switches from the east side of the crest to the west and descends in forest, losing 500 feet in ¾ mile. Now and then Mt. Rainier can be partly viewed through trees; for a better look, walk off the trail 100 feet onto a low, rocky knoll located on the left side of the path soon after passing two small ponds.

At 6 miles the way skirts Buesch Lake, 5081 feet, and reaches a junction with trail No. 56. Follow this a scant ¼ mile to Dumbbell Lake, 5091 feet. Much of the lake is shallow; the rocky shoreline is very interesting. To appreciate its unusual shape, beat through a patch of brush and scramble to the bald summit of 5992-foot Cramer Mountain—and views much broader than merely the lake.

For an alternate return, continue on trail No. 56 to a junction with Cramer Lake trail No. 1106. Follow it down to within ½ mile of Dog Lake, turn west on Dark Meadow trail No. 1107, and finish with a last mile on the Crest Trail. The distance is about the same but most of the way is in forest.

To preserve vegetation, camp at least 100 feet from lakeshores and be gentle walking by. The Forest Service, with volunteer help, has revegetated some of the badly battered shores.

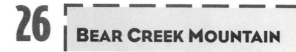

26 | BEAR CREEK MOUNTAIN

Round trip: 7 miles
Hiking time: 4 hours (day hike or
backpack)
High point: 7336 feet
Elevation gain: 1400 feet

Hikable: mid-July through mid-October
Maps: USFS Goat Rocks Wilderness,
Green Trails White Pass (No. 303)
Information: Naches Ranger District,
phone (509) 653-2205

Amble through flowers and lawns and subalpine trees on slopes of a high ridge. Then shift down and ascend lava rocks of the old Goat Rocks volcano to the summit of Bear Creek Mountain, 7335 feet, onetime site of a fire lookout with fabulous views up and down the Cascades.

When the St. Helens cannon went off, it was pointed right at this spot; a month later the surveyor climbed from Conrad Meadows in gray ash-sand that was inches thick atop the snow. Wind, water, and gravity are mingling the Event of 1980 with the many prior Events, but for years the hiker will find stretches of soft "beach."

The flowers are at their best in July and early August, which is nice timing, because the road to the trailhead usually is snowbound until early July; if visiting before then, approach from Conrad Meadows (Hike 27).

Drive US 12 some 9 miles east of White Pass and before reaching Rimrock Reservoir turn right on the paved road signed "Tieton Road" and "Clear Lake." At 3.2 miles cross North Fork Tieton River, and at 6.8 miles turn right on gravel road No. 1204; be careful to stick with this number. At about 11 miles is an unmarked junction; go right (uphill) on a nongravel and maybe rough and rude road. At 13 miles heave a sigh at the road-end and trailhead a few feet from the murky pond humorously called Section 3 "Lake," elevation 6000 feet.

Trail No. 1130 is a dream, traversing wildflowers and Christmas trees

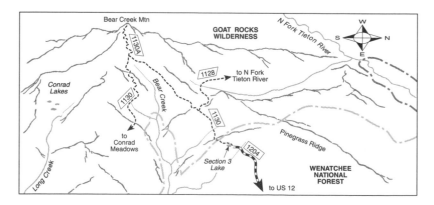

Trail to Bear Creek Mountain

and creeklets and many a lovely camp. At ½ mile is a junction with trail No. 1128 reputedly from the North Fork. At 2½ miles is a junction with the for-sure trail from Conrad Meadows. From here the way winds up through rocks and cold-snowy nooks and various arrays of flowers, passes still more possible camps, and at 3½ miles attains the summit, elevation 7336 feet. Look out to the great volcanoes of Rainier and Adams. Look around you, back down Pinegrass Ridge, across the valley to Darling Mountain and Klickton Divide, and to Devils Horns, Tieton, Old Snowy, and Gilbert, and realize you are smack in the middle of a volcano that was worn out and broken down millennia before St. Helens was so much as a puff of steam in a lowland swamp.

27 | SOUTH FORK TIETON HEADWATERS BASIN

Round trip: 15 miles
Hiking time: allow 3 days
High point: 5500 feet
Elevation gain: 1500 feet
Hikable: July through September

Maps: USFS Goat Rocks Wilderness, Green Trails White Pass (No. 303), Walupt Lake (No. 335)
Information: Naches Ranger District, phone (509) 653-2205

The glaciers on 8184-foot Gilbert Peak, highest of the Goat Rocks, gleam as white as the mountain goats often seen traversing the snows. Cliffs are brilliant: the black and gray and brown of Gilbert and Moon Mountain, the yellow and red of Tieton Peak, and the brick-red of Devils Horns. Warm

Headwater basin of the South Fork Tieton Creek

Lake usually is frozen until late summer. Cold Lake floats icebergs from the Conrad Glacier. All this and much more invites the offtrail explorer. Yet a hiker never need leave a broad and easy path to rejoice in grand views and sublime flowers, following the South Fork Tieton River from Conrad Meadows to its source and making a long, looping swing around the headwaters basin.

Drive US 12 east from White Pass or west from Yakima to just east of Hause Creek Campground and turn south on South Fork Tieton Road, heading westward along Rimrock Reservoir. At 4.5 miles turn left on road No. 1000, signed "Conrad Meadows," and drive 14 miles to a gate at the edge of private property. Park near here, elevation 3900 feet.

Dwarf lupine

South Fork Tieton trail No. 1120 passes the gate and fords Short Creek and Long Creek to a Y. Take the right, trail No. 1120, out into Conrad Meadows, the largest midmontane (subalpine) valley-bottom meadow in the Cascades. The summer after St. Helens blew, when ash kept out the cows, the vastness of lush, table-flat greenery glowed with googols of flowers. Except in the aftermath of major eruptions, however, this Paradise is closely cropped and reekingly flopped.

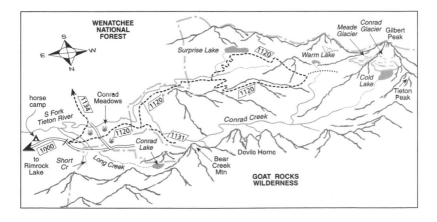

Shoulder of Gilbert Peak

Additionally, in the late 1970s the spindly forest of lodgepole pine edging the meadows was logged—not for big profit (the return was nickels and dimes) but as a hobby. The entirety of the valley starting at Short Creek must be added to the Goat Rocks Wilderness.

Beware of misleading cowpaths in the meadows and gypo cat roads in the wreckage of pine forest. At 1½ miles the trail crosses the gated logging road and resumes on a route built in the late 1980s. The new trail goes through forest beside the South Fork, and bridges Conrad Creek close above its confluence with the South Fork. The way sidehills the ridge separating the two streams and drops to the South Fork valley floor to rejoin the old trail, alternating between meadows and woods.

At about 4 miles, 4300 feet, is a junction, new in the late 1980s. Go right on a new path that begins an interminable series of switchbacks engineered for the heavy cavalry, climbing in deep forest nearly to the crest of the South Fork Conrad divide. At the 5300-foot top of a small, steep meadow (all-summer trickle-creek and delightful camping), the new trail (actually, the reconstruction of an ancient trail that had vanished) com-

mences a gloriously scenic contour around the head of the South Fork, through gardens, by snowmelt-season waterfalls, to an unmarked junction, 7½ miles, 5500 feet.

Meanwhile, at the second junction on the valley floor, the new trail leaves the old one (now abandoned), goes left to a new bridge over the South Fork, and switchbacks forest to Surprise Lake, 6 miles, 5255 feet. No backpacker of refined tastes ever would camp at this hole in the ground filled with fish and ringed by horses; continue upward a bit to the meadows and flowers and broad views and clean air of South Fork Camp. The trail proceeds onward around the basin head, at about 7½ miles reaching that unmarked junction at 5500 feet.

Junction? What appears to be a creek gully actually is the ruins of the old track ½ mile up to a 5600-foot saddle in the South Fork Conrad divide, the start of all-direction off-trail roaming.

The new horse loop gives equestrians a marvelous ride and a camp suitable for big beasts at Surprise Lake. The Forest Service must insist that horses stay strictly to the loop. The rangers claim that there is for horses, as there is for hikers, the possibility of "no-trace camping." It is to laugh! To see the havoc wreaked in these fragile meadows, it is to weep.

The Forest Service exhibited thoughtful sensitivity to the pleasures sought by horse-riders and the fragility of the upper meadows when it revived the ancient trail for a good day loop and conspicuously omitted the signing and reconstruction that would have attracted newcomers to the wonderland above the 5500-foot junction. It has even been urged by some who treasure the wonderland that we delete it from this book. However, this and companion guidebooks are published specifically to protect threatened lands—particularly by making them more friends and defenders.

We urge those new friends to pressure the Forest Service to take further action to preserve the upper parkland. For example, as in the Enchantment Lakes of the Alpine Lakes Wilderness, horses should be banned entirely from the country above the loop, and as population grows, dogs as well, and camping limited by permit. Additionally, the Forest Service and state Department of Natural Resources, manager of the Ahtanum Multiple-Use Area adjoining the national forest, should develop a joint program to restore the ancient trails along the Klickton Divide from the Goat Rocks to Darling Mountain and Blue Slide. The four-wheel and two-wheel motorized machines have driven horses and hikers off that entire ridge of meadows and scenic wonder—thus driving horsefolk into the wilderness to escape the racket.

28 | SHOE LAKE

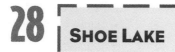

Round trip: 14 miles
Hiking time: 7 hours (day hike)
High point: 6600 feet
Elevation gain: 2200 feet in, 400 feet out

Hikable: mid-July through October
Maps: USFS Goat Rocks Wilderness, Green Trails White Pass (No. 303)
Information: Naches Ranger District, phone (509) 653-2205

Meadows and parklands along the Cascade Crest, grand views of the Goat Rocks and Mt. Adams, and a beautiful lake (absolutely fish-free, which is a mercy) in a green basin. All this on an easy day from the road.

Drive US 12 east from White Pass 0.7 mile to the Pacific Crest Trail parking lot and trailhead opposite White Pass Campground at Leech Lake, elevation 4400 feet.

Spring beauty

(Alternately, for a shorter hike, park at the White Pass ski area, 4400 feet, climb the ski hill 1½ miles, and take a short path that intersects the Pacific Crest Trail at a point 3 miles from the trailhead described above.)

From the official trailhead east of White Pass, the way traverses and switchbacks open forest, touching a ski run at one point, and at 3 miles, 5900 feet, intersects the ridge crest and the path from the ski area.

Now the trail ascends into gardens and scattered alpine trees on

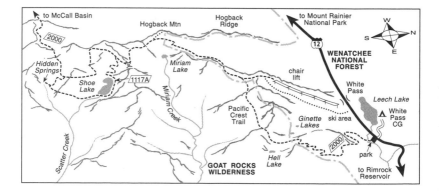

Shoe Lake

the slopes of Hogback Mountain and swings onto the west side of the crest, with a great view of Mt. Rainier. Attaining a 6400-foot saddle, the route contours steep, broad shale slopes on the east side of 6789-foot Hogback (an easy scramble from the trail to the summit) above the basin containing little Miriam Lake and climbs to a 6600-foot saddle, 6½ miles, in a spur ridge—commanding views of the Goat Rocks and Mt. Adams and the bright waters of Shoe Lake.

Take trail No. 1117A and drop 400 feet in ⅓ mile to the lake, 6200 feet, and fields of flowers. Due to damage by past overuse, camping has been banned in the entire basin to give meadows a chance to recover but is permitted ½ mile beyond the lake at Hidden Springs or below the lake. A scar of an old trail climbs the flower-covered hillside and appears to offer a delightful loop around the lake. However, as part of the healing process the route has been deliberately "put to bed" to make it unhikable.

29 | COWLITZ RIVER (CLEAR FORK)

Round trip: to Camp Hagon 13 miles
Hiking time: 8 hours (day hike or
backpack)
High point: 3700 feet
Elevation gain: 200 feet, plus many
ups and downs

Hikable: June through October
Maps: USFS Goat Rocks Wilderness,
Green Trails White Pass (No. 303)
Information: Packwood Ranger District,
phone (360) 494-0600

Trees are the star of this show, miles of Wilderness-preserved forest, cold creeks rattling and babbling in green shadows, and a little meadow-marshy lake thrown in for the bogs and reeds and polliwogs. It's a scene for leisurely ambling and relaxed camping, listening to the thrushes and watching the dippers.

Drive US 12 north from Packwood 4.4 miles and turn uphill 9 miles on road No. 46 to the end, elevation 3400 feet. (In the near future the last steep, rough ¾ mile of road will be abandoned and a new trail constructed beside the cascades of Little Lava Creek.)

Clear Fork trail No. 61 whets (dampens) the appetite with ¼ mile of jeep track through a clearcut before entering virgin forest of the Goat Rocks Wilderness. The way undulates 1¼ miles to Lily Lake, yellow pond lilies blooming in season and hordes of mosquitoes swarming, climbs a bit, and drops at 2 miles to Skeeter Shelter and a junction with trail No. 76 to Sand Lake; go straight ahead. The tread now deteriorates to ankle-tangling roots and the grade repeatedly rollercoasters. At 4 miles is the crossing of Coyote Creek where a massive December 1996 slide wiped out the campground. Cross Chimney Creek at 5 miles. At 6½ miles, where the trail fords Clear Fork, are fine campsites at Camp Hagon, 3600 feet.

Hikers wishing to continue can find safe logs spanning the river. An ascent of 1200 feet in 2½ miles leads to Tieton Pass and the Pacific Crest Trail.

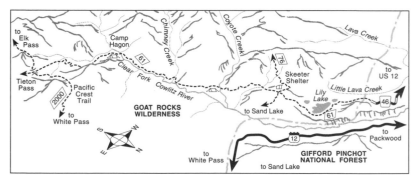

The Cowlitz River trail

30 LOST LAKE LOOKOUT (BLUFF LAKE TRAIL)

Round trip: 14 miles
Hiking time: 9 hours (day hike or backpack)
High point: 6359 feet
Elevation gain: 3400 feet

Hikable: mid-July through September
Maps: USFS Goat Rocks Wilderness, Green Trails Packwood (No. 302)
Information: Packwood Ranger Station, phone (360) 494-0600

Miles of meadows and generous views of the Cascade Crest reward a grueling climb to the highest peak within a 5-mile radius. Oddly, it has no official name. Should it be Coal Creek Mountain, for the long ridge it climaxes? The unofficial name apparently was given by workers who were staying at Lost Lake while building the fire lookout in the 1930s. (The building was removed by the Forest Service in the 1960s.) Backpackers beware: There is no water in the high meadows where you want to camp. You would do better to come via Lost Lake, which is up high and full of it (Hike 31).

Drive US 12 north 4.4 miles from Packwood and turn right on road No. 46. In 1.6 miles go right on road No. 4610. In another 1.5 miles, at an unmarked junction, go sharply left on road No. 4612. At 5.5 miles from the highway is Bluff Lake trail No. 65, elevation 3000 feet.

The trail enters the Wilderness and wastes no time gaining elevation. Fortunately, the beginning is well-shaded by virgin forest. At 1½ miles pass Bluff Lake, 3800 feet, the destination of most hikers. At 2 miles the way steepens and trees thin as the trail switchbacks upward. The agony is relieved by views of Mt. Rainier, so close the crevasses can be seen in the Nisqually Glacier. The trail reaches a ridge top, enters tall trees, and with more ups and a few downs traverses near the crest. At approximately 4 miles the forest becomes more alpine, and flowers outnumber trees as the

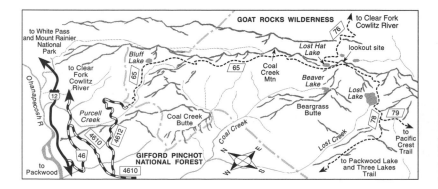

way sets out on a traverse of Coal Creek headwaters. Across the way is 5830-foot Beargrass Butte, a good measuring stick to tell how high you are. In the distance are Johnson Peak and the top of Mt. Adams.

At 6 miles, just level with Beargrass Butte, the path crosses a large, flat meadow; sidetrip the short way for a look down to the cold basin of Lost Hat Lake, frozen most of the year, and trail No. 76 from Clear Fork Cowlitz River. In the next mile the trail overtops Beargrass Butte as it switchbacks up flowers and heather to the plateau summit of the Lost Lake Lookout (mountain), 6359 feet, 7½ miles.

The trail continues on, descending steeply across a slippery scree slope, losing over 1000 feet in 1½ miles to Lost Lake, very tasty.

Unnamed peak, former site of the Lost Lake Lookout

31 | LOST LAKE—THREE PEAKS TRAIL

Round trip: 15 miles
Hiking time: 8 hours (day hike or backpack)
High point: 5165 feet
Elevation gain: 2100 feet in, 300 feet return

Hikable: July through October
Maps: USFS Goat Rocks Wilderness, Green Trails Packwood (No. 302)
Information: Packwood Ranger Station, phone (360) 494-0600

The little lake amid meadows of lupine and lilies and paintbrush and beargrass, ringed by clusters of pointy subalpine trees, is abundant satisfaction. For more flowers—and bigger views—there is the 6359-foot site of an old lookout.

Five trails converge on Lost Lake: Bluff Lake trail (Hike 30) and Coyote Ridge trail are the most scenic; trail No. 76 from Clear Fork gains and loses a lot of elevation; and trail No. 78 from Packwood Lake is crowded. If the meadows around Lost Lake are a hiker's main interest, these routes are less reasonable than Three Peaks trail. The drawback of this route is the first 2 miles are very difficult to follow, weaving in and out of clearcuts, sometimes on road and sometimes on trail; stop at the Packwood Ranger Station for detailed instructions.

Drive US 12 north of the Packwood Ranger Station 1.4 miles and go right on Lake Creek road 0.8 mile and then right on road No. 1266 another 6 miles to the end of the drivable road and the beginning of Three Peaks trail No. 69, elevation about 3100 feet.

The first 2 confusing miles are mostly steep. True trail, when it commences, moderates along the crest of the narrow ridge topped by the three

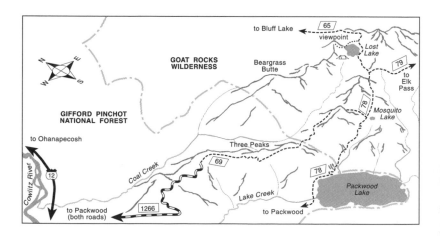

Above: *Mount Rainier from the Noble Knob trail (Hike 8);* left: *calypso, or fairy slipper*

Left: *Both white and red heather;* above: *Shoe Lake and the Goat Rocks (Hike 28);* below: *Mount Rainier from Mount Aix (Hike 20)*

Above: *Mount Rainier from near Shoe Lake (Hike 28);* left: *prince's pine along the Quartz Creek trail (Hike 51);* right: *Blue Lake and Mount Adams from the Craggy Peak trail (Hike 51)*

Clockwise from upper left: *Sunrise on Mount Adams from Sunrise Peak (Hike 49); Indian paintbrush; sego lilies on Juniper Ridge, where eastern and western Cascade flowers meet (Hike 48); beargrass on the side of Sunrise Peak (Hike 49)*

Above: *Mount Adams and Dark Meadow (Hike 52);* below: *a fawn hiding in the forest*

Johnson Peak from the Lost Lake trail

humps for which the trail was named. Occasional windows in the forest give views, including a glimpse of Packwood Lake. At 4 miles is a possible camp. At 5 miles enter the Goat Rocks Wilderness and at 6 miles join Packwood Lake trail No. 78 near Mosquito Lake, 4900 feet.

Go left, gently ascending a small meadow with a huge view of the giant bulk of Johnson Peak. At 7 miles pass Coyote trail No. 79, and at 7½ miles enter the flower carpet edging Lost Lake, 5165 feet. Nice camps.

If not yet satiated with pleasure, continue a steep 1000 feet in 1½ more miles up a cliff to the flower knoll, site of the old Lost Lake Lookout, 6359 feet, with panoramas of the Goat Rocks and other volcanoes.

32 | PACKWOOD LAKE

Round trip: 9 miles
Hiking time: 5 hours (day hike or backpack)
High point: 3200 feet
Elevation gain: 500 feet in, 300 feet out

Hikable: June through November
Maps: USFS Goat Rocks Wilderness, Green Trails Packwood (No. 302)
Information: Packwood Ranger Station, phone (360) 494-0600

A tree-ringed "lake" on the edge of the Goat Rocks Wilderness. From the outlet, look up to 7487-foot Johnson Peak. From the inlet, look back to Mt. Rainier. A wooded island punctuates the picturesque waters.

To the shame of our species, man has done his dirt on this scenic treasure. Washington Public Power Supply System was allowed to dam the outlet to gain a small amount of "peaking" power and in the name of flood control the Federal Power Commission permits the lake level to be lowered 7 feet from September 15 to May 1. Packwood Reservoir. Call it what they have made it.

Additionally, the trail was built so wide and flat and easy that every weekend it is overwhelmed by little walkers, old walkers, and horsemen, all jumbled together. Motorcycles, though forbidden on the trail, race up and down the adjoining pipeline road. Near the outlet are a few campsites—terribly overcrowded. Visit the lake on a weekday; otherwise, pause amid the crowds to enjoy the view, then hike onward.

From Packwood, next to the Packwood Ranger Station, drive east on road No. 1262, in 6 miles coming to a steel tower and, nearby, a large parking lot and the trailhead, elevation 2700 feet.

Trail No. 78 goes gently through big trees with occasional views over the Cowlitz valley toward Rainier. As the lake is neared, the snowy, craggy

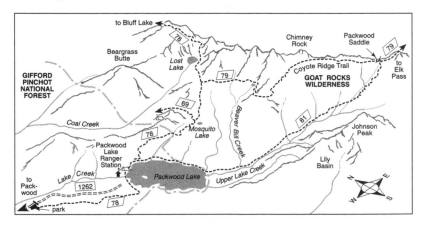

Goat Rocks, dominated by Johnson Peak, can be seen at the valley head. With ups and downs grossing 400 feet but netting only 167 feet, at 4½ miles the trail reaches Packwood Lake, 2867 feet. The campground is across the outlet. Besides the beginning hiker who may be getting his first taste of wilderness, this easy hike attracts people who cannot bear to leave home without their radios, beer, and gas lanterns. For quiet camping continue around the lakeshore to the inlet.

For an extra-special treat, do a 12½-mile loop from Packwood Lake. Hike to Lost Lake (Hike 31) and contour airy miles along 6700-foot Coyote Ridge on trail No. 79 to Packwood Saddle, 5520 feet. Return to Packwood Lake on Upper Lake trail No. 81. About half the distance is in steep meadows high above timberline. The way is little traveled, very peculiar considering the number of people at the lake and the superb scenery of the loop.

Packwood Lake and Johnson Peak

33 | LILY BASIN—HEART LAKE

Round trip: to viewpoint 8 miles
Hiking time: 5 hours (day hike)
High point: 5700 feet
Elevation gain: 1400 feet

Round trip: to Heart Lake 13 miles
Hiking time: 8 hours (backpack)
High point: 6100 feet
Elevation gain: 1700 feet in, 400 feet out

Hikable: late July through mid-October
Maps: USFS Goat Rocks Wilderness,
    Green Trails Packwood (No. 302)

Information: Packwood Ranger Station,
phone (360) 494-0600

Hike a forested ridge to a spectacular view of Packwood Lake and Mt. Rainier, then contour Lily Basin, a high cirque under Johnson Peak, and continue to Heart Lake and views of Mt. Adams. Logging roads to 4500 feet have ripped up the wildland and taken most of the work out of visiting this once-remote corner of the Goat Rocks.

Drive US 12 from the Packwood Ranger Station west toward Randle 1.6 miles, passing the Packwood Lumber Company, and opposite the Cascade Crest Motel turn left on Blakely Road, which becomes poorly maintained road No. 48. At 8.8 miles keep right at an unmarked junction. At 9.8 miles, at another junction, turn left and stay on No. 48 another 1.2 miles to the trailhead, on the right side of the road. Park on a wide shoulder just beyond, elevation about 4300 feet.

The trail is signed "Lily Basin Trail No. 86." Climbing through timber to an old burn, at ½ mile the way enters the Goat Rocks Wilderness and at 1½ miles reaches the crest of a wooded ridge, 4900 feet. The path follows ups and downs of the crest, more ups than downs, occasionally contouring around a bump. At 4 miles, 5700 feet, begin heather and flower meadows with a spectacular view of Packwood Lake and Rainier. At 4½ miles the

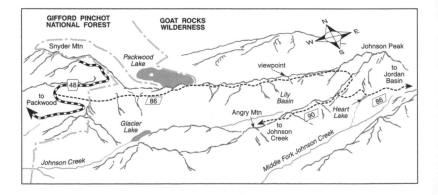

Packwood Lake and Mount Rainier from the Lily Basin trail

trail dips under cliffs and regains the ridge top, proceeding to its very end at the base of Johnson Peak.

Now a mile-long contour around the head of Lily Basin leads over several creeks (the first water of the trip) and a large rockslide. At 6 miles, 6100 feet, the path tops a ridge with a magnificent view of Mt. Adams. Joined here by the Angry Mountain trail, it contours a steep slope and drops to Heart Lake, 5700 feet, 6½ miles, the first logical campsite.

The trip can be extended—trail No. 86 continues to Jordan Basin, Goat Lake, and Snowgrass Flat (Hike 34).

34 | SNOWGRASS FLAT— GOAT RIDGE LOOP

Round trip: to Snowgrass Flat 8 miles
Hiking time: 5 hours (day hike or backpack)
High point: 5830 feet
Elevation gain: 1200 feet
Hikable: July through November

Loop trip: 13 miles
Hiking time: 8 hours (backpack)
High point: 6500 feet
Elevation gain: 1900 feet
Hikable: August through September

Maps: USFS Goat Rocks Wilderness, Green Trails Walupt Lake (No. 335), White Pass (No. 303), Packwood (No. 302), Blue Lake (No. 334)

Information: Packwood Ranger Station, phone (360) 494-0600

Before the 1980 eruption of Mount St. Helens, Snowgrass Flat was one of the most famous flower meadows in the Cascades. The heaviest ashfall in an alpine area except on St. Helens itself buried the west slope of the Goat Rocks. Few flowers bloomed that summer and much of the heather was killed. Since then, paintbrush and lupine have staged a spectacular show. It will be interesting to watch the meadows recover from the blast, as they have from many other blasts—and worse—over the centuries and millennia. Even if there were no flowers, the constant views along the Goat Ridge Loop of Adams, St. Helens, and, of course, the Goat Rocks

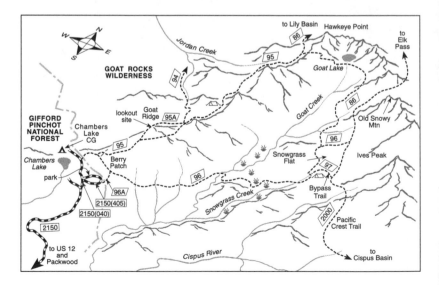

Snowgrass Flat

make the trip a glory. (*Note:* The loop is often snow-covered until some-time in August.)

Drive US 12 south from Packwood 2.5 miles and turn east on Johnson Creek road No. 21. At 15.7 miles, just past Hugo Lake, turn left on road No. 2150, signed "Chambers Lake," and at 18.5 miles turn right on road No. (2150)040, then right again on No. (2150)405 to the hikers' trailhead at Berry Patch, 21.5 miles from Packwood, elevation 4600 feet.

Set out in the woods on Snowgrass Flat trail No. 96A and soon join trail No. 96. At 1¾ miles cross Goat Creek, 4700 feet. Espe-cially in early summer, stop at the bridge to apply insect repellent, lots of it, because here the trail enters ¼ mile of swampy forest alive with the sound of mosquitoes.

At 2 miles the trail begins climb-ing from the valley bottom, leaving behind the swarms of bloodsuckers.

Western anemone

At 3½ miles intersect Bypass Trail; keep left and continue up, emerging occasionally from trees into meadow patches, and at 4 miles finally enter the open expanse of Snowgrass Flat, 5830 feet.

To give nature a chance to repair the damage by horses grazing and hooves and boots pounding, camping is no longer permitted in the Flat. However, sites can be found along Bypass Trail only minutes below and along the first mile of trail No. 86 to Goat Lake. Either makes a fine base for exploratory walks south 2 miles along the Pacific Crest Trail to Cispus Basin and north on the Crest Trail to its 7600-foot high point on the side of Old Snowy (Hike 35).

For the loop, follow trail No. 86 northward from Snowgrass Flat, contouring a steep hillside 3 miles to Goat Lake, 6400 feet, generally frozen until sometime in August. At 3½ miles reach the 6500-foot high point of the loop and a junction with Lily Basin—Heart Lake trail No. 86. From here the trail, now No. 95, contours the west side of Goat Ridge 2½ miles to a junction with Jordan Creek trail No. 94 and a few feet more to a choice of trails. The right fork climbs 300 feet and traverses the 6240-foot site of Goat Ridge Lookout, the views panoramic. The left fork contours below the lookout, rejoins the lookout trail in ½ mile, and descends sharply to the starting point at the Berry Patch trailhead.

Snow-covered Snowgrass Flat from near Goat Lake

35 | GOAT ROCKS CREST

One-way trip: 30 miles
Hiking time: allow 3 to 4 days
High point: 7600 feet
Elevation gain: 5300 feet
Hikable: July through September

Maps: USFS Goat Rocks Wilderness,
Green Trails White Pass (No. 303),
Walupt Lake (No. 335)
Information: Packwood Ranger Station,
phone (360) 494-0600

Walk a rock garden between heaven and earth on a narrow, 7000-foot ridge dividing Eastern and Western Washington. This spectacular section of the Pacific Crest Trail is popular with horse-riders, so try it in the first half of July, when the tread is free enough of snow for safe hiking but not yet passable to horses; tiny alpine flowers are then in bloom, too. The climax portion can be done as a round trip of about 8 miles from Snowgrass Flat (Hike 34), but the route is described here in its full length from White Pass to Walupt Lake.

Drive to White Pass, elevation 4400 feet, and hike 7 miles south on the Pacific Crest Trail to Shoe Lake (Hike 28).

From Shoe Lake the trail crosses a low ridge and drops 900 feet into forest, then ascends and contours to Tieton Pass, 12 miles, and a junction with the North Fork Tieton River trail. Going only slightly up and down, the way proceeds on or near the crest to a Y at 13½ miles. The left (the old Crest Trail) contours 1 mile to a dead end in McCall Basin, 5200 feet, with overused camps and much good off-trail exploring. The right, the new Crest Trail, steeply ascends 2 long miles to Elk Pass, 6600 feet. One great compensation for the energy output is that the entire way is in open country with views of Mt. Rainier and miles of meadowland on the slopes of Coyote Ridge to the west. The last campsites for 3½ miles are in flat meadows before the final drag to the pass, at which is a junction with the Coyote Ridge trail No. 79.

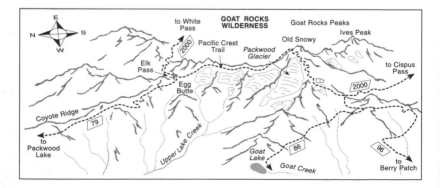

Mount Rainier and Coyote Ridge

Views broaden at the pass—down to Packwood Lake and across the immense depth of Lake Creek to rugged Johnson Peak. The trail follows the ridge several hundred feet higher and then descends. From here one senses the quality of the route ahead. The tread can be seen blasted out of cliffs, gouged in scree slopes; in some places the crest of the ridge has actually been leveled off to give walking room.

The next 2 miles are mostly above 7000 feet, the highest Washington stretch of the Crest Trail and also the most dangerous. Meeting a horse party is bad business, because the horses cannot be turned around and hikers thus must backtrack to a safe turnout. Snowstorms can be expected in any month. Two parties have lost members to hypothermia and there have been several narrow escapes. Don't attempt this section in poor weather.

The trail first contours and climbs to a 7100-foot point with a view of weirdly shaped towers and small glaciers on 8201-foot Gilbert Peak, highest in the Goat Rocks. There is also a fine view of Old Snowy, 7930 feet. Nooks and crannies hold the superb rock gardens, which are in full bloom during early July. The way now follows ups and downs of the narrow crest, sometimes on the exact top and other times swinging around small knobs. From a spot a little beyond the lowest portion, it is possible to avoid a climb by contouring across the Packwood Glacier and rejoining the trail at the saddle on the skyline. The glacier crossing is easy in July but by late August may involve hard ice; the best plan is to stay with the trail on its ascent to the highest elevation at 7600 feet on Old Snowy, a short sidetrip scramble to the 7930-foot summit.

The trail now descends into parkland, at 21 miles intersecting the Snowgrass Flat trail (Hike 34), then contouring into the splendor of Cispus Basin. The route continues in meadows to the Nannie Ridge trail at 24 miles, and via this trail 6 miles to Walupt Lake (Hike 37).

36 | COLEMAN WEEDPATCH

Round trip: 9 miles
Hiking time: 6 hours (day hike)
High point: 5712 feet
Elevation gain: 1900 feet
Hikable: early July through October

Maps: USFS Goat Rocks Wilderness,
    Green Trails Walupt Lake (No. 335)
Information: Packwood Ranger Station,
    phone (360) 494-0600

A grand viewpoint keeps the head turning around and around—from Adams to Rainier to the Goat Rocks—and down 1800 feet to tiny boats on Walupt Lake.

Drive toward Walupt Lake (Hike 37), but 3.2 miles from road No. 21—1.4 miles shy of the lake—find Coleman Weedpatch trail No. 121, elevation 3800 feet.

The first 1½ miles ascend gently in forest, gaining a mere 400 feet. The last 1½ miles tilt, gaining 1000 feet to intersect the Pacific Crest Trail at 5200 feet, 3 miles from the road. Here, continuous forest yields to a mosaic of subalpine tree clumps and little heather-blueberry meadows, the living foreground contrasting with tree-framed glimpses of glaciers of Mt. Adams just 11 miles distant.

Turn north on the Crest Trail an easy 1½ miles to a bluff at 5712 feet. This is the place to unpack the lunch and soak in the scenery and speculate whether or not the fishermen on Walupt Lake are having any luck. Moving about the bluff gives an unrestricted view of Adams.

But, you ask, where is the promised Weedpatch? It can be spotted, a green and squishy meadow-marsh, 500 feet below, and should you descend you'll find all the weeds are flowers. However, there is no trail and the flowers have been good along the way so you likely won't descend. From

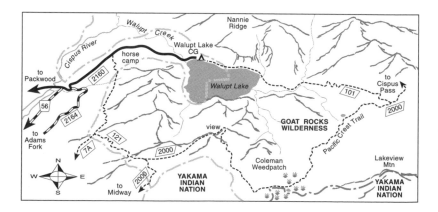

the bluff the Crest Trail is in forest, no views. For a gratifying loop, continue on 4 miles back into meadowland and go left on Walupt Lake Trail No. 101 for 4½ miles to Walupt Lake Campground and walk the road another 1½ miles back to the starting point.

Mount Adams and the Pacific Crest Trail

37 | NANNIE RIDGE — WALUPT CREEK LOOP

Round trip: to Nannie Peak 7 miles
Hiking time: 4½ hours (day hike)
High point: 6106 feet
Elevation gain: 2200 feet

Loop trip: 15½ miles
Hiking time: 9 hours (day hike or backpack)
High point: 5710 feet
Elevation gain: 2300 feet

Hikable: July through September
Maps: USFS Goat Rocks Wilderness, Green Trails Walupt Lake (No. 335)

Information: Packwood Ranger Station, phone (360) 494-0600

Climb a long ridge to views from an old lookout site on Nannie Ridge, to subalpine meadows, to a delightful alpine lake, and then descend to the starting point through more meadowlands to streams and ponds. The trip can be a 15½-mile loop or a 7-mile round trip to the lookout.

Drive US 12 south from Packwood 2.5 miles and turn east on Johnson Creek road No. 21. At 18.5 miles (from Packwood) turn left on road No. 2160 to Walupt Lake at 24 miles. Find the trailhead in the Walupt Lake Campground, elevation 3927 feet.

Start on trail No. 101 and in a few yards turn left on Nannie Ridge trail No. 98 and begin to climb. The first 1½ miles are in timber, passing two small streams. At about 2 miles the trees thin. The next mile is miserably rutted. At about 3 miles the way tops a 5600-foot ridge. On the very crest an unmarked, unmaintained, but quite decent trail climbs ½ mile to Nannie

Steller's jay

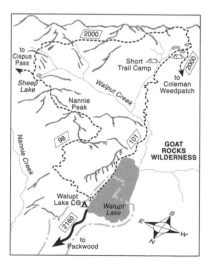

Mount Adams and Sheep Lake

Peak, 6106 feet, site of a former lookout. The summit ridge is ¼ mile of heather, grass, alpine trees, and rocks. Be sure to explore the full length; from the south end are views of Adams and St. Helens and from the north end views of Gilbert Peak and vast meadows.

Those who choose the loop now must lose a discouraging 300 feet as the main trail drops under cliffs. At 3½ miles is a pond (which may dry up in late summer) and another trail, also unmarked, switchbacking to the summit of Nannie Peak. A short bit beyond the pond look down on a small lake, about 500 feet below the trail—a tempting campsite. After passing below more cliffs of Nannie, the way regains the ridge and meadow country and follows ups and downs of the crest to a junction of the Pacific Crest Trail and lovely little Sheep Lake, 5¾ miles, 5710 feet, surrounded by grass and flowers, the camping ideal but limited. Walk around the shore for views of Adams and St. Helens.

To complete the loop, follow the Crest Trail southward, in ½ mile passing more campsites at the crossing of Walupt Creek. At 5 miles from Sheep Lake, near three little ponds, go right on Walupt Lake trail No. 101 a final 4¾ miles to the starting point.

38 ADAMS CREEK MEADOWS

Round trip: 8 miles
Hiking time: 6 hours (day hike or backpack)
High point: 6840 feet
Elevation gain: 2300 feet
Hikable: mid-July through mid-October

Maps: USFS Mt. Adams Wilderness, Green Trails Mount Adams West (No. 366), Blue Lake (No. 334)
Information: Mount Adams Ranger District, phone (509) 395-2501

A grand place it is to sit, gazing to the Goat Rocks, Rainier, and the truncated cone of St. Helens. Green forest ridges (motheaten by clearcuts) contrast with gray ridges that lay in the mainline 1980 blast. A superb place it is to roam, among raw moraines and blocky lava flows, by ponds and waterfalls, in fields of flowers under the Forgotten Giant, the Adams Glacier tumbling a vertical mile from the summit to the edge of the gardens. A great place, too, to watch sunsets and sunrises, seas of valley clouds, swirls of storm clouds arriving from the ocean, and, at night, the monstrous skyglow of Puget Sound City.

From the center of Randle drive the road signed "Mt. Adams" a scant 1 mile south to a split. Veer left on road No. 23, signed "Cispus Center, Mt. Adams, Trout Lake, Cispus Road."

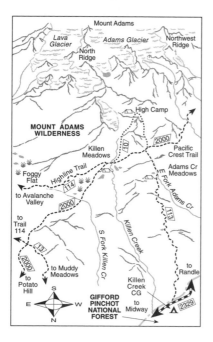

Stay on road No. 23, paved at first, then gravel, to 32 miles from Randle. Turn left on road No. 2329. In 2 miles pass the sideroad to Takhlakh Lake and at 6 miles (37.7 miles from Randle) find the parking area at the Killen Creek trailhead, elevation 4584 feet.

Killen Creek trail No. 113 (which never goes near Killen Creek) enters the Mount Adams Wilderness, ascends open pine forest brightly flowered by beargrass in early summer, and at 2½ miles, 5840 feet, opens out in a broad meadow brilliant early on with shooting star, avalanche lily, and marsh marigold, later with paintbrush and heather, cinquefoil and phlox. Here is the first water, East Fork Adams Creek, and nice camps.

The trail ascends lava-flow steps

to cross the Pacific Crest Trail, 3 miles, 6084 feet. Above the Crest Trail intersection is the uprise of a spur ridge that ultimately joins the North Cleaver, a customary route to the summit of Adams. Continue upward from the Crest Trail on High Camp trail No. 10 for 1 long mile from the Crest Trail to a broad meadow swale, 6840 feet, called High Camp, Mountaineers Camp, Adams Glacier Camp, take your pick. No campfires are allowed above the Crest Trail.

The one flaw of High Camp (other than the punishment it takes in storms, evidenced by the streamlined clumps of trees) is that on any fine summer weekend it's a mob scene. But there's no need to put up with crowding. Throughout the vast meadowlands of Adams Creek Meadows on one side of the spur and Killen Meadows on the other are innumerable private nooks. Visit High Camp—and go someplace else to camp. But please use an existing site rather than creating a new one.

Mount Adams from Adams Glacier Meadow

39 | AVALANCHE GLACIER VIEW

Round trip: 12 miles
Hiking time: 8 hours (day hike or backpack)
High point: 6100 feet
Elevation gain: 1900 feet
Hikable: July through October

Maps: USFS Mount Adams Wilderness, Green Trails Mount Adams West (No. 366)
Information: Mount Adams Ranger District, phone (509) 395-2501

Very nice, if small, meadows and broad vistas of hinterland forests chewed by chainsaw moths are rewarding. Made more so by a recent geologic event are the close-up views of the White Salmon Glacier and the Avalanche Glacier, scene of a 1997 massive landslide. The access to the devastation, and to other explorations high in the moraines, is quick and excellent. A sidetrip adds a fillip for those intrigued by the names of Madcat Meadow and Lookingglass Lake.

Drive from Trout Lake on the road signed "Mount Adams Recreation Area/Randle." In 1.2 miles turn left on road No. 23 ("Randle"), and at a sign that says it is 10 miles from Trout Lake turn right on road No. 8031. In 0.4 mile from road No. 23 go left on road No. (8031)070, pass unsigned sideroads, and beware of deep, axle-busting waterbars. At 3.1 miles from road No. 23 go right on road No. (8031070)120 and at 3.9 miles find Stagman Ridge trail No. 12, elevation 4193 feet.

The trail begins in a clearcut, enters virgin forests of Mount Adams Wilderness, and for some 1½ miles follows the long, gentle, wooded crest of Stagman Ridge, rounded on the west side, on the east an 800- to 1000-foot

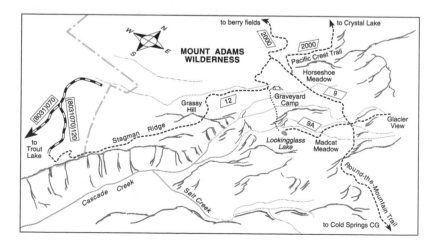

cliff to Cascade Creek. The way leaves the ridge and at about 3½ miles comes to an unmarked fork, 5600 feet. (An unmaintained easy-to-miss shortcut trail goes straight ahead a few feet to Graveyard Camp, 5700 feet. Drop a bit and contour east, still in timber with occasional windows on Adams, saving over a mile to Lookingglass Lake.)

The Stagman Ridge trail continues to its end at the Pacific Crest Trail, 4⅓ miles. Follow the Crest Trail upward ½ mile, then go right 1 mile on Round-the-Mountain Trail No. 9 to a high point of 6100 feet. For unobstructed views of the glaciers climb above the trail; a basecamp hereabouts would give time for wandering to the uppermost meadows and to moraine crests so high as to be veritable mountains in their own right.

For a look at tiny Lookingglass Lake, go right on trail No. 9A, dropping past Meadow Camp and Madcat Meadow a mile to the lake, 5580 feet. Very limited camping space.

Madcat Meadow and Mount Adams

Now, about the Avalanche Glacier. According to a newspaper report, "It's not there anymore." Well, that's an exaggeration. The nourishing snow will fall and the ice mass will grow again. But it surely staged a show August 30 and 31, 1997, tumbling ice and rock 3 miles down the slopes, the largest avalanche (except for those of St. Helens) on a Cascade volcano in a third of a century. It came by its name honestly. In 1921 it dumped off about 4 million cubic meters of ice, snow, and rock. Near the end of the eighteenth century it sent 15 million cubic meters, the Salt Creek lahar, down to the meadows and forests; about 6000 years ago it spewed some 66 million cubic meters into Trout Lake valley.

These lofty masses of volcanic rock weakened by hot acidic vapors are prone to this sort of thing when soaked by rain and snowmelt. On the other side of Adams, a series of avalanches, beginning October 20, 1997, dropped from the summit of The Castle, part of Battlement Ridge, rumbled down onto the Klickitat Glacier, and stirred chunks of ice to join the rock debris, after a run of 3 miles finally halting at 5600 feet, for a time damming Big Muddy Creek.

40 | MOUNT ADAMS HIGHLINE

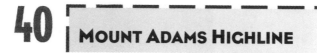

One-way trip: from Cold Springs to
Devils Gardens 24½ miles
Hiking time: allow 3 to 4 days
High point: 7760 feet
Elevation gain: approximately 4000 feet
Hikable: mid-July through September

Maps: USFS Mount Adams Wilderness,
Green Trails Mount Adams West (No.
366), Blue Lake (No. 334)
Information: Mount Adams Ranger
District, phone (509) 395-2501

The 34-mile timberline circuit of Mt. Adams is one of the greatest highland walks in the Cascades. Foregrounds of parkland and flowers and waterfalls rise to lava jumbles that look like yesterday's eruptions, and to a succession of glaciers tumbling from the 12,276-foot summit (including the Avalanche Glacier that tumbled itself to death in August 1997 and the Klickitat Glacier that made a similar big mess that October). By day, hikers look out to miles of forested ridges and three other massive volcanoes. By night they gaze to megalopolitan skyglows of Puget Sound City, Yakima, and Portland.

The Mazama Glacier and Hellroaring Canyon, the missing link of the Around-the-Mountain Trail

However, you can't hardly do it. The Great Gap, the 4½ miles between Avalanche Valley and Bird Creek Meadows, has a half-dozen major glacial torrents to cross, including the formidable Big Muddy. There never has been and never can be a trail—not without huge expenditures and a miles-long detour down the valley to where bridges could be built (and annually rebuilt).

Moreover, 8 miles of the circuit— including The Gap—lie in the Yakama Nation and require a permit from the tribal council in Toppenish, a process as complicated as crossing the Big Muddy. For reasons of safety

Marmot

and politics, we advise starting the journey not at Bird Creek Meadows, in Yakama land, but at Cold Springs, on South Climb trail No. 183.

From Trout Lake drive north on the road signed "Mt. Adams Recreation Area." At 1.3 miles pass road No. 23. At 2 miles go straight ahead on road No. 80, signed "South Climb," then left on road No. 8040 to Morrison Creek at 12 miles, then right again on No. (8040)500 to the road-end, elevation 5600 feet.

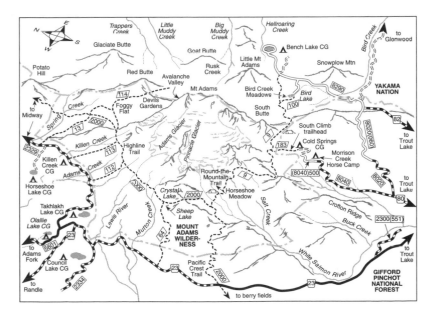

Hike 1 mile on trail No. 183 to
the Mount Adams Wilderness and
a bit more to Round-the-Mountain
Trail No. 9, elevation 6200 feet.

To the right the trail contours 2
miles to the reservation boundary
and legendary Bird Creek Meadows; the Yakamas allow day-use
here for a fee. An off-trail, meadow-
contouring mile leads to a viewpoint at 6512 feet, an overlook of
Hellroaring Valley, this end of the
Great Gap.

To the left the trail goes upsy-
downsy, mainly in subalpine forest
but with many meadow interludes
and many vistas and many tempting sidetrips up to moraines and
glaciers. Creeks and camps are frequent, though some of the glacial
torrents are muddy, requiring the
water to be settled in a pot; these
streams are not the Ganges and a
little clean glacier milk never hurt
anyone and adds body to the drink.
At 7¼ miles from the road-end, the
Pacific Crest Trail is joined at Horseshoe Meadow, 5900 feet; a promontory just beyond gives a four-
volcano vista, including the trip's last look at Hood.

Sidetrips continue to beckon as the Crest Trail proceeds north below
little Crystal Lake and above little Sheep Lake, beyond the awesome Mut-
ton Creek lava flow. At 14½ miles, 6100 feet, is the headwater creek of the
Lewis River; for a supreme basecamp, amble up the slope to meadowlands
and settle down for days of exploring country below the Pinnacle and
Adams Glaciers. At 16 miles, 6084 feet, is a junction with Killen Creek trail
No. 113 (Hike 38), 3 miles from the road; for hikers wishing to focus on
Avalanche Valley, this is the proper approach.

At 17 miles cross Killen Creek (near several campsites). In ¼ mile more
Round-the-Mountain Trail, now called Highline trail No. 114, departs to
the right from the Crest Trail, at 19½ miles entering the green of Foggy Flat,
6000 feet, a lovely meadow traversed by a clear brook. Now a stern uphill
commences, from forest to the lava chaos below the Lava Glacier—whose
meltwater torrents may be impossible to cross—and at last, at 24½ miles,
tops out in the vast tundra barrens of Devils Gardens, 7760 feet. What a

Mount Adams from near Foggy Flat

spot! Above are icefalls of the Lyman and Wilson Glaciers, below is the volcanic vent of Red Butte. The winds they do howl up here, and the clouds do roll; though giant cairns mark the route, to attempt this saddle in a storm is to court hypothermia. Here, too, is the reservation boundary.

With necessary permits one can proceed 2 miles to the lonely wonder and sublime campsites of Avalanche Valley. What's to say about this green vale where cold springs gush from lava tubes and meander through the flowers beneath cold walls of the Wilson and Rusk Glaciers, beetling crags of Battlement Ridge, Victory Ridge, The Spearhead, The Castle, and the hanging glaciers on Roosevelt Cliff? Well, when good little hikers finally check in their boots, this is where they go. Bad little hikers spend eternity in the 4½ miles of The Gap, staggering from moraine boulder to boulder, leaping Big Muddy and Hellroaring, trying to find the one and only semi-easy way over the Ridge of Wonders, never quite attaining Bird Creek Meadows at 34 miles to complete the circuit.

41 | MOUNT BELJICA, GOAT LAKE, AND GLACIER VIEW

Round trip: to Mount Beljica 4 miles
Hiking time: 5 hours (day hike)
High point: 5478 feet
Elevation gain: 1300 feet in, 600 feet out

Round trip: to Glacier View 6 miles
Hiking time: 3 hours (day hike or backpack)
High point: 5450 feet
Elevation gain: 1100 feet

Hikable: mid-July through October
Maps: USFS Glacier View and Tatoosh Wilderness; Green Trails Mount Rainier West (No. 269)

Information: Packwood Ranger Station, phone (360) 494-0600

Mount Rainier—The Mountain—perhaps must be climbed to the crater, or at least explored in the zone of glacier snouts and moraines and lava cleavers, to be fully *felt*. But it is best *seen* at something of a distance, where the neck doesn't get a crick from bending back. An old fire lookout and watch site provides a connoisseur's perspective, superior to any in the Paradise vicinity. On a summer day, when the hikers on trails of Mount Rainier National Park outnumber the flowers, dodge away to Glacier View Wilderness. If the meadows and lakes don't quite match those in the park, the relative solitude and unsurpassed view of The Mountain more than compensate. It is close enough to see crevasses in the mighty

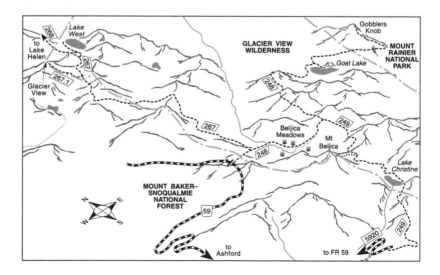

Gobblers Knob from near Mount Beljica

Tahoma Glacier, yet far enough away to appreciate the vertical length of the tumble from summit ice cap virtually to forests.

Drive SR 706 (the way to the park's Nisqually entrance) 3.8 miles past Ashford and turn left on Copper Creek road No. 59. At 3.4 miles from the highway, keep left at a junction. If Beljica is the destination, at 5 miles turn right on road No. 5920, and in 6.5 miles reach the Lake Christine trailhead, elevation 4400 feet. If Goat Lake or Glacier View is the destination, continue on road No. 59, at 7.6 miles from SR 706 cross a ridge with an outstanding view, and at 9 miles reach the Glacier View-Goat Lake trailhead, elevation 4400 feet.

Beljica trail No. 249 sternly ascends a ridge, then eases to traverse a very steep sidehill to Lake Christine, 1 mile, 4802 feet. Continue past the small, meadow-ringed lake and climb a scant ½ mile to an unmarked and easy-to-miss junction. Turn left on the unmaintained trail ½ mile to the summit of 5478-foot Mt. Beljica. Fill your eyes and exhaust your camera film. Anonymous until climbed in 1897 by members of the Mesler and LaWall families, the peak's name consists of the first letters of Burgon, Elizabeth,

Mountain phlox

Mount Rainier from the Glacier View Lookout site

Lucy, Jessie, Isabel, Clara, and Alex. Trail No. 249 continues, losing 600 feet to Beljica Meadows and Goat Lake trail No. 248.

From the Glacier View-Goat Lake trailhead, a short path climbs to intersect trail No. 267, which parallels the road a bit, often a stone's throw from clearcuts, and enters the Glacier View Wilderness at the start of a ridge extending northward.

A junction presents alternatives. The right fork, trail No. 248, goes ½ mile, losing 200 feet, crosses ½ mile of 4400-foot Beljica Meadows, a cozy marsh-meadow at the foot of Mt. Beljica, then goes right an up-and-down 1½ miles on trail No. 248 to forest-surrounded Goat Lake, and finally climbs to Gobblers Knob.

When trail No. 248 goes right, stay left on No. 267, signed "Glacier View," along the ridge, with some small dips and lots of ups, swinging around the forested slopes of one of its summits and around the meadowy-rocky-woodsy slopes of another, to a saddle 2½ miles from the road. Here the trail splits. The right fork drops 600 feet in a scant mile to tiny Lake West.

The left fork proceeds ⅓ mile along a splinter of andesite to the 5450-foot summit, once the site of the Glacier View Lookout. Get out your map to identify the monster ice streams of the Puyallup and Tahoma Glaciers, the rock cleavers of Sunset Ridge and Tokaloo Rock and Success Cleaver, and the meadows of Klapatche and St. Andrews Parks.

42 | TATOOSH RIDGE

Round trip: to viewpoint 6 miles
Hiking time: 4 hours (day hike)
High point: 5400 feet
Elevation gain: 2600 feet
Hikable: July through September

Maps: USFS Glacier View and Tatoosh
Wilderness, Green Trails Packwood
(No. 302)
Information: Packwood Ranger Station,
phone (360) 494-0600

This long ridge, with its flower meadows and beautiful lake, is in nature's plan an integral part of Mt. Rainier. However, in man's plan (a sorry and silly story, too involved to tell here) it is not in Mount Rainier National Park. (Not *yet*.) The ridge gives views not only of The Mountain but also the backside of the Tatoosh Range, whose peaks are familiar as seen from Paradise but, except for Pinnacle, are difficult to recognize from here. On the highest point is the site of the Tatoosh Lookout, made famous in the 1940s by Martha Hardy's bestselling book *Tatoosh*, the story of her years as a fire lookout. (The book was reprinted in the 1980s.) The wildland vista Martha Hardy celebrated was at long last (by the 1984 Washington Wilderness Act) accorded the protection of the Tatoosh Wilderness.

The trail extends the full length of the ridge, starting in the south near Packwood, climbing beside Hinkle Tinkle Creek, and ending in the north on a logging road near the park boundary. If transportation can be arranged, the entire distance can be done on one trip. It is described here from a north-end start because that way has 1000 feet less elevation gain.

From the Packwood Ranger Station at the north end of Packwood, drive west on Skate Creek road No. 52. In 0.5 mile cross the Cowlitz River. (To start on the south end of the ridge, cross the bridge and turn right on Cannon Road, which eventually becomes road No. 5290. Follow this upriver 9 miles. At an intersection turn right, continuing on road No. 5290 for 1.2 miles to the trailhead.) For the north end continue on Skate Creek road 4

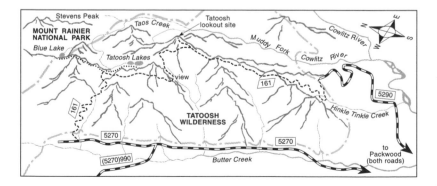

Tatoosh Lake and Mount Rainier

miles from the ranger station (sign says "3"), turn north on road No. 5270, drive 5.8 miles to a junction, and there continue ahead on No. 5270 for 1.5 miles to the trailhead, elevation 2800 feet.

Trail No. 161 sets off at a steep grade, gaining about 1800 feet, climbing from Douglas fir forest to Alaska cedar and mountain hemlock; slopes of alpine meadows begin, in season a mass of colorful blossoms. The trail makes three short switchbacks up a small stream, the only water on the main route—and in late summer, maybe none. At 2½ miles the way comes to the crest of the ridge and a junction. The unmaintained trail to the left goes to the park boundary and a possible dry campsite. Go right. Shortly beyond is a junction to Tatoosh Lakes. Proceed straight ahead but keep the junction in mind for later reference. Tread may be lost in lush greenery and soft pumice; just keep going and eventually gain a ridge shoulder, 5400 feet, and a spectacular view of Mt. Adams, St. Helens, and the Cowlitz valley. To the north Mt. Rainier looks down like a benevolent old lady, very fat.

After soaking up views, there are things to do, more to see. For one, continue on the trail 1½ miles and find the mile-long spur trail climbing to the Tatoosh Lookout site at 6310 feet, highest point on the ridge outside the park. Second, retrace steps to that junction and follow a bootmade path to Tatoosh Lakes, a small one and a large one, on the east side of Tatoosh Ridge. From the aforementioned junction, a trail of sorts switchbacks up, crosses a 5500-foot saddle, and drops to the lakes near the outlet. But the trail can be hard to follow and cliffs make crosscountry tricky. No camping allowed near the lakes.

43 | HIGH ROCK

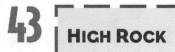

Round trip: 3 miles
Hiking time: 2 hours (day hike)
High point: 5658 feet
Elevation gain: 1400 feet

Hikable: June through October
Map: Green Trails Randle (No. 301)
Information: Packwood Ranger District,
    phone (360) 494-0600

A short but steady climb to a lookout with a breathtaking view of Mt. Rainier. The cabin sits on a point of rock that juts out in the sky like the prow of a ship. Once this was a challenging hike, but now, in common with most Forest Service trails south of Rainier, it is barely an afternoon walk— or better, a morning walk, when the lighting is more striking. A good trip for small children, but hold their hands tight on the last bit to the summit. A note of caution: The Forest Service irrationally allows mountain bicycles on the steep, hazardous trail. Should you see cars at the trailhead with empty bike racks, it would be wise to go elsewhere to avoid the risk of the tiresome procedures inevitable in a police investigation.

Drive SR 706 east from Ashford a long 2 miles and turn right on Kernahan Road, signed "Big Creek Campground-Packwood." From this junction drive about 1 mile to a steel bridge crossing the Nisqually River. At 1.5 miles is a junction. The easiest way to the trailhead is to go right on road No. 85 about 6 miles, then 5 miles more on No. 8440 to Towhead Gap, elevation 4301 feet. (In 1998 this road was damaged and may not be re-opened until 1999; check with rangers.) If road No. 85 is closed, or sidetrips

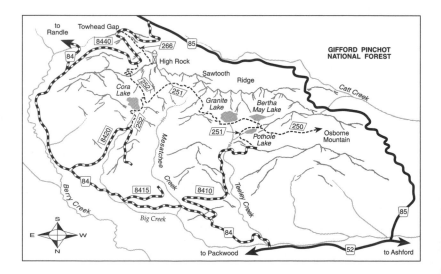

to Cora, Bertha May, or Granite Lakes are contemplated, go left on road No. 52, signed "Packwood." At 4.3 miles turn right on road No. 84, cross Big Creek, and start climbing. At 11.3 miles keep right on road No. 8440 and at 14 miles reach Towhead Gap.

Trail No. 266 starts on the north side of the gap, ascends a clearcut a few hundred feet, and enters forest. The first mile is mostly through trees, gradually thinning. The final ½ mile to the lookout is fairly open, with views to Mt. Adams and Mount St. Helens.

Climaxing all is the eye-popping panorama of Mt. Rainier. Nowhere in the national park does one get this magnificent sweep from Columbia Crest down to the Nisqually Entrance. Observe the outwash from the catastrophic 1947 flood of Kautz Creek. Note hanging ice on the Kautz Glacier. Pick out peaks of the Tatoosh Range and Mt. Wow. See the green gardens of Indian Henry's Hunting Ground. When your eye shifts from The Mountain to your feet, hang on! Cora Lake is 1750 feet below, almost in spitting distance.

Air view of the High Rock Lookout

At midday Rainier is a big, flat curtain of white. The best views are when the sun slants over the face of the mountain, the contrast of bright light and dark shadows delineating every ridge and valley, even the trees in the parklands and crevasses on glaciers. Therefore plan to be at the lookout before 10:00 in the morning or after 4:00 in the afternoon.

To while away the heat and flat light of midday, before or after the summit climb, visit lovely Cora Lake, reached by a ½-mile trail from road No. 8420, a spur from Big Creek road No. 84, or Bertha May and Granite Lakes, reached by a 1-mile trail from Teeley Creek road No. 8410. A very nice 3-mile trail runs along under Sawtooth Ridge, connecting the lakes, but logging roads are so close, and trail bikes so numerous, that the lakes are mobbed by noisemakers. A dirty shame.

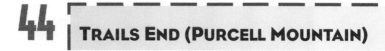

44 | TRAILS END (PURCELL MOUNTAIN)

Round trip: via Lookout Trail 7 miles
Hiking time: 5 hours (day hike)
High point: 5442 feet
Elevation gain: 2600 feet

Hikable: mid-June through November
Map: Green Trails Randle (No. 301)
Information: Packwood Ranger District,
phone (360) 494-0600

A basin of subalpine trees and a large flower-covered meadow, topped by 5442-foot Purcell Mountain, site of the Trails End Lookout. Nothing remains except melted glass, nails, a few bits of rusty iron, a heliport, and a panorama of the South Cascades.

A few years back the Forest Service built a logging road to the 3500-foot level. Hikers complained but were ignored—or were they? Since then roading has been partly replaced by helicopter logging, poor solace for ancient forest but a small mercy for the trail system.

The 16-mile-long Purcell Mountain trail, traversing the entire length of the mountain, starts on private land in someone's backyard and until the trailhead can be moved the trail is closed. However, the Lookout trail, which climbs directly to the summit, is maintained. Snow remains on the longer route until early July, but the direct route can be hiked in mid-June with only a few snowpatches up high.

For the Lookout trail, from Randle drive US 12 eastward 5.9 miles, turn left on an unmarked paved road (the old highway), and in 1 mile turn left on road No. 63. In a mile look over the side of the Davis Creek bridge into a spectacular canyon. At 4.5 miles from the paved road (11.5 miles from Randle) bear left on road No. 6310, in 0.5 mile cross Davis Creek, and a short distance farther find the trailhead, elevation 2800 feet.

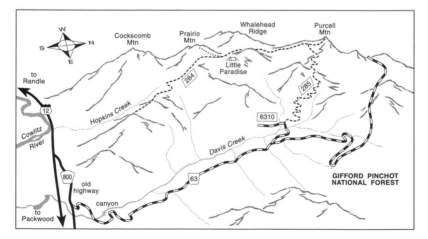

Pre-1980 photo of Mount St. Helens from the Purcell Mountain trail

The route starts on an abandoned road. In about ⅓ mile the trail doubles back to the right, off the road, and zigzags upward through a 1980s clearing, then forest. At 2½ miles the way reaches meadows. At 3 miles, 5000 feet, just before the junction with the Purcell Mountain trail, is a possible camp. A final ½ mile climbs to the summit panoramas.

What to do now? One choice is to follow the Purcell Mountain trail down past the Lookout trail junction to Little Paradise, 4800 feet, a small meadow surrounded by tall trees; water and camps can be found a bit below the meadow. From here wander the short distance up 5065-foot Prairie Mountain; all but the summit and steep south side are wooded. Farther down the Purcell Mountain trail, at 4400 feet, under Cockscomb Mountain, are springs and open meadows.

45 | KLICKITAT TRAIL

One-way trip: 21 miles
Hiking time: allow 2 to 3 days
High point: 5656 feet
Elevation gain: 4000 feet
Hikable: mid-July through October

Maps: Green Trails McCoy Peak (No. 333), Blue Lake (No. 334)
Information: Packwood Ranger District, phone (360) 494-0600

Tradition says this is on the route taken by the Klickitats on trading excursions from their homes east of the Cascades, climbing from the Klickitat River to Cispus Pass (Hike 36), then descending to Puget Sound country. But the European has come, and though the trail is lonesome, seldom is it beyond sight or sound of logging. The way is paralleled by logging roads, hacked by several clearcuts, and intersected once by a road at Jackpot Lake.

The trail is here described the whole length, starting at the west end, but it makes more practical sense to start on road No. 20 near Jackpot Lake and explore westward to Cispus Butte, Castle Butte, and Pompey Peak, then eastward to Horseshoe Point and St. Michael Lake. Following are descriptions of three starting points:

To reach the east terminus, drive Johnson Creek road No. 21 to the junction just beyond Hugo Lake (Hike 34), go right another 0.8 mile, and then right on road No. 22 and drive 2 miles to the Klickitat trailhead, elevation 4400 feet.

To reach the west terminus, drive 6 miles from Randle on road No. 23, then take a left and go 8.5 miles on road No. 55, then take a right and go 1.5 miles on road No. 5508, then go left on No. (5508)023 a few feet and right 1.7 miles on road No. (5508)024 to the trailhead, elevation 4300 feet.

For Jackpot Lake, drive US 12 east 12.7 miles from Randle (3.7 miles

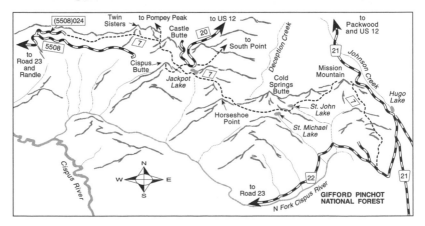

Mount Rainier from Cispus Butte

west of Packwood) and turn uphill on Smith Creek road No. 20 and go a little over 12 miles to where it intersects the east segment of the Klickitat Trail. In 0.2 more mile pass Jackpot Lake and go another 0.2 mile to the far side of a large clearcut and the unmarked west segment of the trail, elevation 4600 feet. A map is needed to figure out where road meets trail. There are some old mile markers along the route, but no indication where the counting starts.

From the west terminus, trail No. 7 climbs 500 feet, follows the ridge top, and in a bit more than 1 mile drops steeply to a clearcut. The way then passes under 5805-foot Twin Sisters and at about 4 miles, 5200 feet, comes to a junction with the Pompey Peak trail.

The next 1½ miles are glorious alpine meadows and forest groves, Castle Butte towering above. At 5½ miles, an absolute must is the ½-mile sidetrip to 5656-foot Cispus Butte, site of an old lookout surveying Rainier, Adams, St. Helens, Hood, and ridge upon ridge of the gigantic "tree farm" where nevermore again will trees grow to the giant size the Klickitats knew.

The trail descends into timber, dropping almost 1000 feet to the large clearcut and road No. 20 at Jackpot Lake, 6 miles, 4500 feet, and another clearcut. A traverse near the top of a 5500-foot butte has more views. At 8 miles the route drops to headwaters of Deception Creek, crosses clearcuts, and at 9 miles contours under Horseshoe Point and gradually ascends to a saddle below 5733-foot Cold Springs Butte. The tread here is particularly faint. The short sidetrip to the summit of the butte is well worth the effort.

The path drops through forest to campsites at St. Michael Lake, 10½ miles, 4700 feet, contours past tiny St. John Lake, climbs nearly over the top of 5683-foot Mission Mountain, and goes downward in trees, and at 17 miles reaching the east terminus on road No. 22.

46 | BLUE LAKE HIKERS TRAIL

Round trip: 5 miles
Hiking time: 4 hours (day hike or backpack)
High point: 4058 feet
Elevation gain: 1800 feet in, 100 feet out

Hikable: late June through October
Map: Randle Ranger District
Information: Randle Ranger District, phone (360) 497-1100

Columnar basalt above the Blue Lake Hikers Trail

Experienced hikers who can handle the built-in hazards will find a delightful stream between a steep forested hill on one side and an impressive cliff of columnar basalt on the other, the trail climaxing at mile-long forest-ringed Blue Lake, an ideal destination for Boy Scout troops, church campouts, gimpy old fishermen, and tremulous novices.

However, the Forest Service has in its infinite wisdom converted the whole Blue Lake trail system to motorcycles and ATVs (all-terrain vehicle). Seeking to appease irate hikers, in 1993 it built the Blue Lake Hikers Trail. In further multiple-use-confused wisdom, it designed

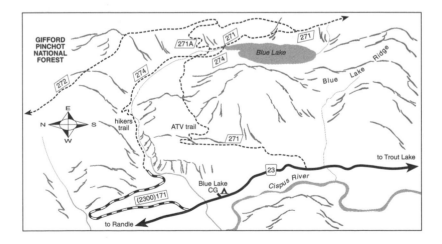

Blue Lake

hazards into the trail, presumably in a misguided effort to deter trespassing wheels, but effectively eliminating the majority of hikers the trail was meant for, who must hike the dusty, noisy, smelly motorcycle / ATV "trail" (road).

From Randle (Hike 47) drive road No. 23 some 15 miles and go left on steep, rough, narrow road No. (2300)171 another 3.3 miles to the road-end and trail No. 274.

After climbing 200 feet in the first ⅓ mile, the trail skinnies along a narrow ledge across a near-vertical cliff and ascends a stone staircase where a mishap could be tragic. Safely beyond, the trail then descends to Blue Lake Creek and a fascinating 250-foot wall of columnar basalt. At about 2 miles the way levels, crosses the four-wheel-drive ATV "trail" No. 271 (road, motorway, but not a trail) and reaches lakeshore, campsites, and a delightful sandy beach, 4058 feet, supposedly motorfree (tracks show otherwise).

47 | TONGUE MOUNTAIN

Round trip: 3½ miles
Hiking time: 3 hours (day hike)
High point: 4750 feet
Elevation gain: 1300 feet

Hikable: late June through September
Map: Green Trails McCoy Peak (No. 333)
Information: Randle Ranger District,
phone (360) 497-1100

The Cispus River twists and turns through the forest 3300 feet beneath your toes, Rainier and Adams loom big and icy in the distance, the perfumes of the flowers overpower the reek of your sardine sandwiches. The rocky jut of Tongue Mountain from the north end of Juniper Ridge once was the site of a fire lookout, sufficient recommendation. Juniper Peak has bigger views and more wildflowers but this hike looks straight down on the Cispus River and takes about half the time and energy, a real bargain.

Turn south in Randle, cross the Cowlitz River, and drive 1 mile. Turn left on road No. 23 and in 9 miles (from Randle) turn right on road No. 28. At 10 miles leave pavement and go straight ahead on road No. 29. In 14 miles turn left on road No. 2904 and at 18 miles from Randle find trail No. 294 on the north side of the road, elevation about 3600 feet.

Set out in young forest dating from a forest fire in the early 1930s. Gain 500 feet in an easy up-and-down mile to a junction. The straight-ahead fork drops 5 miles to McCoy Creek (Hike 48); go right, uphill, on trail No. 294A, leaving the motorcycles behind. Short switchbacks ascend a rock garden of blue lupine and penstemon, yellow wallflower, and orange paintbrush, at 2 miles topping out in a saddle, 4750 feet. Views, flowers, the spot to open the sardine can.

The horses that used to carry supplies to the lookout cabin atop Tongue Mountain, 4838 feet, stopped here, and so should you. The footpath the final hundred feet to the summit long since has slid out, leaving a rock scramble very simple for a climber, but for a hiker, one false move and he's in the Cispus River.

Tongue Mountain and Mount Rainier

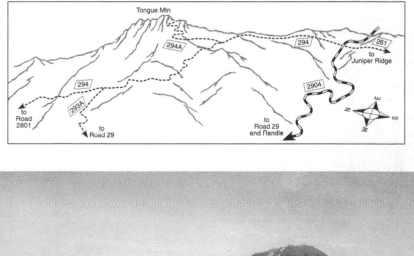

48 JUNIPER RIDGE

Round trip: to Juniper Peak 8 miles
Hiking time: 5 hours (day hike)
High point: 5611 feet
Elevation gain: 2000 feet
Hikable: mid-June through November

Round trip: to Boundary Trail 23 miles
Hiking time: allow 3 days
High point: 5611 feet
Elevation gain: 3100 feet in, 2300 feet
out, plus sidetrips to peaks
Hikable: July through October

Map: Green Trails McCoy Peak (No. 333)
Information: Randle Ranger Diistrict,
phone (360) 497-1100

A classic hike with dramatic views up the Cispus River to Mt. Adams, out to Mt. Rainier and Mount St. Helens, and over endless forested hills and valleys—all while walking a long ridge, sometimes on open hillsides covered with huckleberries, sometimes in young forest just getting established after the great Cispus fires of 1902 and 1918. The route provides a variety of trips: an easy afternoon stroll to a 4500-foot saddle (the trail this far generally is free of snow in early or mid-June); a day hike to Juniper Peak; an overnight backpack; or a long approach to the Boundary Trail. Except for snow patches in early July, the ridge is dry, ruling out backpacking. For this reason the five high points are also described as day hikes to Tongue Mountain (Hike 47), Sunrise Peak—Jumbo's Shoulder (Hike 49), Dark Divide (Hike 50), and Juniper Peak, here. The nearby Indian Heaven, Goat Rocks, and Mount Adams Wildernesses are so thronged

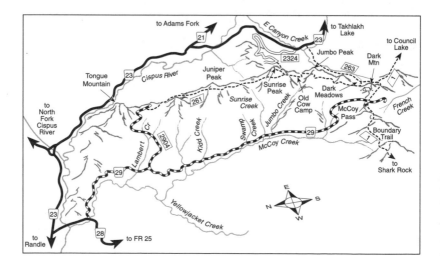

Mount Adams and flowers on Juniper Ridge

that the Forest Service is encouraging hikers to go elsewhere. Juniper Ridge is among the best substitutes—or would be, except motorcycles are allowed on the trail and few hikers can stand the racket and stench. However, you owe it to the trail—and yourself—to do it once, go home and write a letter, and eventually you'll be able to come again and again, quiet and happy.

Drive to the Tongue Mountain trailhead (Hike 47), elevation 3600 feet.

Trail No. 261 goes a few hundred feet through a clearcut, enters post-fire forest, and climbs under two prominent knolls, ascending steadily, with frequent views, 2¼ miles to a 4500-foot saddle. The trail continues climbing, gaining 1100 feet to within a few feet of the top of 5593-foot Juniper Peak, 4 miles, and views far and near, a good turnaround for day-hikers.

For the full length, continue southward, dropping about 400 feet to pass beneath cliffs. At 5½ miles is a super-great huckleberry patch—outstanding even in an area famous for huckleberries. At 5¾ miles pass a tiny lake, dry in summer; until then, campsites.

At 7 miles is the Sunrise Peak trail, a ¼-mile sidetrip to the 5880-foot site of a former lookout (Hike 49). At 7¾ miles, after losing almost 1000 feet to a broad saddle, is Old Cow Camp (no water). The trail again climbs, at 9 miles passing beneath cliffs of 5788-foot Jumbo Peak (Hike 49), and descends to the Boundary Trail at Dark Meadow, 12 miles, 4300 feet; campsites here possibly with water (Hike 50). From Dark Meadow the Boundary Trail leads in 2 miles to road No. 29 at McCoy Pass.

Note the many sawn stumps along the ridge to Juniper. These are not from logging but the cutting of snags, which in the philosophy of the old forestry had to be eliminated lest they attract lightning and flame like torches. The new forestry teaches that snags are the feeding and nesting headquarters of many important birds, as well as creatures lower on the food chain that feed them, and ultimately those of us at the top of the food chain.

49 | SUNRISE PEAK— JUMBO'S SHOULDER

Round trip: to Sunrise Peak 4 miles
Hiking time: 3 hours (day hike)
High point: 5892 feet
Elevation gain: 1600 feet

Hikable: July through October
Map: Green Trails McCoy Peak (No. 333)

Round trip: to Jumbo's Shoulder 7 miles
Hiking time: 4 hours
High point: 5500 feet
Elevation gain: 1600 feet in, 400 feet out

Information: Randle Ranger District,
phone (360) 497-1100

Walk miles of subalpine meadows aglow with wildflowers and, in season, blueberries, to a 5500-foot high point on famous Juniper Ridge, or huff and puff a steep trail to a climax of the ridge, the site of a 1930s fire lookout, and revel in more fields of flowers. Both trips give views north and south to St. Helens, Hood, Adams, and Rainier. The two can be done in a day but both cry out for a slow pace, which probably means two trips.

Turn south in Randle on a road signed "Mount St. Helens and Trout Lake," cross the Cowlitz River, and drive 1 mile. Turn left on road No. 23 signed "Trout Lake" and drive 19 miles to the junction with road No. 21. Stay right on road No. 23 another 4.6 miles and go right on road No. 2324. At 4.2 miles from road No. 23, at an unmarked junction, go sharply right. In another mile go left on road No. (2324)063. At 5.6 miles from road No. 23 find Sunrise Peak trail No. 262, elevation 4300 feet. (Motorcyclists are still allowed on the Sunrise Peak trail but they prefer the faster straight stretches of the ridge trail and are not too often an infernal nuisance here.)

The trail crosses a clearcut and climbs steeply in forest, at ½ mile breaking out to meadows and views of Mt. Adams and Mt. Rainier. The way follows the ridge a short bit and then traverses the slope to a junction at 5000 feet, 1 mile from the road. For Jumbo, go straight ahead, as described

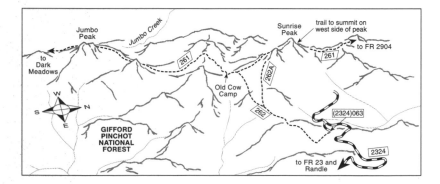

Jumbo Peak from Sunrise Peak. The Juniper Ridge trail can be seen crossing the foreground ridge and the one in the distance.

below. For Sunrise Peak, turn right on trail No. 262A, climbing very steeply up the south side of the peak, crossing to the west side, and returning to the south side, where switchbacks attain the summit rocks. The lookout's iron handrail used for a grip, the last 30 feet are an easy scramble to the summit, 5892 feet, 2½ miles.

For Jumbo's Shoulder, back at the junction go straight ahead on trail No. 262, losing 300 feet, and at 1½ miles join Juniper Ridge trail No. 261. Go left into the saddle of Old Cow Camp; no campsites and no water. The tread, deeply rutted by motorcycles, climbs 200 feet, rounds a ridge, contours headwaters of Jumbo Creek, and ascends more severe ruts to a large basin. The way levels off and climbs a snowbank, which may last through July, to Jumbo's Shoulder, 5500 feet, 3¼ miles from the road. Until the snow is gone and water dries up, campsites can be found in the basin. The summit of 5801-foot Jumbo Peak is only 300 feet higher, attained by a very steep, obscure trail; near the top, stay on the west side of the ridge, away from cliffs.

50 | DARK DIVIDE — JUNIPER RIDGE

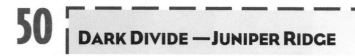

Round trip: 8 miles
Hiking time: 6 hours (day hike or backpack)
High point: 5400 feet
Elevation gain: 1500 feet in, 200 feet out

Hikable: July through October
Map: Green Trails McCoy Peak (No. 333)
Information: Randle Ranger District, phone (360) 497-1100

The esteem for Dark Divide and its flower-covered meadows and its dramatic views along the procession of Cascade volcanoes from Hood to Rainier, these many years urgently proposed for dedication as Wilderness, can be measured by the attention given in this guidebook (especially Hikes 48 and 49). No wildland in the state of such magnitude and national importance is being so cavalierly shrugged off by the cavalier shruggers of the Forest Service and Congress, and that's why the Washington Trails Association is devoting major energies there to preserving and restoring motorfree trails. As always, boots are crucially important in making their (and your) case.

The aversion hikers have to sharing trails with motorcycles has played into the Forest Service's hand. When there are no hikers there are no nasty letters; therefore, say the shruggers, hikers have no interest in these trails, so let the machines roar. That's why more hikers must grit their teeth and do some suffering, even if they feel like missionaries sent to convert the cannibals.

The hike starts on an abandoned trail that is a bit hard to locate. Drive

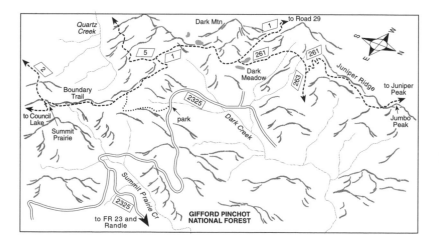

road No. 23 south from Randle and at 0.9 mile past milepost 24 turn right on road No. 2325. The road climbs to 4000 feet (views of Juniper Ridge), descend 100 feet into Dark Creek valley, a tributary of East Canyon Creek, and at 5.3 miles from road No. 23 find the start of the unsigned trail beside a small stream, elevation 3900 feet.

The way climbs 550 feet in a scant mile through trees, then huckleberry meadows, to intersect the Boundary Trail No. 1 at 4550 feet. Go right on the wooded ridge with occasional views, descending 200 feet, steeply at times on trail deeply rutted by ORVs. The trail, which is sometimes on the narrow divide and other times in large meadows, reaches 4400-foot Dark Meadows and a fork some 2½ miles from the road. The left fork, the Boundary Trail, proceeds to road No. 29. The right, trail No. 261, crosses Dark Creek (possible camping) and climbs to the crest of Juniper Ridge and a high point on the shoulder of Jumbo Peak (Hike 49).

Dark Meadow and Mount Adams

51 | QUARTZ CREEK

Round trip: to Quartz Creek Camp 9 miles
Hiking time: 7 hours (day hike or backpack)
High point: 2500 feet
Elevation gain: 500 feet, plus innumerable ups and downs

Hikable: June through November
Map: Green Trails Lone Butte (No. 365)
Information: Mount St. Helens National Volcanic Monument Headquarters, phone (360) 247-5473

Trees 3 and 4 feet and even 8 in diameter line the trail, rising straight without a limb for 100 feet, probably among the best sawlogs remaining in Gifford Pinchot National Forest, but from another perspective seen as a magnificent example of an increasingly rare ecosystem—the ancient lowland forest. The creek usually is out of sight in a deep canyon but never out of sound. Three stream crossings add excitement.

From Pine Creek Information Center at the north end of Swift Reservoir, drive 17.5 miles up Lewis River road No. 90 to the Quartz Creek bridge and trail No. 5, elevation 1800 feet.

The trail is seldom level, repeatedly climbing steeply over obstacles and dropping just as steeply. The first ⅔ mile is along the river on an old "mining" road, the trees here as yet unmolested. Above the trail, just before dropping into Platinum Creek, is the rusted old machinery of the "mine" (no minerals, just fantasies). Platinum Creek is the first interesting stream crossing, difficult when the water is high.

The way climbs steeply, traverses a 1970s clearcut, and at 2 miles comes to Straight Creek. A large log with ax-flattened top spans the flood; a nervous person might feel better scooting across in a sitting position. On the far side is a good camp and just downstream are Quartz Creek Falls; other falls are upstream on Straight Creek.

The trail ascends a clearcut and at 2½ miles reenters forest, coming at 4 miles to Snagtooth Creek, another log bridge, and more camps. At 4½ miles is an unsigned junction. The main trail, marked by two blazes, goes left,

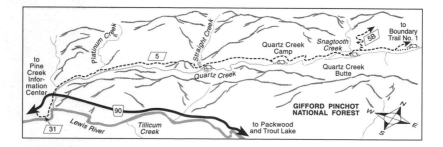

Quartz Creek Falls

uphill. Take the right, marked by four slash-line blazes, and drop ¼ mile to delightful Quartz Creek Camp, surrounded by magnificent trees, elevation 2300 feet.

Although it lacks the loving care evident to here, the Quartz Creek trail continues. At 6 miles is a junction with the Snagtooth Mountain trail leading to road No. 9341. At 10½ miles the way intersects Boundary Trail No. 1 near road No. 2325.

52 | LEWIS RIVER

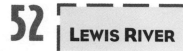

One-way trip: 9½ miles
Hiking time: 6 hours (day hike or backpack)
High point: 1600 feet
Elevation gain: 400 feet upstream

Hikable: March through November
Map: Green Trails Lone Butte (No. 365)
Information: Mount St. Helens National Volcanic Monument Headquarters, phone (360) 247-5473

The Forest Service belatedly (conscience-stricken?) has proposed a "wild and scenic" designation for a wide corridor along the Lewis River to preserve as much of the natural condition as still exists. This trail runs through it, one of only three lengthy low-elevation valley paths surviving in the Gifford Pinchot National Forest. The 9½-mile sample described here—the huge firs, cedars, and maples of the forest canopy, the understory of shrubs, the forest-floor carpet of Oregon grape, vanilla leaf, oxalis, and moss— would serve as a poignant reminder of the hundreds and hundreds of miles of such splendor that we inherited and in a few decades have squandered.

The trail can be hiked in either direction. Parties that can arrange transportation to allow a one-way trip would be well advised to start at the top, which is 400 feet higher than the bottom. However, parties making a round trip should start at the bottom and thus be sure to cover at least the lower 3 miles, where the best trees are; for this reason direction are given bottom-to-top.

Drive either road No. 25 from Randle or road No. 90 from Cougar. At the north end of Swift Reservoir, just past the Pine Creek Information Center, keep to road No. 90 for 5.2 miles. Turn left on road No. 9039 and go 1 mile to the Lewis River bridge. Park here and find the lower trailhead across the bridge, elevation about 1100 feet.

To reach the upper trailhead, from the junction of road Nos. 90 and 9039

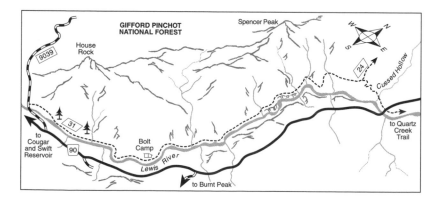

The Lewis River trail

continue on No. 90 to a concrete bridge over the Lewis River at 14.5 miles from the information center. A few yards from the west end of the bridge find the trailhead, elevation about 1400 feet.

From the lower beginning, cross the bridge and find Lewis River trail No. 31 on the upstream side of the road. Enter the magnificent forest. The way winds along bottomland flats, climbs a small bench, and emerges into an old clearcut at 1 mile. To somewhat beyond 1½ miles the path follows the margin of the logging before reentering virgin trees. After a few steep ups and downs, at just under 2½ miles is Bolt Camp; the shelter here is amazingly well-preserved considering it was built in the early 1930s. (In 1979 a Forest Service employee spent his days off reshaking the cabin.) At 4 miles the valley narrows to a canyon, a good turnaround for round-trip hikers, because from this point the trail goes up and down a lot but never again reaches river level.

At 7 miles the trail climbs a 300-foot bluff. At 7½ miles find a viewpoint a few feet off the tread and look down to the canyon sliced in columnar basalt. From here on the river is unseen. At 9 miles cross Cussed Hollow and climb over the last bump to the upper trailhead and road No. 90 at 9½ miles, 1400 feet.

Want more? The Lewis River trail crosses the highway and goes another 5½ miles to the Quartz Creek trail (Hike 51), passing five waterfalls as it travels between the river and the road.

53 | CRAGGY PEAK

Round trip: to Boundary Trail 13 miles
Hiking time: 5 hours (day hike or backpack)
High point: 5300 feet
Elevation gain: 1700 feet
Hikable: mid-July through early November

Maps: Green Trails Lone Butte (No. 365), McCoy Peak (No. 333)
Information: Mount St. Helens National Volcanic Monument Headquarters, phone (360) 247-5473

Follow a wooded ridge above a mountain lake to 2 miles of alpine meadows and views, and views, and views. Try this trip early in July; if conditions are right, there may be miles of beargrass in bloom.

The trail is harassed by machines and jeopardized by logging, including a timber sale ½ mile from Blue Lake. Logging at these high elevations is particularly shocking because the timber has relatively little commercial value—a quarter or more of the trees are left on the ground to rot after being cut and a new forest may be 200 years or more growing.

From Pine Creek Information Center at the north end of Swift Reservoir, drive north on road No. 25. At 5.6 miles, at the first switchback after leaving the Muddy River, turn right on road No. 93. Watch all intersections carefully; during logging operations some sideroads are used more than the main road. At 18.7 miles the pavement ends. Go left on road No. 9327 another 0.3 mile to Craggy Peak trail No. 3, elevation 3600 feet.

The trail crosses clearcuts and at one point is only ½ mile from road No. 9331 (the road is gated). At 2½ miles pass close to a clearcut, which could be used as a shortcut; to reach this alternative starting point, walk

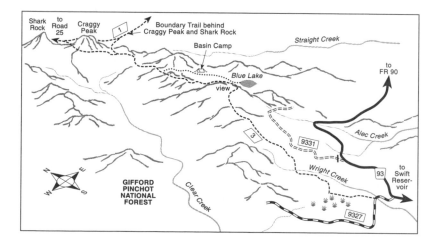

Blue Lake and Mount Adams from the Craggy Peak trail

road No. 9331 about 1½ miles and go left on an unmarked spur.

In the next 2 miles the trail climbs gently, eventually ascending a wide ridge. The vistas begin. At a little over 4 miles the ridge becomes quite narrow and at times the hillside is steep. At 4½ miles, 5200 feet, the way contours around a high point. The timber thins, the trail enters meadows. At 5 miles, 5200 feet, is a spring and a possible campsite. For better sites find a way trail descending 400 feet to Basin Camp. Better yet, go all the way down to Blue Lake at 4553 feet. (This also can be reached by walking road No. 9331 some 2½ miles and finding a path of sorts to the lake.)

The Craggy Peak trail crosses a 5300-foot high point and contours under the green slopes of Craggy Peak to join the Boundary Trail, elevation 5100 feet, 6 miles from the trailhead. For widest views (including a closeup of Shark Rock, the most impressive hunk on the Dark Divide), take a faint boot-built path from the Boundary Trail up the east ridge of Craggy to the 5725-foot summit.

54 | BADGER PEAK

Round trip: 10 miles
Hiking time: 7 hours (day hike or backpack)
High point: 5664 feet
Elevation gain: 1600 feet

Hikable: late July through September
Map: Green Trails McCoy Peak (No. 333)
Information: Mount St. Helens National Volcanic Monument Headquarters, phone (360) 247-5473

The Forest Service blasted off the top of the peak for a flat space to erect a fire-lookout cabin. The cabin is gone, along with a lot of the forests it was there to help protect, but the views haven't quit. South is Mt. Hood, east are Mt. Adams and jagged crags of Shark Rock Scenic Area, north is Mt. Rainier, and west is a close-up look at the smoldering remains of Mount St. Helens. However, the hike is not unmixed glee because loggers are working both sides of the route, a forested ridge. Furthermore, much of the tread is inches deep in 1980 pumice, as slow going as dry sand. Finally, hikers not equipped with ice ax and knowledge of how to use it must not attempt the peak in early summer, when a dangerous snow gully blocks the trail near the summit. This hike can also start from Mosquito Meadows trail No. 292 on road No. 28; the distance is a bit shorter, but the elevation gain is greater.

Drive road No. 25 to Elk Pass, 24 miles from Randle, 40 miles from Cougar, and find the parking area for Boundary Trail No. 1 on the west side of the highway about 200 feet north of the pass, elevation 4080 feet.

Find the trailhead across the highway. The trail sets out in woods along ups and downs of the ridge crest, at 2 miles passing Mosquito Meadows trail No. 292, the alternate approach. The way ascends ridge slopes to a junction at 4 miles, several hundred feet from Badger Lake, 4940 feet.

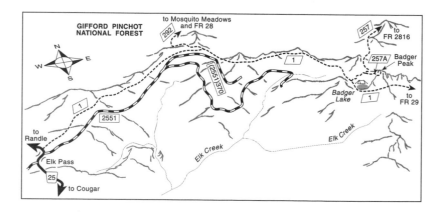

Mount Rainier from the top of Badger Peak

Campsites here rely on the spring-fed lake for water, to be kept in mind should you be of a mind to take a swim.

The summit of Badger Peak is a scant 1 mile from the lake. Climb from the junction in soft pumice, contouring a steep slope. In ¼ mile pass Badger Ridge trail No. 257 from road No. 2816. (Two game traces as good as the built trail also ascend the ridge.) Just below the summit is a steep gully, unworthy of notice when snowfree, but when full, one slip and you're 300 feet down the mountain, battering the boulders.

Aside from that, simply remember to beware of active volcanoes.

55 | LAKE WAPIKI

Round trip: 9 miles
Hiking time: 6 hours (day hike or backpack)
High point: 5685 feet
Elevation gain: 1700 feet in, 500 feet out
Hikable: late July through October

Maps: USFS Indian Heaven Wilderness/ Trapper Creek Wilderness, Green Trails Lone Butte (No. 365), Mount Adams West (No. 366)
Information: Mount Adams Ranger District, phone (509) 395-2501

Every hiker of Indian Heaven has a favorite trip. Some like to immerse themselves in bushels of lakes, as in Hike 56. Others home in on a single choice spot, such as Placid Lake or Junction Lake. But all connoisseurs agree that Lake Wapiki, walled by cliffs on three sides, 5925-foot Lemei Rock towering above, is outstanding. The route described here throws in high viewpoints and wildflowers; the hiker not interested in these can use a slightly shorter access from road No. 24.

For a shorter round-trip of 7 miles, minus the wildflowers and views, from Cultus Creek Campground drive east on road No. 24 to Little Goose Campground and hike Filloon Trail No. 102, then Lemei trail No. 34, and finally trail No. 34A to the lake.

By driving road No. 24 to Indian Berry Fields, Cultus Creek Campground can be reached from Carson or Randle. The Trout Lake route described here is the shortest from a state highway. In Trout Lake drive past the Forest Service ranger station and follow signs to Berry Fields and Carson Road. Within a mile the road makes a left turn and passes road

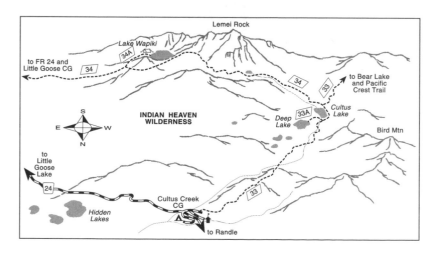

Lake Wapiki

No. 88. Stay on Carson Road, which for a stretch takes on a second identity, road No. 24. At about 7.5 miles Carson Road goes straight ahead and road No. 24 makes an abrupt right turn. Don't miss it, stay on No. 24. In another 6.5 miles pass the Little Goose Campground, the alternate starting point. At 8.5 miles go left into Cultus Creek Campground. Find the trailhead at the back of the campground, parking space for three or four cars, elevation 3988 feet.

Begin on trail No. 33, climbing 1000 feet in 2 miles—steeply in spots—to Cultus Lake, 5100 feet. Round the shores and go left on trail No. 34, through heather, avalanche lilies, blueberries, with views of Adams and Rainier, climbing to a 5685-foot high point just 250 feet below the summit cliffs of Lemei Rock, and a promontory 500 feet above Lake Wapiki. To the afore-mentioned views add Hood, beyond the Columbia River, miles and miles of forest, and, in the distance, farm fields.

The trail descends ½ mile to a junction 4 miles from Cultus Creek Campground. Go right on trail No. 34A, gaining 100 feet in ½ mile to Lake Wapiki, a great place to camp (100 feet from water)—but be aware that some hikers also think it's a great place to swim so don't forget your iodine.

56 | INDIAN HEAVEN LOOP

Short loop trip: 10 miles
Hiking time: 6 hours (day hike or
  backpack)
High point: 5237 feet
Elevation gain: 1700 feet
Hikable: July through October

Maps: USFS Indian Heaven Wilderness/
  Trapper Creek Wilderness, Green
  Trails Lone Butte (No. 365), Wind
  River (No. 397)
Information: Mount Adams Ranger
  District, phone (509) 395-2501

A fascinating portion of the Pacific Crest Trail, twenty-three lakes big enough to have names and some 100 lakelets, ponds, and tadpole pools, all in an area at about 5000 feet elevation. Foregrounds of continuous forest, groves of subalpine trees, and flat, grassy meadows are complemented by glimpses of glaciered volcanoes.

Indian Heaven has been well known to hikers and horsemen for many years, but remoteness long kept use to a minimum. In recent years logging roads have come close, giving easy access to the innermost lakes and meadows. Then, in 1984, Congress designated the Indian Heaven Wilderness, which protects the area from wheels and chainsaws. This designation has brought with it the problems inherent in national fame. Trails built in the soft pumice by trappers and the Forest Service for occasional use

*Bear Lake in the Indian Heaven
Wilderness*

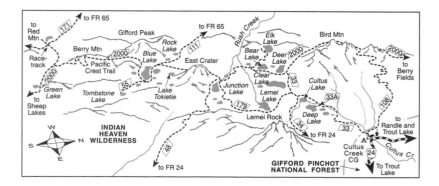

Lemie Lake

were unable to withstand the increased recreational use, especially the heavy
pounding by horses. The Forest Service therefore built new trails on soil that
can better withstand impact and abandoned the former trail system.

The new trails can be sampled on a 1-day, 10-mile loop hike, an overnight
18-mile loop, or by spending several days to visit more lakes. They usually
melt free of snow early in July, but since Indian Heaven is also called "Mosquito Heaven," the trip is recommended for late August or September when
the bugs are gone and, incidentally, the huckleberries are ripe.

The starting point is Cultus Creek Campground, elevation 3988 feet, reached from Trout Lake on road No. 24 (Hike 55).

Whatever the chosen trip, start on trail No. 33, thus avoiding a very steep and hot ascent of 1200 feet on trail No. 108, which is better used for the return leg of the loop.

Trail No. 33 begins in forest, climbing 600 feet in the first mile. At 1¾ miles make the short sidetrip on trail No. 33A to Deep Lake for the view of Mt. Adams rising over treetops, then proceed to Cultus Lake at 2 miles, 5050 feet; typical of many of the lakes, it has trees around half the shore, meadows around the rest. To the southeast is 5925-foot Lemei Rock and to the northwest 5706-foot Bird Mountain; one or the other of these peaks can be seen from a number of the lakes. The way climbs 100 more feet, then descends to meet Lemei Lake trail No. 179. For the short loop, keep right, staying on trail No. 33; pass within a few yards of Clear Lake and come to the Pacific Crest Trail near Deer Lake, 4 miles. Head north on the Crest Trail. At about 8 miles turn right on trail No. 108, climb over a 5237-foot saddle in Bird Mountain (a great view of Mt. Rainier), and drop steeply 1½ miles to Cultus Creek Campground.

For the longer loop that adds another 4 or more miles, along with more lakes and large meadows, from Cultus Lake follow trail No. 33 up and over a wooded saddle. In ½ mile from the lake go left on trail No. 179, passing Lemei Lake; at some 2½ miles from Cultus Lake reach Junction Lake and the Pacific Crest Trail. Turn south on the Crest Trail for a possible 2-mile (each way) sidetrip to Blue, Sahalee, and Tyee Lakes; in another 4 miles is the Indian Racetrack.

For the loop, from Junction Lake go north on the Pacific Crest Trail, passing Bear Lake, to intersect trail No. 33 near Deer Lake. Either return on trail

Sawtooth Mountain and Mount Rainier

No. 33 to Cultus Lake or continue on the Crest Trail to cross the Bird Mountain saddle as described above.

Don't be fooled by the seemingly flat terrain—the paths have many short ups and downs. Campsites are numerous, some by lakes and others by streams; campers should stay 100 feet from water. The pumice soil is very fragile, so camp in the forest or in already established campsites. The lakes and streams have a very small flow of water, so to avoid contamination wash dishes and bodies far away from the water's edge. Remember the iodine.

57 | RACETRACK

Round trip: 7 miles
Hiking time: 4 hours (day hike)
High point: 4300 feet
Elevation gain: 800 feet
Hikable: mid-July to October

Maps: USFS Indian Heaven/Trapper
Creek Wilderness, Green Trails Wind
River (No. 397)
Information: Mount Adams Ranger
District, phone (509) 395-2501

In 1853 naturalist George Gibbs wrote (as quoted by Harry M. Majors in *Exploring Washington*), "The racing season is the grand annual occasion of these tribes. A horse of proved reputation is a source of wealth or of ruin to his owner. On his steed he stakes his whole stud, his household goods, clothes, and finally his wives. . . . They ride with skill, reckless of all obstacles, and with little mercy to their beasts, the right hand swinging the whip at every bound. . . . The Indians ride with ham-rope knotted around under their jaw for a bridle. The men use a stuffed pad, with wooden stirrups."

The Klickitat and Yakama peoples came here in late summer to pick huckleberries and dry them in the sun. The highland then was a vast berry field, whether because the harvesters regularly set fires to burn encroaching forests, or because the Little Ice Age had kept the treeline at lower elevations, or a combination. For centuries, perhaps millennia, they traveled (perhaps) the trails we now walk, to places suitable for combining the berry harvest with picniclike socializing. Having at some time in the eighteenth century acquired horses from neighbors (ultimately, from the Spanish in Mexico), they began to bring along their nags for the sport Gibbs observed. In the Racetrack meadow they wore a rut 2000 feet long; only a few hundred feet can now be seen, trees having invaded most of the meadow; and despite modern horse-riders who like to run their mounts along it, the rut

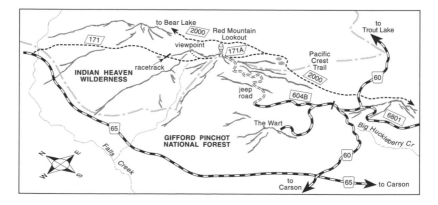

Indian Race Track is the black line across the meadow, with Mount St. Helens in distant haze.

is mere inches deep. This isn't a place to see history. But if you sit a spell picking huckleberries you can feel it.

The trailhead can be reached from Trout Lake by way of road No. 24. At 7.5 miles from Trout Lake go straight ahead on road No. 60, pass Goose Lake, Red Mountain Road, and go right on road No. 65 to Racetrack trail No. 171, elevation 3500 feet. From the south drive north from Carson 6 miles on Wind River Highway; go right on road No. 65, signed "Panther Creek Campground," and drive 15 miles on road No. 65 to the trailhead.

In ¼ mile the trail reaches Falls Creek, the only all-summer water on this route, and in early summer too much water, the boulder-hop crossing not rationally possible. However, since the huckleberry time of September is the usual time of a hike (unless one wishes to see the acres of beargrass blooming in mid-July), the creek generally is more pleasing than repelling. For 1 mile the trail climbs rather briskly, then levels off and drops a bit to the Racetrack, 2½ miles, 4300 feet, near a pond that dries up in summer.

For an airplane-wing overview of the Racetrack meadow, continue on trail No. 171, climbing in woods toward the Red Mountain Lookout to the top of the first hill. Leave the trail and ascend north on pumice slopes to a bare knoll, 4700 feet, 3½ miles from road No. 65.

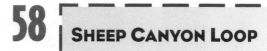

58 | SHEEP CANYON LOOP

Loop trip: 7 miles
Hiking time: 4 hours (day hike)
High point: 4700 feet
Elevation gain: 2400 feet
Hikable: July through October

Map: Green Trails Mount St. Helens
(No. 364)
Information: Mount St. Helens National
Volcanic Monument Headquarters,
phone (360) 245-5473

Be properly awed and somewhat spooked, visualizing what it would have been like to be here that catastrophic Sunday in May 1980. Walk across giant mudflows, pass rows of trees laid flat by the 300mph winds that accompanied the eruption and standing skeletons of trees killed by heat. Find evidence of prior eruptions. And yet, for most of the way, hike in tall trees that have escaped the many eruptions during their 300 years since seedlinghood. And explore alpine meadows with flowers as colorful as they've ever been.

From road No. 90, near the south end of Swift Reservoir, turn uphill on road No. 83 for 3 miles, then left 5 miles on road No. 81, and finally go right on road No. 8123 and drive 10.5 miles to the road-end trailhead, elevation 3360.

Sheep Canyon trail No. 240 climbs an easy ½ mile to Sheep Canyon, stripped of vegetation by the mudflow. At a junction go left on trail No. 238, crossing Sheep Creek on a bridge. Climb back into forest, descend 600 feet to a crossing, approximately 2900 feet, of a stream below Crescent Ridge, and skirt the enormous mudflow of South Fork Toutle River to a junction with Loowit Trail No. 216, 1¾ miles from the road. Before 1980 this valley was a deep forest of 300-year-old trees; all were carried away by the turmoil of rock and water from melted glaciers. Go right on the Loowit Trail, climbing almost 2000 feet in forest with occasional views of the mudflow. Finally, reach trees killed by superheated air estimated to have been

Clark's nutcracker

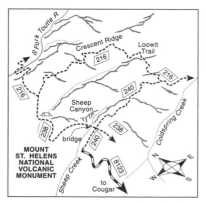

Sheep Canyon and Mount St. Helens

480 degrees Fahrenheit. The way climbs flower gardens, with views of alpine meadows and snowfields of Mount St. Helens, to a 4700-foot high point about 3½ miles from the start, then drops to scorched forest, traversing headwaters of Sheep Canyon. At approximately 5½ miles is the junction of Sheep Canyon trail No. 240. Either descend 2 miles back to the starting point or, if the day is still young, explore southward a mile or two along the Loowit Trail, ascending again into meadowland before backtracking and descending the Sheep Canyon trail.

59 | LOOWIT TRAIL

Loop trip: 28 miles
Hiking time: allow 3 days
High point: 4800 feet
Elevation gain: 4100 feet
Hikable: mid-July through September

Map: Green Trails Mount St. Helens
(No. 364)
Information: Mount St. Helens National
Volcanic Monument Headquarters,
phone (360) 247-5473

To fully appreciate the cataclysm of May 18, 1980, there's no substitute for the complete circuit, all the way around what's left of Mount St. Helens, marveling that it used to be known as the Fujiyama of the West, and by the Original Inhabitants was called Loowit, for the beautiful young girl turned into a beautiful mountain. But you gotta have heart. And guts. Not to mention legs and a lot of experience. The trail traverses fields of ankle-twisting lava blocks and pumice slopes as tiring as soft snow. It descends steep walls and deep gullies and climbs, climbs, climbs back up. Rain and snowmelt and gravity ceaselessly work at destroying the tread. (So do feet; stay with the trail. Hikers are prohibited from wandering more than 10 feet from the trail anywhere in the Spirit Lake Basin to protect the sensitive ecosystems and the hundreds of research plots there.) Many miles are shadeless and exposed to sun, wind, and dust storms of volcanic ash. Campsites with water are rare. Yes, you really gotta do it, don't you?

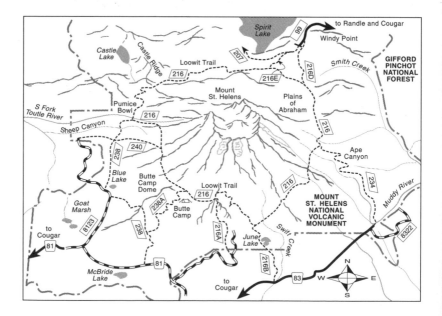

Clockwise from upper left: *Mount St. Helens, and driftwood on Spirit Lake (Hike 60); Mount St. Helens from Mount Margaret (Hike 70); Clark's nutcracker; avalanche lily pushing through a slowly melting snowbank*

Overleaf: *The Lewis River trail (Hike 52)*

Above: *Avalanche lilies and
Mount Olympus from High Divide
(Hike 87)*; right: *Olympic marmot*;
left: *Blue Glacier (Hike 90)*

Left: *Hoh Rainforest (Hike 90);* above: *Lake La Crosse (Hike 96);* below: *Mildred Lake and Sawtooth Ridge (Hike 72)*

Above: *Sea stacks (Hike 100)*; right: *driftwood and sea stacks from Third Beach (Hike 100)*

So where do you start? The seven possibilities all have disadvantages: one they share is that to the 28 miles of loop must be added a minimum of 6 in-out miles on access trail, since no road touches the Loowit. Another is the entrance fee to the National Volcanic Monument, varying from access to access but everywhere high because management expenses are very heavy, what with masses of pilgrims comparable to Japan's Fuji. The highest fees of all are at Windy Point, described (but not necessarily recommended) here, and that would argue for starting at the cheaper Butte Camp trailhead, reached from Merrill Lake road No. 8100; however, the fee system is too new for the kinks to be worked out and is subject to change.

Loowit Trail crossing pumice fields on the north side of Mount St. Helens

Beargrass

If daunted by the prospect of carrying a pack over this suburb of Hell, keep in mind that by use of two cars the loop can be done in day-hike segments, a cooler full of iced root beer in each car.

From road No. 25, between Randle and Cougar, drive road No. 99 some 16 miles to its end at Windy Point, elevation 4000 feet.

Walk the gated service road signed "Truman Trail No. 207" 2 miles toward the mountain, climbing a bit, then dropping to a dry wash. Leave the road-trail here and climb 1 mile on obscure Windy trail No. 216E to intersect Loowit Trail No. 216 at 4500 feet.

Head west, in and out of numerous dry gullies. Look down on Spirit Lake, up at the gaping crater, and out to miles and miles of barren hills denuded by the blast in the blowdown zone that extended 14 to 17 miles to the west. At approximately 7 miles reach Castle Ridge.

Drop steeply in loose ash of the Pumice Bowl to a crossing of the South Fork Toutle River. A bit farther is an intersection with Sheep Canyon trail No. 238, at about 3200 feet. For an excellent campsite follow this trail a scant ½ mile to a stream.

The Loowit climbs from the blast area and switchbacks up Crescent Ridge into scorched trees and to flower fields, attaining a 4700-foot high point at the edge of meadows. The best stretch of the trail ensues, descending in subalpine forest. With many ups and downs, the way ascends again to timberline and at approximately 5½ miles from the South Fork Toutle reaches a junction with Butte Camp trail No. 238A. If the hour is late, take the 1¼-mile sidetrip and 800-foot elevation loss for a night at Butte Camp.

In the next 5 miles the pace becomes slower and the routefinding tricky, the trail often obscure as it crosses lava fields, losing 1400 feet to a junction with June Lake trail No. 216B; a ⅓-mile sidetrip leads to campsites at June Lake. The next 4¾ miles are equally difficult, traversing more cruel lava flows to a junction with Ape Canyon trail No. 234. Matters then improve and the remaining 4 miles across the Plains of Abraham to the final junction are generally smooth sailing. Turn right on No. 216D to road No. 99 (gated) and 2 miles back to Windy Point.

Log-covered Spirit Lake and Mount St. Helens from Norway Pass

60 | NORWAY PASS—MOUNT MARGARET —JOHNSTON RIDGE OBSERVATORY

Round trip: to Norway Pass 5 miles
Hiking time: 3 hours (day hike)
High point: 4508 feet
Elevation gain: 900 feet
Hikable: July through September

Round trip: to Mt. Margaret 11 miles
Hiking time: 6 hours (day hike)
High point: 5858 feet
Elevation gain: 2300 feet
Hikable: August through September

Map: Green Trails Spirit Lake (No. 332)

Information: Mount St. Helens National Volcanic Monument Headquarters, phone (360) 247-5473

The Boundary Trail provides the best easy vantage to survey the devastation of May 1980, the crater blasted from the former perfect symmetry of Mount St. Helens, the new (and ghostly) Spirit Lake. Be prepared for hot sun—there is no shade (no trees) on the trail. Carry water and perhaps a parasol. Also be warned that steep snow slopes below Mt. Margaret may not be safe for hikers until late summer.

Drive road No. 25 either 22 miles from Randle or 44 miles from Cougar and turn uphill on road No. 99, signed "Mount St. Helens—Windy Ridge Viewpoint." At 8.9 miles from road No. 25 turn right on Ryan Lake road No. 26 and in 1 mile reach the Boundary Trail/Norway Pass trailhead, elevation 3600 feet.

The trail switchbacks up through blown-down timber. Note that on slopes where the blast of hot gas and ash blew straight from the mountain, the trees lie flat in tidy parallel lines; where the blast eddied in the lee of a hill, they are piled one atop the other in a haphazard jackstraw. The feature of interest

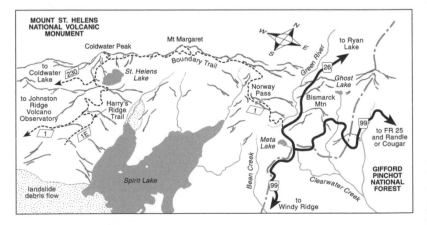

Mount St. Helens from Mount Margaret

near the pass used to be the old mining machinery; that all disappeared, though there is a badly dented boiler from the Camp Fire Girls' camp on Spirit Lake. The view, of course, is now the thing. Look down to Spirit Lake, half-filled with logs. Note how a giant "tidal" wave (the technically accurate term is *seiche*) washed away the forest 500 feet above the shore.

From the pass continue westward, doing several substantial ups and downs, into the flower gardens of Mt. Margaret and views to the Mt. Margaret backcountry lakes—first Grizzly Lake, then Boot and Obscurity Lakes. At about 5½ miles a short spur leaves the Boundary Trail and climbs to within 20 feet of the 5858-foot summit of Mt. Margaret, with aerial views of Spirit Lake and St. Helens. To the north is Rainier, east Adams, and south Hood.

The Boundary Trail continues 10 miles to the Coldwater Peak trail, which climbs ¾ mile from the Boundary Trail to the summit. The Boundary Trail turns south, looping above St. Helens Lake along the east slope of the ridge, then switches to the west side through a natural rock arch which frames a view of Mt. Adams. A descent leads to the intersection of the Harry's Ridge trail, which goes a long ½ mile to a viewpoint above Spirit Lake. The Boundary Trail proceeds to where a portion of the massive debris avalanche crossed the North Fork Toutle River, swept upward 1500 feet, and spilled over the ridge into the Coldwater drainage. At 15½ miles from road No. 26 is Johnston Ridge Volcano Observatory.

The 15½ miles from road No. 26 to the Observatory are a tempting one-way day hike, except the road distance between the two trailheads is some 140 miles, making a two-car switch difficult. Now, if a non-hiking friend is available. . . .

61 | GOAT MOUNTAIN

Round trip: to Deadmans Lake 11 miles
Hiking time: 5¾ hours (day hike or
  backpack)
High point: 5300 feet
Elevation gain: 1900 feet in, 1000
  feet out

Hikable: July through mid-October
Map: Green Trails Spirit Lake (No. 332)
Information: Mount St. Helens National
  Volcanic Monument Headquarters,
  phone (360) 247-5473

Among the most exciting ridge walks in the South Cascades is the 2½-mile crest of Goat Mountain, through meadows of soft pumice spotted with flowers, huckleberry bushes, and subalpine trees, by little spring-fed lakelets ringed by fields of grass, to ½-mile-wide, forest-ringed Deadmans Lake. Views open south to depths of the Green River valley, to the Mt. Margaret backcountry topped by Mount St. Helens, and north out the Quartz Creek valley to Rainier.

Drive south from the center of Randle on the road signed "Cispus, Mt. Adams, etc." Cross the Cowlitz River and at a junction in 1 mile keep straight on road No. 25. At 8.7 miles cross the Cispus River to a junction. Continue straight ahead on road No. 26, signed "Ryan Lake." At 22.5 miles from Randle turn right on road No. 2612 and at 22.8 miles find the trailhead, No. 217, just beyond the Ryan Lake parking area, elevation 3400 feet.

The trail begins with a ¾-mile walk over the fairly level Devastated Area, then turns steeply upward, switchbacking in and out of the Blast Area, and at 1¾ miles, 4600 feet, tops the crest of Goat Mountain, which, by the chances of the eruption, escaped the catastrophe.

The way follows the ups and downs of the crest. At 2 miles it passes above the first of the lakelets, at 3 miles contours around a 5600-foot high

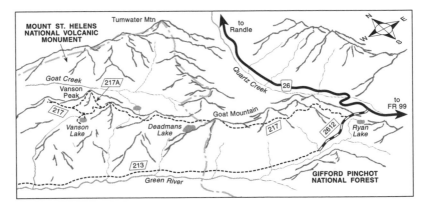

Tarn on Goat Mountain with Mount Rainier in the distance

point, and at 3¾ miles, 5200 feet, crosses from the south side of the ridge to the north, directly above two more lakelets. Now begins a 900-foot descent to Deadmans Lake, 5½ miles, a wonderful spot for a basecamp. The trail can be followed another 2¾ miles to 4948-foot Vanson Peak, site of a former lookout; a sidetrip leads to Vanson Lake.

62 | OBSERVATION (TRAPPER) PEAK LOOP

Loop trip: from Government Mineral Springs 13 miles
Hiking time: 8 hours (day hike)
High point: 4207 feet
Elevation gain: 2900 feet

Round trip: from road No. 58 6 miles
Hiking time: 3 hours (day hike)
High point: 4207 feet
Elevation gain: 1600 feet in, 300 feet out

Hikable: June through September
Maps: USFS Trapper Creek Wilderness, Green Trails Lookout Mountain (No. 396), Wind River (No. 397)

Information: Mount St. Helens National Volcanic Monument Headquarters, phone (360) 247-5473

There are two ways to climb 4207-foot Observation Peak, site of the old Trapper Lookout, for its panoramic view of the Wind River Valley. One is a loop starting low, in the valley bottom, and ascending forest. The easier other starts high, following the ridge through meadows.

For the loop trip, drive Wind River Highway 15 miles north from Carson toward Government Mineral Springs. Cross the Wind River and in 0.2 mile turn right on road No. 5401 for 0.4 mile to the trailhead, elevation 1300 feet.

Parallel a summer-home road 1 mile on Trapper Creek trail No. 192 and go right on Observation trail No. 132, steeply climbing the south side of Howe Ridge. At 3 miles cross a small stream, which may be the last water. At 4½ miles swing around the north side of the ridge. At 6 miles turn left on Observation trail No. 132A for a final ½ mile to the peak and views, views, and more views. For the return go back to the junction with No. 132, follow it west ½ mile, and descend Big Hollow trail No. 158 to Dry Creek trail No. 194, which ends at the same trailhead you started from.

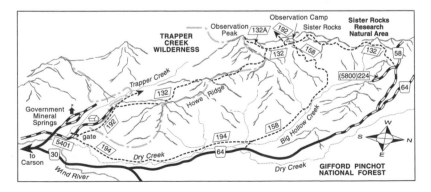

For the upper ridge walk, drive Wind River Highway, which is now road No. 30, north 2 miles past the turnoff to Government Mineral Springs, turn left on Dry Creek road No. 64 for 6 miles, and go left 2 more miles on road No. 58; find the trailhead on the west side of the road at the junction with road No. (5800)224, elevation 3200 feet.

Observation trail No. 132 sets out in virgin forest of Sister Rocks Research Natural Area, gaining 800 feet. At about 1 mile it enters an old burn grown up in huckleberries and flowers and drops 300 feet along the ridge connecting Sister Rocks to Observation (Trapper) Peak. At 1¾ miles are trail No. 158 and Observation Camp (water is sometimes to be found in a spring on the north side of the ridge). At 2½ miles is the junction with trail No. 192 from Government Mineral Springs; go left. A final ½ mile climbs the peak.

For an interesting sidetrip, wander meadows of flowers and huckleberries to the top of Sister Rocks, 4261 feet. Near the top are traces of an old trail, a few telephone poles, and bits of melted glass, all that remains of the Sister Rocks Lookout.

Trapper Peak and Mount Hood

63 | SIOUXON CREEK

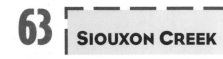

Round trip: 6 miles
Hiking time: 3 hours (day hike or backpack)
High point: 1300 feet
Elevation gain: 400 feet in, 300 feet out
Hikable: March through November

Map: Green Trails Lookout Mountain (No. 396)

Loop trip: 13½ miles
Hiking time: 8 hours (day hike or backpack)
High point: 4106 feet
Elevation gain: 3000 feet in, 300 feet out
Hikable: July through October

Information: Mount St. Helens National Volcanic Monument Headquarters, phone (360) 247-5473

The canopy is interwoven branches of tall firs, hemlocks, and maples. The floor is moss, oxalis, and ferns. The trail was reconstructed in 1990 to skirt the exciting waterfalls for which the valley is famed, and to stay in sight and sound of the ripples and tumbles of Siouxon Creek, a lowland stream whose limeade pools invite a person to mingle with the fish. Joyous camps are plentiful. Should a person feel energetic, the summit of 4108-foot Huffman Peak is handy for views of St. Helens and plenty more.

Siouxon Creek is an oasis between private and public tree farms, and it, too, was intended for the saw. The road was designed to go the length of the valley and the first 4 miles were completed and paved, but thanks to the concern of Forest Service employees, it was never finished. This may be the only remote trail with a paved road to the trailhead. The Forest Service has recommended the Siouxon for a Wild and Scenic River

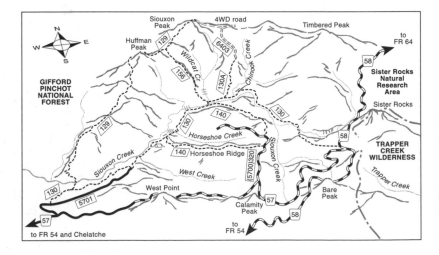

Falls on Siouxon Creek

classification, which could give the valley the preservation it deserves.

Drive to the headquarters of Mount St. Helens National Volcanic Monument on SR 503 between the towns of Amboy and Cougar. A few feet north at Chelatche Prairie General Store go east on Healy Road. At 2.4 miles the county road becomes road No. 54. At 9 miles from headquarters go left on road No. 57. In another 1.2 miles go left again on road No. 5701. At 11 miles from headquarters, the road switchbacks, intersecting the onetime beginning of the trail. Drive on to the road-end and new trailhead 14 miles from headquarters, elevation 1500 feet.

Siouxon Creek trail No. 130 plummets 300 feet to the banks of Siouxon Creek and a bridge across West Creek, then winds upstream on the valley floor by inviting campsites. In 1 mile pass Horseshoe Ridge trail No. 140, which ascends to road No. (5700)320 and a 3495-foot promontory, former site of the Horseshoe Ridge Lookout. At about 1½ miles the way climbs above a 60-foot waterfall on Horseshoe Creek, then traverses above a steep bank overlooking Siouxon Creek. In a scant 2 miles is the deep plunge-basin pool of a waterfall. At 3 miles is a crossing of Siouxon Creek on a bridge and a great turnaround point for a valley walk. Before returning, hike trail No. 156 up Wildcat Creek ½ mile to a waterfall tumbling into a rock cirque.

Sidetrip for the energetic: Cross Siouxon Creek and go left on trail No. 156, a steep 1300-foot climb 2½ miles up Wildcat Ridge to Siouxon Ridge, then go west on Huffman trail No. 129 in trees, meadows, and rocky slopes to 4106-foot Huffman Peak, a former lookout site. The sidetrip is 3½ miles each way and gains 2700 feet, a lot.

For a loop: From Huffman Peak continue 5 miles down the ridge on trail No. 129 to Siouxon Creek and 2 more miles back to the start.

64 | DOG MOUNTAIN

Round trip: "Old Trail" 6 miles
Round trip: "New Trail" 7½ miles
Loop trip: "Newest Trail" 9 miles
Hiking time: 5 hours (day hike)
High point: 2948 feet
Elevation gain: 2848 feet

Hikable: March to January
Map: Green Trails Hood River (No. 430)
Information: Columbia River Gorge
National Scenic Area,
phone (541) 386-2333

The Columbia Gorge is a national scenic treasure if there ever was one. Downcutting by the River of the West has kept pace with the uprising of the Cascade Range across its path, thus the river is older than the mountains. Local private-property extremists still demand their "rights" and most politicians are quick and eager to compromise the game away. A hiker can go far toward judging the relative merits of positions by walking a former stretch of the Cascade Crest Trail to a former lookout with views across the gorge to Mt. Hood and up and down the river.

Three trails lead to the top. The "old trail," which serviced the Puppy Dog Lookout from the 1930s, served as part of the Cascade Crest Trail until the Pacific Crest Trail was relocated near the Bridge of the Gods. Because the old trail was a very steep 3 miles, a "new trail" with switchbacks was built about 1980, still very steep but taking 3.8 miles to do the climb. Now the "newest trail" does it in 4.5 miles and thus is only moderately steep. Great opportunities exist for loops, though the Old is so difficult to maintain it may be abandoned.

Don't be confused by the trailhead sign for the Newest, "Dog Mountain trail 3.7 miles—Augsperger Mountain 7 miles." Augsperger is spelled wrong and the sign distance to the top is actually 4.5 miles. A half-mile up

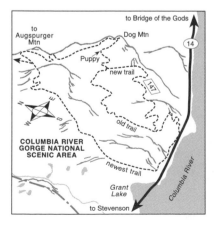

Newest is a crossing of what appears to be a very old and very steep wagon road, trees growing in the middle that look 50 or more years old. For some reason the Scenic Area is trying to hide the probable historic road.

Drive US 14 on the Washington side of the Columbia 9 miles east from Stevenson. Between mileposts 53 and 54 (MP 53.8) find a large parking area for the Dog Mountain trail, elevation 186 feet. Watch for snakes and poison oak, both beautiful but best enjoyed at a distance.

The Columbia River from the Puppy Lookout site

The two new trails both have good views. Higher elevations lead to the prairie-subalpine steppe, gaudy in spring with buttercups and asters, lupine and paintbrush, and scores of other blossoms. At 3 miles, 2505 feet, on the "Old" and "New" trails is the site of the Puppy Lookout, so-called because it was only partway up Dog Mountain. The cabin was on a shelf dug from the hillside. Here are the best river views; only the tip of Hood can be seen.

For more wildflowers as the season progresses, and bigger views of Hood, the Old and New trails continue ½ mile to the top of Dog Mountain, 2948 feet, 3 miles, and join the Newest trail. Do you have any remaining doubts about the worthiness of the Columbia Gorge to be preserved for the nation?

65 | SILVER STAR MOUNTAIN

Round trip: from south side 11 miles
Hiking time: 7 hours (day hike)
High point: 4390 feet
Elevation gain: 2000 feet
Hikable: May through October

Maps: USGS Larch Mtn., Bobs Mtn.,
  Dole Mtn., Gumboot Mtn.
Information: Wind River Ranger
  District, phone (509) 427-3200

The road approach is a nightmare for the family car, but the path through miles of flowers is a dream for hikers. The absence of forest and the abundance of meadowland are the result of the largest fire in the recorded history of the state, the Yacolt Burn of 1902. The sky was so dark in Seattle, 140 miles away, that street lights were turned on during the day. When rains finally damped the blaze, thirty-five people had been killed, hundreds of homes lost, and 238,000 acres blackened. The lower elevations soon reforested and are now being logged. Centuries must pass before forest advances foot by foot, year by year, to the heights. So it goes in the way of Nature. Nigh onto a century later, hikers glory in miles of ridge-top meadows carpeted with flowers, only an occasional rotting stump to remind that there was once a forest here. The climax is Silver Star Mountain, site of a former lookout.

Five great trails lead to the summit. The route recommended here gives the most miles of meadows and has the option of a looping return. Finding trailheads in the maze of county, Department of Natural Resources, and Forest Service roads is a challenge, and some of the roads are atrociously bad. A Forest Service map is essential.

From the town of Washougal on the Columbia River, drive the Washougal River Road, SR 140, some 10 miles. At a small country store

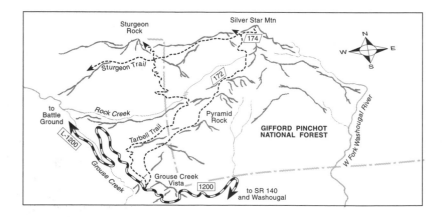

Silver Star Mountain

where the road makes a right turn and crosses the river, go straight ahead for 0.5 mile, then left on Sky Road 3.7 miles. At the county line turn right on the Skamania Mine road. A bit shy of 0.5 mile from the turn, go right, lose elevation, and cross a bridge; the road now narrows and starts climbing. At 2.8 miles from Sky Road go left on road No. 1200 another 4.3 miles to what the map calls Grouse Creek Vista, elevation 2375 feet. The trailhead sign only says Tarbell Trail (don't confuse with the Tarbell Camp on the west side of Silver Star).

On the north side of the road are two trails. To the left is Tarbell Trail, the possible return loop; the recommended route, to the right, trail No. 172, was part of the 1930s lookout road. Though ORVs have been barred for some time, signs prohibiting them are missing; both motorcycles and 4WDs climb over the barricade, so the first steep mile is badly chewed by machines. At 1 mile the way moderates and enters meadowland miles of beargrass, which blooms here in mid-May. Looking back, see Mt. Hood looming above the Columbia River. At 2 miles skirt Pyramid Rock. At 3¾ miles pass another CCC road-turned-4WD track. At 4½ miles note the Sturgeon Trail. A short bit farther go right up a steep, eroded roadbed to the 4390-foot high point on Silver Star and to views of Rainier, St. Helens, Adams, and more miles of meadows.

A return on the Sturgeon and Tarbell Trails is about the same distance. The big views and flower meadows are missing but an added attraction is a waterfall, a delightful grace note in the dryland.

66 | PACIFIC CREST TRAIL

The Pacific Crest National Scenic Trail, which extends from Mexico to Canada, is also known in the northernmost 250 miles by its older name, the Cascade Crest Trail. The 246-mile portion between the Columbia River and Snoqualmie Pass traverses highlands past three grand volcanoes and through the spectacular ruins of a fourth. The way isn't all pure fun because it also goes through lower, forested sections of the Cascade Range, where logging roads and clearcuts have savaged the wilderness solitude. However, the feeling of accomplishment gained by traveling the full length of the crest cannot be spoiled even by the worst of the messed-up parts.

Few hikers complete the route in a single effort; most do the trail in short

Mount Adams and the Pacific Crest Trail above Snowgrass Flat

bits over a period of years. Those taking the whole trip at once can start at either end; the south-to-north direction is described here.

At many places the trail is being relocated for the sake of easier grades or better scenery. The following brief summary is intended merely to provide a general impression of the route. For details of mileages and campsites, consult the Forest Service map and log of the Pacific Crest Trail, available from any Forest Service office.

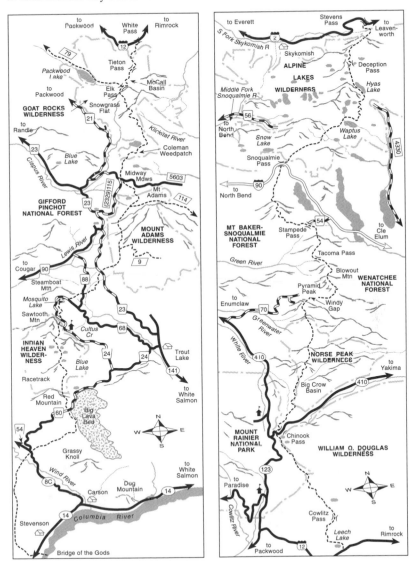

Columbia River to White Pass

One-way trip: about 148 miles
Hiking time: allow 15 days minimum
High point: 7620 feet
Elevation gain: about 24,900 feet

Hikable: the first 27 miles in May, mid-July for the rest
Map: USFS Pacific Crest National Scenic Trail—Washington State Southern Portion

Begin beside the legendary "River of the West," skirt the slopes of giant Mt. Adams, enjoy views to what's left of graceful Mount St. Helens, and walk the airy crest of the Goat Rocks Wilderness—the most difficult, as well as one of the most dramatically beautiful, segments of the entire Crest Trail.

Drive US 14 east from Vancouver to the Bridge of the Gods and locate the trailhead parking lot on the north side of the highway, elevation 186 feet.

Mount Adams and Adams Glacier Meadows near the Pacific Crest Trail

Hike through forest and lava flows with occasional views. The route is interrupted by logging roads, clearcuts, powerlines, and pipelines. Go up and down several times. Unless from the sky, there is no water the first 12 miles. The trail crosses the Wind River and, shortly after, road No. 30. The way climbs to Big Mountain and then drops to road No. 60 and a dry camp. *Distance from the Columbia River to road No. 60 about 45 miles; elevation gain 7900 feet; hiking time 5 days.*

From road No. 60 climb miles of woods to Red Mountain and Blue Lake and the pond-dotted meadows and famous huckleberry fields of Indian Heaven (Hike 56). Pass near Bear Lake, go almost over the top of Sawtooth Mountain, cross road No. 24, and continue through Huckleberry Meadows to Mosquito Creek. Cross road No. 8851 and traverse the east side of Steamboat Mountain to a crossing of road No. 88 and to road No. 23. *Distance from road No. 60 to road No. 23 about 26 miles; elevation gain about 2900 feet; hiking time 3 days.*

The next stage is climaxed by the alpine gardens and glacial streams on the flanks of Mt. Adams. Cross road No. 23, traverse Swampy Meadows, and at 12 miles join the Mount Adams Highline Trail (Hike 40). At 22 miles leave the Highline Trail and at 23½ miles leave the Mount Adams Wilderness at Spring Creek and cross road No. 5603 to road No. 2329 at Midway Meadows. *Distance from road No. 24 to Midway Meadows about 29 miles; elevation gain about 3500 feet; hiking time 3 days.*

Now starts the first long stretch of roadless country, most of it in the Goat Rocks Wilderness, including a couple of miles that can be dangerous. From Midway Meadows go a short bit along a rough road, round a lava flow, and at 6 miles enter the Wilderness. Proceed past Coleman Weedpatch, intersect the Walupt Lake Trail, and pass above Snowgrass Flat (Hike 34). Carefully, bewaring of hazards, climb the ridge above the Packwood Glacier and traverse the shoulder of Old Snowy to Elk Pass (Hike 35). The route crosses above McCall Basin to Tieton Pass and Shoe Lake (Hike 28), at 34 miles leaving the Wilderness and descending to White Pass. *Distance from Midway Meadows to White Pass about 38 miles; elevation gain about 6100 feet; hiking time 4 to 5 days.*

White Pass to Snoqualmie Pass

One-way trip: about 98 miles
Hiking time: 13 days
High point: 6500 feet
Elevation gain: about 20,400 feet

Hikable: mid-July through October
Map: USFS Pacific Crest National Scenic Trail—Washington State Southern Portion

North from White Pass extend miles of marvelous meadows and lakes and large views of Mt. Rainier in the William O. Douglas and Norse Peak Wildernesses, then a lower and more wooded (and road-marred) section of the crest leading to Snoqualmie Pass.

The first stage rarely leaves meadows and panoramas for long and passes numerous small lakes—too many to name here. From White Pass Highway, hike to Sand Lake (Hike 25), Cowlitz Pass, Fish Lake, and the Mount Rainier National Park boundary at 15½ miles. Weave in and out of the park, following the crest by Two Lakes and Dewey Lakes, and around the side of Naches Peak to Chinook Pass and SR 410; here leave the national park. *Distance from White Pass to Chinook Pass about 25 miles; elevation gain about 2400 feet; hiking time 3 days.*

The opening third of the next part lies in alpine terrain as before, and the remainder in woods broken by roads. Climb from Chinook Pass to Sourdough Gap (Hike 11), traverse to Bear Gap and around Pickhandle Point and Crown Point, with views to the Crystal Mountain Ski Area, ascend the crest, contour below the summit of Norse Peak, and drop into Big Crow Basin. Proceed to Little Crow Basin, a junction with the Arch Rock Trail, Arch Rock Camp, and Rod's Gap. Pass Government Meadows, cross the Naches Wagon Trail, and contour under Pyramid Peak to Windy Gap. *Distance from Chinook Pass to Windy Gap about 27 miles; elevation gain about 2500 feet; hiking time 3 days.*

Now comes a portion with few views except in clearcuts. From Windy Gap follow the crest nearly to the top of Blowout Mountain, descend in

Small pond on the Pacific Crest Trail near Frying Pan Lake

Sheep Lake near Chinook Pass

woods and clearcuts to Tacoma Pass and a logging road, and travel onward under Snowshoe Butte to Lizard Lake and road No. 54 at Stampede Pass. *Distance from Windy Gap to Stampede Pass about 27 miles; elevation gain about 1100 feet; hiking time 3 days.*

More forest travel—but much of the private land is being logged so the path is not always easy to find and not always pleasant, despite increasingly mountainous views northward. From Stampede Pass hike to Dandy Pass, then Mirror Lake, contour Tinkham and Silver Peaks (Hike 3) to Olallie Meadow and Lodge Lake, climb to Beaver Lake, and drop down ski slopes to Snoqualmie Pass. *Distance from Stampede Pass to Snoqualmie Pass about 18 miles; elevation gain about 1400 feet; hiking time 2 days.*

From Snoqualmie Pass the Pacific Crest Trail continues 253 miles to Allison Pass in Canada. See *100 Hikes in Washington's Alpine Lakes, 100 Hikes in Washington's North Cascades: Glacier Peak Region,* and *100 Hikes in Washington's North Cascades: Mount Baker Region.*

67 | SUNDOWN PASS

Round trip: about 17 miles
Hiking time: 10 hours (day hike or backpack)
High point: 4103 feet
Elevation gain: 2800 feet in, 300 feet out
Hikable: late July through October

Maps: Custom Correct Enchanted Valley—Skokomish, Green Trails Mount Tebo (No. 199), Mount Steel (No. 167), Mount Christie (No. 166)
Information: Hood Canal Ranger District, phone (360) 877-5254

Looking for solitude? Here it is!

Good trail follows a loud river through big-tree forest, then poor trail ascends to heather meadows and a delightful lakelet. The lower valley invites day hikes. Riverbank camps tempt a person to lounge overnight, listening to the water, looking at the trees and trying to understand why the South Fork Skokomish River was omitted from the Wonder Mountain Wilderness established in 1984.

Drive US 101 between Shelton and Hoodsport to 0.6 mile south of the Skokomish River bridge, turn upvalley on Skokomish River Road and drive 5.5 miles, then go right on road No. 23. Stick with it through many surprising twists and turns, taking care to dodge sideroads to Browns Creek Campground, Spider Lake, and Pine Lake. At 19 miles from the highway, go left on road No. 2361, pass a trailhead to the Lower South Fork Skokomish River trail, and at 24.5 miles come to the end of the road and the South Fork Skokomish River trail No. 873, elevation 1300 feet, the trailhead for both the lower and upper river trails.

Take the upper trail, walking an abandoned road about ¾ mile, and enter

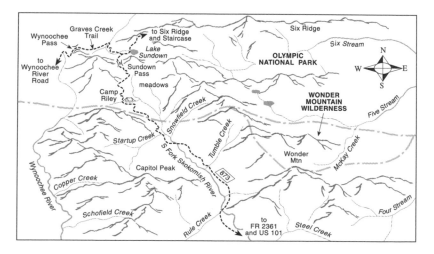

Snow patch on Sundown Pass

deep forest interspersed with huge boulders that in the dim past were thousands of feet above, part of Wonder Mountain. At 1¾ miles cross Rule Creek and the South Fork on logs; by now, observing the beautiful large trees, you see why they were not given protection by the Washington Wilderness Act of 1984 (the Lumber Barons had their eyes on them) and why they are on our agenda for Wilderness Act II. At 2 miles recross the river on a log. At a scant 4 miles a log may span Startup Creek to the last riverside camp. The trail starts up, for sure, and then contours steep slopes to the boundary of Olympic National Park, about 5 miles, 2800 feet. The good news is that here begins wilderness protection. What not everyone will consider even better news is that the wilderness is guarded not only by statute but by the end of good trail; the way trail beyond here receives little maintenance, is easy to lose, and shouldn't be attempted until all the snow melts, revealing boot-beaten tread, a help in routefinding.

Sometimes ascending ladderways of roots, other times traversing, the way is marked by metal tabs on trees and plastic ribbon. About ½ mile into the park is Camp Riley, in soggy meadows trampled by a herd of elk, many of whose trails are better than the official one. Cross the greenery and search for signs; if you go more than a few hundred feet with no definite sign of humanity, return to the last landmark and try again.

Beyond the meadows the trail climbs steeply, then levels out in a nice subalpine meadow. The trail appears to be intent on crossing the meadow but in fact only skirts it a bit before turning right, back into the woods; be wary, watch for tread. The trail tilts up and traverses to the right, ascending heather meadows dotted by small tarns. Above the highest, look for faint tread and ascend to Sundown Pass, 4103 feet, approximately 7 miles from the road.

Good tread descends 300 feet in ½ mile to a junction with the Graves Creek trail and in a level mile reaches Lake Sundown, 8 miles.

68 | MOUNT ELLINOR

Round trip: to summit 4½ miles
Hiking time: 5 hours (day hike)
High point: 5944 feet
Elevation gain: 2100 feet
Hikable: mid-July through October

Maps: Custom Correct Mt. Skokomish—
Lake Cushman, Green Trails Mt. Steel
(No. 167), The Brothers (No. 168)
Information: Hood Canal Ranger
District, phone (360) 877-5254

From the top of Mt. Ellinor, Puget Sound and Hood Canal are laid out like a map, Rainier, Adams, and St. Helens on the horizon. In the other direction are Mt. Olympus, the twin ears of Mt. Stone, the double top of The Brothers, and the impressive cliffs of Mt. Washington. Look down in the Jefferson Creek valley to an inviting lake called Ellinor Pond, 2000 feet below.

From 1853 to 1857 George Davidson surveyed Puget Sound, working from the brig *R. H. Fauntleroy,* named for his superior, the head of the U.S. Coast and Geodetic Survey. Needing names for the maps he was making, he drew upon the Fauntleroy family, calling the southernmost peak on the Olympic skyline Ellinor, for the youngest daughter, the double-summited peak for her brothers, and the highest point for her older sister Constance. Later, Davidson and Ellinor were married. However, subsequent mappers shifted Ellinor to a lower peak, replacing her with Mt. Washington.

The camera-packing co-author grew up nearby and Ellinor was the first real mountain he bagged, back when he was 12 years old. In those days the route began with a 5200-foot climb from Lake Cushman. Then, as now, the official trail ended at the first meadow. From there to the top was a

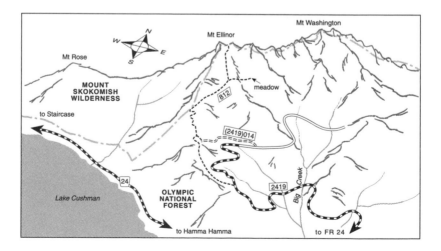

wild and dangerous rock scramble. A logging road has shortened the trail to a mere 1½ miles, bringing the summit scramble in reach of folks with no experience and less sense. In 1990, thanks to volunteers Frank Maranville (age 71), Frank Heuston (76), Tom Weilepp (61), with help by the Olympia Branch of The Mountaineers and Olympic National Forest, a new, safe (relatively) trail has been built to the top. Even now (1998) the three are still maintaining it. The trail is sketchy in places, steep all the way, but much less dangerous than it was.

Drive US 101 along Hood Canal to the center of Hoodsport. Turn west and go 9 miles on the Lake Cushman road to a junction. Turn right 1.6 miles on road No. 24, then left on Big Creek road No. 2419. At 4.8 miles from road No. 24 pass the lower trailhead (for use when the road is blocked above) and at 6.4 miles go left on road No. (2419)014 another 0.7 mile to the road-end and trailhead, elevation about 3500 feet. Carry a full canteen; the slopes are dry.

Find the path, climbing very steeply up the nose of the ridge. In ¼ mile is a junction with the lower trail. At a long 1 mile, as the first heather appears, is a Y; straight ahead ⅓ mile is a small meadow, 4500 feet, and vistas of lowlands and Cascades as good as those from the summit.

From the Y the summit trail steeply climbs heather meadows, forest, rockslides, scree slopes, and flower gardens in a scant 1½ mile,

Mountain goat on top of Mount Ellinor

gaining 1100 feet to the 5944-foot top. In several rocky stretches the tread is faint. The final 50 feet are a scramble. Watch your feet. Also take care to note where the trail ends, lest on the way down you end up on cliffs.

69 | FLAPJACK LAKES

Round trip: to lakes 16 miles
Hiking time: 10 hours (day hike or backpack)
High point: 4000 feet
Elevation gain: 3200 feet
Hikable: mid-June through October

Maps: Custom Correct Mount Skokomish—Lake Cushman, Green Trails Mount Steel (No. 167)
Information: Olympic National Park Wilderness Information Center, phone (360) 452-0300

Park Service Wilderness Reservation required for overnight stay

Two subalpine lakes set side by side like flapjacks in a frying pan. Above the waters and the forests rise sharp summits of the Sawtooth Range, a group of peaks noted among climbers for the odd texture of the rock, which largely consists of "pillow lava" erupted under the surface of an ancient sea and now eroded into weird shapes.

Drive US 101 along Hood Canal to Hoodsport. Turn west, pass Lake Cushman, go left on road No. 24, and follow the North Fork Skokomish River road to the Staircase Ranger Station and trailhead, elevation 800 feet.

The trail follows an abandoned road the first 3¾ miles, where really-truly trail goes right and ascends moderately but steadily in cool forest to Madeline Creek, 5¼ miles; campsites across the bridge. The way steepens to campsites and a junction at Donahue Creek, at 7½ miles. A way trail goes left to Black and White Lakes in 1⅓ miles, Smith Lake in 2¼ miles.

The right fork switchbacks another very long ¾ mile to Flapjack Lakes, 3850 feet. One lake is quite shallow, the other is deeper and ringed by rock

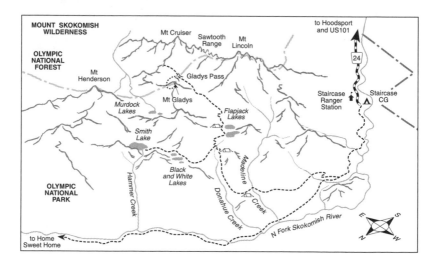

Flapjack Lakes and Sawtooth Range

buttresses; the two are separated by a narrow isthmus. The most striking Sawtooth summit from the lakes is The Horn—known to a party of hikers who saw it on an autumn night years ago with the full moon (made of green cheese, then) touching its yearning snout, as "The Mouse." Other hikers have seen it as "Chipmunk."

Actually, the trip only just begins at the lakes. For high and wide meadows and broad views, walk the Mt. Gladys way trail 1½ more miles up a lovely valley of rocks and flowers and bubbling water to Gladys Pass, 5000 feet, between a rounded garden peak and a vicious finger of lava. Roam the gardens to the 5600-foot summit of Mt. Gladys. Stare at the frightening walls of 6104-foot Mt. Cruiser ("Bruiser"), whose tower is visible from Seattle, standing like a boundary monument on the southeast corner of Olympic National Park.

Popularity has forced stringent restrictions on camping: Between Memorial Day and Labor Day the nightly limit is 30 persons at the lakes and above; stoves-only at the lakes and above. If the quota is full, day hike from Donahue Creek.

70 | HOME SWEET HOME

Round trip: to Camp Pleasant 13 miles
Hiking time: 8 hours (day hike or backpack)
High point: 1600 feet
Elevation gain: 800 feet out
Hikable: May through November

Round trip: to Home Sweet Home 27 miles
Hiking time: allow 2 days
High point: 4688 feet
Elevation gain: 4000 feet in, 500 feet out
Hikable: July through October

Maps: Custom Correct Mount Skokomish—Lake Cushman, Green Trails Mount Steel (No. 167)

Information: Olympic National Park Wilderness Information Center, phone (360) 452-0300

Park Service backcountry use permit required for overnight stay

In early May, when a small elk band is still in the Skokomish valley and trillium and calypso orchids are in bloom, walk the gentle trail to Nine Stream. In summer, climb from the valley to First Divide and broad views,

Mount Steel, taken on a springtime hike to Home Sweet Home

then drop to Duckabush River drainage and the lupine meadows of Home Sweet Home.

Drive US 101 to the center of Hoodsport (Hike 68) and turn west, pass Lake Cushman, and go left on road No. 24 to the Staircase Ranger Station, elevation 800 feet.

The North Fork Skokomish River trail follows a revegetated abandoned road; thanks (no thanks) to the 1985 man-caused Beaver Burn, there are several views. At 3¾ miles the way becomes an honest-to-golly trail to Big Log Camp, 6 miles, a spacious area beside the stream. At 6½ miles the path crosses the river on a bridge over a deep, quiet pool. Immediately beyond is a junction; go right. The trail climbs slightly to Camp Pleasant, 7 miles, 1600 feet, on a large maple flat. This appropriately named spot makes a good overnight stop for springtime backpackers.

At 10 miles, 2091 feet, is Nine Stream and the end of level walking. In the next mile the trail ascends at a comfortable rate through a big meadow, then forest. After that the way is continuously steep and often rough. Flower gardens become more frequent. Mt. Hopper and Mt. Stone appear, Hopper to the east and Stone to the southeast.

At 12½ miles the trail reaches a meadow below Mt. Steel, turns sharply right, and climbs to the crest of 4688-foot First Divide, 13 miles, and views across the Duckabush valley to Mt. La Crosse, White Mountain, and the greenery of La Crosse Pass.

A ½-mile descent from First Divide brings happy travelers to Home Sweet Home, 4198 feet, and blossoms of avalanche lilies or lupine or whatever the season has to offer. The view of 6233-foot Mt. Steel is superb.

Many hikers continue, losing 2000 feet to the Duckabush River trail. From here they go upstream, gaining 2500 feet to Lake La Crosse, and cross O'Neil Pass to the Enchanted Valley trail (Hike 95), or downstream 1½ miles and then climb over 5566-foot La Crosse Pass to Honeymoon Meadows on the Dosewallips (Hike 76). Only the vast meadows at the pass make this grueling 3000-foot ascent on a waterless south-facing slope worth the effort.

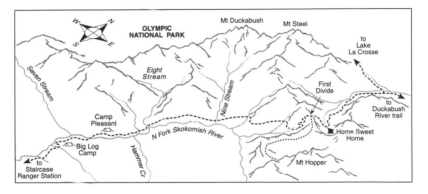

71 | UPPER LENA LAKE

Round trip: to upper lake 14 miles
Hiking time: 12 hours (day hike or backpack)
High point: 4600 feet
Elevation gain: 3900 feet
Hikable: to lower lake April through November, to upper lake July through October

Maps: Custom Correct The Brothers—Mount Anderson, Green Trails The Brothers (No. 168)
Information: Olympic National Park Wilderness Information Center, phone (360) 452-0300

Park Service backcountry use permit required for overnight stay

Hike an easy trail, free of snow most of the year, through splendid forest to popular and often crowded Lena Lake, which should have been included in 1984 in The Brothers Wilderness but was omitted because a kilowatt-crazed utility was scheming for a hydroelectric project. Both the Forest Service and environmental groups are protesting the project. But to add immediate insult to possible injury, the Forest Service has opened the trail to bicycles, thus effectively closing it to peaceful walking.

Drive US 101 along Hood Canal some 14 miles north of Hoodsport, cross the Hamma Hamma River bridge, and 0.5 mile beyond Waketickeh Creek turn left on the Hamma Hamma River road No. 25 and drive 8 miles to the trailhead, elevation 685 feet.

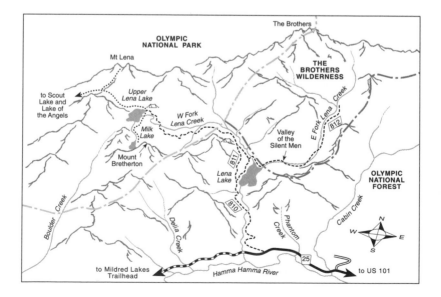

Upper Lena Lake and Mount Bretherton

The wide trail, No. 810, switchbacks gently and endlessly in forest shadows. At 1½ miles it crosses the dry stream bed of Lena Creek, which runs underground most of the year. At 3 miles is Lena Lake, 1800 feet. Here the trail splits. The right fork drops to campsites by the lake and rounds the west shore ½ mile to more. For a great sidetrip, at a junction turn right to follow East Fork Lena Creek (trail No. 812) into the Valley of the Silent Men, crossing and recrossing the stream many times, toward The Brothers, a principal summit of the Olympic horizon seen from Seattle. This ancient prospectors' trail is mainly used by fishermen and climbers but is well worth exploration by hikers who enjoy loitering beside cold water frothing and sparkling through rapids, swirling in green pools, all in the deep shade of old forest.

For Upper Lena Lake, stay left, following West Fork Lena Creek on trail No. 811, entering Olympic National Park at 4 miles. At about 5 miles, 2700 feet, the trail crosses a creek, which can be hazardous during the spring runoff.

As the trail climbs, the vegetation changes to subalpine forest. Heather and huckleberry appear along with Alaska cedar. Occasional views open down the valley toward The Brothers. The steepness ends abruptly at Upper Lena Lake, 4600 feet, 7 miles. A rough up-and-down way trail rounds the north side.

Camps are inviting but have been beaten bare by overuse; some are closed, being revegetated by the Park Service. Camp only at designated sites; stoves only. A privy is located near the inlet. The shore demands roaming, as do the meadows and screes ringing the cirque. For more ambitious explorations scramble to the summit of 5995-foot Mt. Lena, or ascend the creek falling from little Milk Lake, tucked in a quiet pocket and generally frozen until late summer, or follow a boot-beaten track over a 5000-foot ridge near Mt. Lena to Scout Lake, or follow the ridge by its numerous tarns toward Mt. Stone and Lake of the Angels.

72 | MILDRED LAKES

Round trip: 10 miles
Hiking time: 9 hours (day hike or backpack)
High point: 4100 feet
Elevation gain: 2300 feet in, 600 feet out
Hikable: mid-July through mid-October

Maps: Custom Correct Mt. Skokomish—Lake Cushman, Green Trails Mt. Steel (No. 167)
Information: Hoodsport Ranger District, phone (360) 877-5254

Three mountain lakes beneath the startling basalt spires of Sawtooth Ridge, well worth a visit—as they'd darn well better be, after the struggle. To keep the area primitive, the trail (way) is not maintained by the Forest Service, and on certain wooded slopes is so obscure the hiker may not recognize it. What "trail" there is has been hammered into hillsides and over countless logs by the boots of generations of fishermen, hikers, and climbers. The distance is only 4½ miles to the first lake, but that doesn't include detours around wooden barricades. Nor does the figure given here for elevation gain include the ups and downs over logs and rocks and bumps. These are just extra dividends. But don't complain—even more than the official designation by Congress in 1984, they make it *real* wilderness.

Drive some 14 miles north of Hoodsport and go left on the Hamma Hamma Recreation Area road No. 25 (Hike 71) to the end at a concrete bridge over the Hamma Hamma River, elevation 1900 feet. Find Mildred Lake trail No. 822 at the far side of the bridge and enter the Mount Skokomish Wilderness.

In the first mile a little work has been done—logs cut, the tread occasionally graded. Such gestures end in the second mile as the way climbs steeply over a 3200-foot ridge and drops 300 feet to a delightful camp beside Huckleberry Creek, approximately 2 miles. The trail is easily lost here amid false paths made by elk and confused hikers.

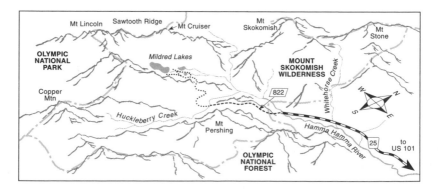

Upper Mildred Lake and Sawtooth Range

Cross the creek, stay level several hundred feet, then climb—and climb, with only an occasional respite, 1000 feet, mostly straight up on the stretch known as "Bailey's Boulevard." At 4100 feet is a ridge top of heather and alpine trees and great views that tempt a party to call it quits. Don't. The madding crowd has been left behind. The end is near. Drop 300 feet to Lower Mildred Lake at 4½ miles, follow the path along the shore to the lakehead, and near the inlet find the trail (again amid many false paths) climbing a bit in ⅓ mile to the upper lake and great views and great camps, 5 miles from the road.

The third lake, about the same elevation, is off toward Mt. Cruiser. The path starts from the outlet of the upper lake. Despite the formidable approach, so many undaunted boots have tramped here that the lakeshores are being revegetated; be kind to the plants.

If time permits, ascend (with some bushwhacking) a 5000-foot knoll below Mt. Lincoln. The effort is repaid with a view of Mt. Washington, Mt. Pershing, and a score of other Olympic peaks.

73 | DUCKABUSH RIVER

Round trip: 10 miles
Hiking time: 6 hours (day hike or backpack)
High point: 1700 feet
Elevation gain: 1300 feet in, 800 feet out
Hikable: May through November

Maps: Custom Correct The Brothers—Mount Anderson, Green Trails The Brothers (No. 168)
Information: Hoodsport Ranger District, phone (360) 877-5254

Park Service backcountry use permit required for overnight stay in park

The Duckabush River Trail is 20 miles long, wildland all the way to Lake La Crosse and O'Neil Pass (Hike 96) in the heart of the Olympics, and the hiker who takes this respectful approach through valley forest truly earns the highland flowers. However, the lower stretch of trail, in 200- to 400-year-old firs and hemlocks, with sumptuous riverside camps, is a trip on its own, particularly enjoyed in late spring and early summer when the snow is still deep on the heights but is gone here, replaced by the blooms of bead lily and calypso orchid. It's not all a garden path; there are two major obstacles, Little Hump and Big Hump, but, for reasons to be explained, you shouldn't complain.

Drive US 101 some 22 miles north of Hoodsport to 0.2 mile past the Duckabush River bridge, and at milepost 310 turn west on the Duckabush River road which at 3.7 miles becomes road No. 2510. At 6 miles pass the horse corral, turn right on road No. (2510)011, and go the 0.1 mile to the Duckabush River trail No. 803, elevation 500 feet.

The trail gets directly to business, climbing the first obstacle on a long-abandoned road, gaining 400 feet in 1 mile to the boundary of The Brothers Wilderness atop Little Hump, which weeds out the pikers among the hikers.

The way drops 200 feet (oh! oh!) to river level and for 1 mile of flat valley

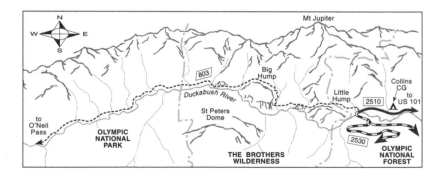

Along the Duckabush River valley

bottom follows an old logging railroad grade through second-growth dating from the 1920s and 1930s. At 2¼ miles is a good camp.

Excellent if steep trail now tackles the main job. While toiling up it 1000 feet, bless the Big Hump for stopping the railroad loggers in the 1930s, as well as the truck loggers of later decades, saving this forest—which you will notice is virgin—for wilderness designation in 1984. So, no complaints, give thanks for your sweat. At 3½ miles a false summit gives views across the valley to St. Peters Dome and downstream, and at 4 miles is the true top of Big Hump, 1700 feet. The way promptly drops 600 feet (no complaints!) to the river and a great campsite at 1100 feet, about 5 miles from the road. A scant 1½ miles lead to the park boundary and more camps.

74 | MOUNT JUPITER

Round trip: 14 miles
Hiking time: 10 hours (day hike)
High point: 5701 feet
Elevation gain: 3600 feet
Hikable: June through October

Map: Custom Correct The Brothers—
Mount Anderson
Information: Hoodsport Ranger
District, phone (360) 877-5254

Look from Seattle across Puget Sound to the Olympic horizon; right smack between The Brothers and Mt. Constance is Jupiter. Actually, the peak does not deserve rank in such distinguished company, but it stands so far out in the front of the range as to seem bigger than it really is. But give old Jupe his due: The peak offers unique combination views of lowlands and mountains. The summit ascent, however, is long and strenuous and usually dry and hot. Most hikers are content to climb to the views and leave the summit to compulsive peakbaggers. Carry a loaded canteen—there is no water on the way.

(*Note:* Due to a maze of logging spurs on state and private land, the correct road is hard to stick with and the private logging company may gate the road without notice.) Drive US 101 along Hood Canal some 22.5 miles north of Hoodsport, to a scant mile past the Duckabush River bridge. A bit south of the Black Point road, turn west on the Mount Jupiter road 0.2 mile to a junction; go right on road No. (2610)010 (not signed as such) which becomes (2610)011. At 0.8 mile stay left at the Juniper/Madrona junction, then pass up Love Road, stay left at 1.7 miles, signed (sometimes) "Mt. Jupiter Trail," and ascend the steep and tortuous zigzag way under powerlines. At 2.4 miles reach the gate, signed "No motor vehicles. Gate may be closed without notice." (The Forest Service has an easement but

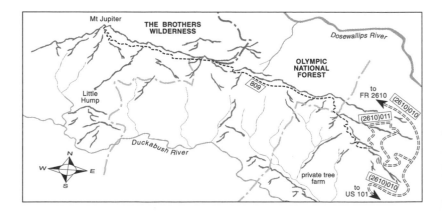

The Brothers and cloud-filled Duckabush River valley from the Mount Jupiter trail

the company has the right to close the road.) Whether or not to continue is the driver's choice. The road steepens and comes to more junctions; most of the time the correct way is obvious or signed. At 5.4 miles stay left and at 5.8 miles reach a wide parking area near the trailhead, elevation 2150 feet.

The first mile switchbacks up south slopes of the ridge dividing the Duckabush and Dosewallips Rivers. At 1 mile, 2850 feet, the trail reaches the ridge crest and here leaves state land and enters Olympic National Forest. The hike to this point, with splendid panoramas, can be done in late May and early June, when the trip is really the most pleasant, especially since rhododendrons are then in bloom along the lower trail.

However, for those willing, the way goes on, following the ridge crest up and down, up and down, at 5 miles entering The Brothers Wilderness. A final very steep mile attains the summit, 7 miles, 5701 feet.

From summit or the trail the views are glorious. North beyond the Dosewallips is Mt. Constance, and south beyond the Duckabush are the double summits of The Brothers. Westward is the grandeur of Olympic National Park. Eastward across Hood Canal and the Kitsap Peninsula are Seattle, the Space Needle, suburbia, smog, civilization.

75 | LAKE CONSTANCE

Round trip: to the lake 4 miles
Hiking time: 7 hours (day hike or backpack)
High point: 4750 feet
Elevation gain: 3300 feet
Hikable: mid-June through October

Maps: Custom Correct Buckhorn Wilderness, Green Trails Tyler Peak (No. 136), The Brothers (No. 168)
Information: Olympic National Park Wilderness Information Center, phone (360) 452-0300

Park Service Wilderness Reservation required for overnight stay

A classic tarn in a secluded cirque, the deep blue waters ringed by alpine trees and heather gardens and sheer cliffs of Mt. Constance. But the way there does not fit any official, rational definition of "trail," nor could it be made such without enough explosives to fight a medium-size war. The Park Service classifies it as a climbers' route—super-steep, dangerous in spots, and not recommended for beginners or small children or the fainthearted or anyone who quails at gaining 3300 feet in only 2 miles.

Drive US 101 along Hood Canal to the Dosewallips River road just north of Brinnon. Turn west 14 miles to 0.5 mile inside the park boundary and the several wide spots that serve as the trailhead parking area at Constance Creek, elevation 1450 feet.

The first mile is brutal, virtually without switchbacks, gaining some 2000 feet to a short, level stretch and a good forest camp at the 1-mile marker. The second mile seems even steeper, though this is purely an optical illusion caused by the ladderways of tree roots and the short rock cliffs. Feet must be placed with care and thank-god handholds thoroughly tested. Caution is especially essential on the descent. At 2 miles, 4750 feet, the trail abruptly flattens into the cirque.

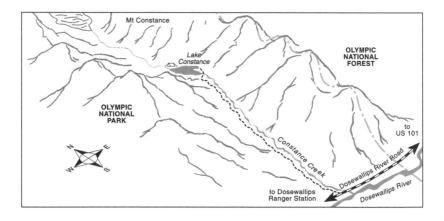

Lake Constance

Popularity among the innocent and the undaunted has forced stringent restrictions: Camping *by reservation only*; a nightly limit of 20; use designated sites only; no fires; *please use the privies.*

Impressive as the lake is, the truly awesome scenery lies higher, beyond the portals of what Boy Scouts of old, feeling spooky, called "Dead Man's Gap." Follow a boot-beaten climbers' track above the lake, up talus, through the gap into Avalanche Canyon, a mile-long glacier trough between the higher east peak of Constance and the west peak ("Inner Constance"). Solemn and spectacular it is, a place of crags, cliffs, and scree, snowfields and moraines. Hikers can walk safely to the canyon head at about 6000 feet.

The geology adds fascination. The weird, bumpy-looking walls of the canyon consist of "pillow lava" formed by molten rock erupting under the sea and cooling into these odd, rounded shapes. Heat and pressure metamorphosed limestone into pastel-colored rocks, often in variegated fault breccia of striking beauty. Hot mineralized solutions deposited green crystals of epidote intermixed with the white of quartz and calcite.

76 | ANDERSON GLACIER

Round trip: to Anderson Glacier 22 miles
Hiking time: allow 3 days
High point: 5000 feet
Elevation gain: 3500 feet
Hikable: mid-July through October

Maps: Custom Correct Buckhorn
Wilderness, Green Trails Mount Steel
(No. 167), The Brothers (No. 168)
Information: Olympic National Park
Wilderness Information Center,
phone (360) 452-0300

Park Service backcountry use permit required for overnight stay

Follow a long trail to the edge of one of the largest glaciers in the eastern Olympics. Enjoy glorious views down the Dosewallips River to Mt. Constance, over Anderson Pass to Mt. La Crosse and White Mountain, down into the Enchanted Valley at the head of the Quinault River, and, of course, across the Anderson Glacier to the summits of Mt. Anderson. In early August a wild array of flowers blooms, including small fields of lupine and paintbrush that stand out dramatically against the rugged background.

Drive US 101 along Hood Canal to just north of Brinnon and turn west on the Dosewallips River road, coming to the end of pavement in 4.7 miles, Elkhorn Campground junction at 10.7 miles, Constance Creek at 13.5 miles, and at 15 miles the road-end and trailhead at Dosewallips Campground and Guard Station, elevation 1540 feet.

The trail starts in deep forest with a showing of rhododendrons in late

The Anderson Glacier

June and, after going up and down a bit, reaches a junction at 1½ miles. Turn left to Dose Forks Camp and cross the river. At about 2½ miles the way again crosses the river, now the West Fork Dosewallips, this time on a bridge perched spectacularly some 100 feet over the water. The trail climbs steeply to dry forests high above the stream, which flows in so deep a gorge that often it cannot be heard.

The trail descends a bit to campsites at 5 miles, then climbs again, and with minor ups and downs reaches the small opening of Diamond Meadow at 6¾ miles, 2692 feet. Pleasant campsites by the stream. At 7½ miles the trail once more crosses the river and begins a steady ascent, at about 8 miles climbing steeply beside the raging torrent as it tumbles through a narrow gorge. At 8¾ miles, 3627 feet, the valley opens into the broad, flat expanse and good camps of Honeymoon Meadows, named years ago by a Seattle couple who long since have celebrated their golden wedding anniversary. (Here and above, stove-only camping. And the valley is a happy hunting ground for a number of bears, so watch your groceries.) One final time the trail crosses the river, here a jump wide (a big jump), and ascends to Camp Siberia at 10 miles and Anderson Pass at 10½ miles, 4464 feet.

The Anderson Glacier Overlook way trail climbs steeply from the north side of the wooded pass, emerging from trees and in ¾ mile ending at a small tarn amid boulders and meadows. A few feet farther are the edge of moraine and the views, 5000 feet.

The West Fork Dosewallips trail to Anderson Pass often is included in longer trips: a 27-mile one-way hike down Enchanted Valley (Hike 95); a 49-mile one-way hike to O'Neil Pass and out the Duckabush River (Hike 96); a 36½-mile one-way hike out the North Fork Skokomish River; and a 41-mile loop trip via O'Neil Pass and the upper Duckabush, returning to the Dosewallips via a grueling 3000-foot climb to La Crosse Pass.

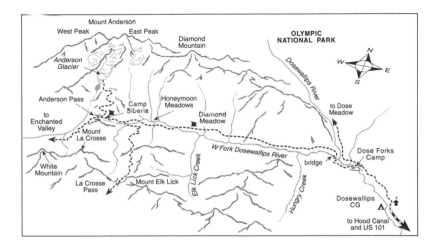

77 | HAYDEN PASS

Round trip: to Hayden Pass 31 miles
Hiking time: allow 3 to 4 days
High point: 5847 feet
Elevation gain: 4250 feet
Hikable: July through October

Maps: Custom Correct Gray Wolf—
Dosewallips, Green Trails The Brothers
(No. 168), Tyler Peak (No. 136),
Mount Angeles (No. 137)
Information: Olympic National Park
Wilderness Information Center,
phone (360) 452-0300

Park Service backcountry use permit required for overnight stay

Miles of marvelous forest, then alpine meadows waist-deep in flowers, where fragrance makes the head swim on warm days, where a quiet hiker may see deer, elk, marmots, or bear. All this and impressive views too, plus numerous fine campsites at short intervals along the trail. The pass makes a superb round-trip destination or can be included in an across-the-Olympics journey to the Elwha River, or in a giant 10-day loop over Low Divide, returning via Anderson Pass.

Drive US 101 along Hood Canal to the Dosewallips River road just north of Brinnon. Turn west and go 15.5 miles to the road-end campground and trailhead, elevation 1540 feet (Hike 76).

A gentle 1½ miles through open forest in a dense groundcover of salal and rhododendron (the latter blooms in late June) lead to Dose Forks. A bit beyond is a junction with the trail to Anderson Pass (Hike 76); take the right fork and start climbing. At 2 miles note animal tracks at Soda Springs. Cross many little streams, nice spots for resting. At 2½ miles the Sunnybrook sidetrail heads up to supremely scenic but far-above Del Monte Ridge and Constance Pass.

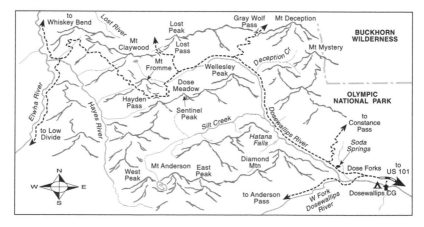

As the path ascends, Diamond Mountain appears across the river; from a well-marked point, see Hatana Falls. At about 8 miles the valley widens and the trail crosses a series of meadows. At 9 miles pass the sidetrail to Gray Wolf Pass and continue in steadily more open terrain, with wider views, to Dose Meadow at 13 miles, 4450 feet; a sidetrail ascends to Lost Pass.

Beyond the meadows a bridge crosses a small canyon of a creek-size river with a lion-size roar. At 13½ miles, 4600 feet, the way enters the vast garden basin of the headwaters, surrounded by high peaks. The trail crosses the river one last time and switchbacks to Hayden Pass, 15½ miles, 5847 feet. In early summer a steep snowbank blocks the tread; be cautious.

Hayden Pass is the low point on the skinny ridge connecting Mt. Fromme and Sentinel Peak. North is Mt. Claywood, east are Wellesley Peak and the Dosewallips valley, south is glacier-covered Mt. Anderson, and west are the Bailey Range and distant Mt. Olympus.

Down from the pass 1 mile on the Elwha River side, just before the trail enters forest, find a delightful campsite by a bubbling creek.

For the across-the-Olympics hike, continue 9 miles and 4200 feet down from the pass to the Elwha River trail and then 17 miles more to the Whiskey Bend road-end (Hike 85).

No wood fires are permitted above 4000 feet; carry a stove or a lot of baloney sandwiches.

Avalanche lilies at Hayden Pass (John Spring photo)

78 | MARMOT PASS

Round trip: to Marmot Pass 10½ miles
Hiking time: 9 hours (day hike or backpack)
High point: 6000 feet
Elevation gain: 3500 feet

Hikable: July through mid-November
Maps: Custom Correct Buckhorn Wilderness, Green Trails Tyler Peak (No. 136)
Information: Quilcene Ranger District, phone (360) 765-3368

Before World War II, in an era when Boy Scouts were perhaps the principal wanderers of the Olympic wilderness, the "Three Rivers Hike" was among the most popular trips from old Camp Parsons. Thousands of scouts now getting quite long in the tooth vividly recall their introduction to highlands on the grueling "Poop Out Drag," climbing steeply and endlessly along a sun-baked south slope, arriving in late afternoon at Camp Mystery, then taking an after-dinner walk through flower gardens and broad meadows to Marmot Pass and thrilling evening views down to shadowed forests of the Dungeness River, 3000 feet below, and beyond to Mt. Mystery, Mt. Deception, second-highest in the Olympics, and the jagged line of The Needles, all etched in a sunset-colored sky.

Drive US 101 along Hood Canal to 0.9 mile south of the Quilcene Ranger Station and turn west on Penny Creek Road. At 1.4 miles go left on a road signed "Big Quilcene River Road," which becomes road No. 27. At about 10 miles, go left on No. 2750, signed "Big Quilcene Trail"; in another 5 miles, find the start of Big Quilcene trail No. 833, elevation 2500 feet.

Warrior Peak and Mount Constance from Marmot Pass

The trail immediately enters the Buckhorn Wilderness and follows the river through intensely green forest, all moss and ferns and lichen, crossing numerous step-across creeks, passing many close-up looks at the lovely river. At 2½ miles is Shelter Rock Camp, 3600 feet, and the last water for 2 miles.

Now the way turns steeply upward from big trees to little, the hot, dry scree alternating with flowers, on the famous (or infamous) Poop Out Drag. At 4½ miles the suffering ends as the trail abruptly flattens out at Camp Mystery, 5400 feet, with two delightful springs and campsites in alpine trees. Except for snowmelt there is no water above, so if a camp with solitude is desired, load up the water-carrier here and continue to a private nook on high.

The trail continues upward, passing under a cliff and opening into a wide, flat meadow, marmots whistling up a storm. At 5½ miles, 6000 feet, the way attains the Buckhorn Botanical Area and, a bit farther, Marmot Pass and panoramas westward, as well as back down east to Hood Canal.

The Three Rivers Hike of saga and myth descended the trail 1½ miles to Boulder Shelter, followed trail No. 833 to Home Lake and Constance Pass in Olympic National Park, climbed Del Monte Ridge, and plunged down the interminable short switchbacks of the Sunnybrook trail to the Dosewallips River trail, and thence to the road. The trip is still extremely popular, using a two-car shuttle.

Fine as the views are from Marmot Pass, nearby are even better. For a quick sample, scramble up the 6300-foot knoll directly south of the pass. For the full display, at the pass turn north on trail No. 840, leading to Copper Creek, and along the 1½ miles to Buckhorn Pass take one of several boot-beaten paths to the 6950-foot west summit of Buckhorn Mountain. Especially striking are the dramatic crags of 7300-foot Warrior Peak and 7743-foot Mt. Constance and the views north to the Strait of Juan de Fuca and Vancouver Island.

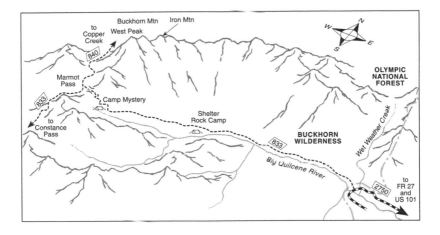

79 | MOUNT TOWNSEND

Round trip: 8½ miles
Hiking time: 6 hours (day hike or backpack)
High point: 6280 feet
Elevation gain: 2880 feet

Hikable: June through November
Maps: Custom Correct Buckhorn Wilderness, Green Trails Tyler Peak (No. 136)
Information: Quilcene Ranger District, phone (360) 765-3368

Climb to a northern outpost of the highlands. Look down to the Strait of Juan de Fuca, Puget Sound, Hood Canal, and across the water to Mt. Baker, Glacier Peak, and faraway Mt. Rainier. In the other direction, of course, see the Olympic Mountains. The steep southeast slopes of the trail route melt free of snow in early June, and usually only a few easy patches are encountered then. Mid-June is best, though, when the entire forest road is lined with rhododendron blossoms, spring flowers are a-blooming in the lowlands and summer flowers on the south-facing rock gardens high up. This trail is especially popular when others are still in snow, often on a fine day drawing a hundred hikers.

Two trails lead to the summit. The one from Townsend Creek, ascending the southeast side with two separate trailheads, is described here. The other, the Little Quilcene trail from Last Water Camp, is perhaps cooler walking in midsummer but is harder to maintain and less used.

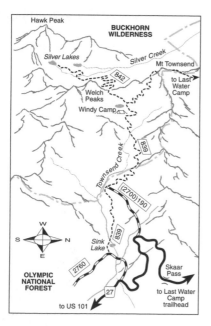

Because of three trailheads, road signs can be confusing. Drive US 101 to 0.9 mile south of the Quilcene Ranger Station and go west on Penny Creek Road. At 1.4 miles go left on "Big Quilcene River Road," which becomes road No. 27. At 13.4 miles pass up road No. 2760, the lower of the two starts. About 14 miles, at a switchback go left on road No. (2700)190 to Mt. Townsend trailhead No. 839, elevation 3400 feet.

For the Little Quilcene trail from Last Water Camp, drive road No. 27 another 5 miles and turn left on road No. 28 for 2 miles, then left on road No. 2820 for 3 miles to the Little Quilcene River trailhead, elevation 4000 feet.

Headwaters of Silver Creek from Mount Townsend

The Mt.Townsend trail No. 839 ascends steadily in timber ½ mile, and then opens out and steepens somewhat to Windy Camp, 2¼ miles, 5300 feet. Pleasant camping around little Windy Lake.

The way continues upward in parkland with a scattering of small flower gardens. At 2½ miles is a junction. The left fork, trail No. 842, climbs over a saddle, drops into Silver Creek, and climbs again to campsites at Silver Lakes, a sidetrip of 2½ miles each way; one small lake is on the trail and the other is hidden. The right fork heads up the mountain, topping the ridge at 3¼ miles, 6000 feet, then following the crest, passing 100 feet below the first summit at 3¾ miles and running to the most northerly part of the ridge and the second summit, connecting there with the Little Quilcene trail and a trail down to Silver Creek.

Which summit is the higher? They are so evenly matched—the north, 6212 feet, the south, 6280 but seeming lower—you must do both. Soak up the view over the waters to the Cascades and over the rolling meadow ridges of the Olympics. The rugged peaks to the south are Mt. Constance and its neighbors and, farther away, The Brothers.

80 | TUBAL CAIN MINE

Round trip: to Buckhorn Lake 12 miles
Hiking time: 7 hours (day hike or backpack)
High point: 5300 feet
Elevation gain: 2000 feet

Hikable: late June through October
Maps: Custom Correct Buckhorn Wilderness, Green Trails Tyler Peak (No. 136)
Information: Quilcene Ranger District, phone (360) 765-3368

In the 1890s the Tubal Cain Mine promoters began selling stock like crazy and hiring mules to haul tons of machinery, steel pipe, 10-inch wooden pipe, and such truck as elaborate bedsteads to the prospecting operation, hauling out just enough "High Grade" ore samples to keep the stock sales going. Originally supplies were brought in over Marmot Pass, but in the 1920s the route shifted to the Dungeness River, on a 14-mile trail starting at packer Charley Fritz's farm. The digging (first claimed to be for copper, later for manganese) pooped along by fits and starts until the 1950s and likely isn't ended yet; old mines never die, they just are acquired by fresh gangs of stock peddlers. The frantically paced logging of the 1960s and 1970s has shortened the trail to a mere 3 miles. Hike the trail in late June or early July when rhododendrons are blooming the first 2 miles and the alpine meadows are flowered red, white, blue, and yellow.

Drive US 101 to 0.1 mile south of the entrance to Sequim Bay State Park and turn left on Louella Road. At 0.9 mile go left and follow the Palo Alto Road (past Charley Fritz's farm), which eventually becomes road No. 28. At 7.4 miles from US 101 keep right on road No. 2860. Pass East Crossing

The Buckhorn Pass trail near Copper City

Campground, cross the Dungeness River, and start climbing. At 12.3 miles is a switchback and intersection with road No. 2870. Keep left on No. 2860. At 17.2 miles the road dips downward; at 18.8 miles recross the Dungeness River, pass through a gate (closed in winter), and at 22.7 miles reach the trailhead for Tubal Cain Mine trail No. 840, elevation 3300 feet.

Cross Silver Creek and in ¼ mile enter Buckhorn Wilderness, walking beneath 10-foot high rhododendrons—the best part of the trip. At about 3 miles, just a bit above the trail, is a small mine shaft. A rough way trail (No. 841) leads from here to the site of another Tubal Cain mining operation and a World War II plane wreckage in Tull Canyon, thought by some to be well worth the 3-mile round-trip sidetrip. At 3½ miles reach Copper Creek and the site of the Tubal Cain Mine operation, elevation 4350 feet. The heavy iron pipe, 10-inch wooden pipes wrapped in steel wire, remains of old stoves, and a water heater, all were carried in by pack train. The buildings collectively known as Tull (or Copper) City have rotted into the soil or been burned up in campfires (or some of them, on a memorable Fourth of July in the 1930s, blown sky-high by larking youngsters who found the absent miners' cache of dynamite). As a tourist attraction, the "city" is lame. The history is all in the imagination. The scenery is blocked by forest. Ghost towns in the wet Northwest have a short afterlife.

Boulder-hop Copper Creek and break out of the woods to lush herbaceous meadows, the bright green gaudy-spotted with blossoms, and switchback a mile up steep slopes to about 5½ miles and a junction in a grove of trees. The left fork goes in ½ mile of ups and downs to forest-ringed Buckhorn Lake, 5300 feet, 6 miles. Excellent camps near a stream a hundred feet above the lake.

The right fork is the entry to the sky, climbing meadows to the long, broad tundra ridge of Buckhorn Pass at 7 miles, 5700 feet, and views of valleys and mountains and salt water, then sidehilling rock gardens to Marmot Pass, 8¾ miles (Hike 78).

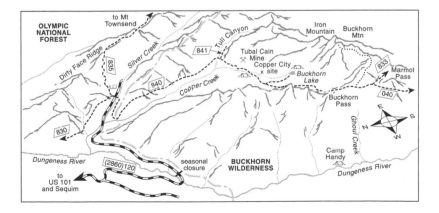

81 | ROYAL BASIN

Round trip: 14 miles
Hiking time: allow 2 days minimum
High point: 5100 feet
Elevation gain: 2600 feet
Hikable: mid-July through October

Maps: Custom Correct Gray Wolf—
Dosewallips, Green Trails Tyler Peak
(No. 136)
Information: Olympic National Park
Wilderness Information Center,
phone (360) 452-0300

Park Service backcountry use permit required for overnight stay

Splendid forests and streams, an alpine lake and fields of flowers, surrounded by some of the highest and craggiest peaks in the Olympics. Allow plenty of time for the entry hike because the last several miles are rough and in places quite steep. Plan at least an extra day for roaming.

Drive US 101 to 0.1 mile south of the entrance to Sequim Bay State Park and turn left on Louella Road. At 0.9 mile go left and follow the Palo Alto Road, which eventually becomes road No. 28. At 7.4 miles from US 101, keep right on road No. 2860. Pass East Crossing Campground, cross the Dungeness River, and start climbing. At 12.3 miles is a switchback and intersection with road No. 2870. Keep left on No. 2860. At 17.2 miles the road dips to the upper Dungeness trail No. 833 at 18.8 miles, elevation 2500 feet.

The trail follows the water, always within sound and often in sight. At 1 mile, 2700 feet, is a junction of streams and trails; take the right fork, Royal (originally Roy) Creek trail No. 832. In ½ mile enter Olympic National Park. This far the way is entirely through forest, including beautiful specimens of fir, the floor sometimes a soft mattress of moss and other times a broad green carpet of vanilla leaf. At around 4 miles the trail begins traversing

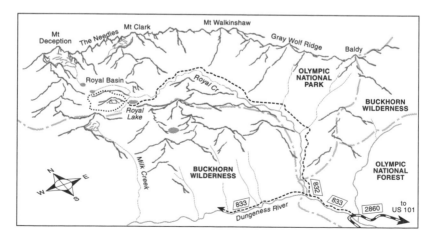

View from near Royal Lake

small flower meadows, each larger than the last. The path also steepens and becomes rougher. Ahead are glimpses of Gray Wolf Ridge and crags of The Needles.

The valley bends sharply southward and narrows. At about 6 miles, 4700 feet, the trail climbs a little cliff and enters the lower part of Royal Basin, an interfingering of groves of subalpine trees, small meadows, and thickets of scrub willow. The trail crosses Royal Creek and several tributaries on flimsy poles; note the milkiness of the main creek, which carries glacier-milled rock flour. A final steep climb culminates at Royal Lake, 7 miles, 5100 feet. On the far shores are numerous campsites in the woods. Near the sound of a waterfall directly west is a large camp under the huge overhang of Shelter Rock; to find it, follow a path around the upper end of the lake and over a small knoll.

Several boot-beaten tracks lead to upper Royal Basin's high gardens. Any will do, but take care to skirt certain green, flat meadows which in fact are bogs. Make a grand tour to the very top of the basin. Below huge piles of moraine, find a tiny milk-blue lake fed by the small glacier on the side of 7788-foot Mt. Deception. Continue to the ridge crest and look down to the fairyland of Deception Basin.

82 | GRAND RIDGE

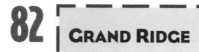

One-way trip: 7¾ miles
Hiking time: 5 hours (day hike)
High point: 6600 feet
Elevation gain: 1900 feet, loss 750 feet
Hikable: mid-July through September

Maps: Green Trails Mt. Angeles (No. 135),
    Custom Correct Hurricane Ridge
Information: Olympic National Park
    Wilderness Information Center,
    phone (360) 452-0300

Park Service backcountry use permit required for overnight stay

Never is the term "between heaven and earth" more appropriate than when walking the crest of Grand Ridge. On one hand lies the deep Grand Creek valley, the Olympic Mountains beyond; on the other is the deeper Cox valley, the Strait of Juan de Fuca, ocean-going ships, and mills of Port Angeles. However, "heaven" demands a stern effort, the trail climbing up and down, up and down high points of the ridge.

There is no water except drips from the lingering snowbanks of very early summer, so a party must either carry about a gallon a day apiece or make it a day hike. A round trip of 15½ miles and a total of 2650 feet elevation gain is a hard day in the hot sun, so a one-way trip is recommended. Ideally a friendly driver would leave you off at one end and pick you up at the other; switching two cars around adds hours of driving. Logic says start at the high point, Obstruction Point, on the west end of the ridge and finish at the low point, Deer Park, on the east end. However, you will be tripping yourself up, constantly looking back to see the view, so the heck with logic. Start at Deer Park and look as you walk.

To reach Obstruction Point, the destination, from US 101 on the east side of Port Angeles, drive Olympic National Park Highway 18 miles to Hurricane Ridge. Just before the lodge turn left on a rough, steep, narrow, and scenic road 7.9 miles to its end, elevation 6200 feet.

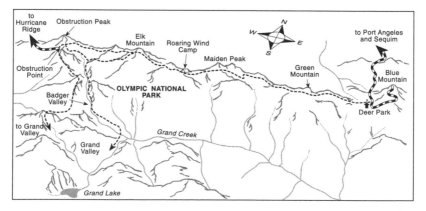

For Deer Park, drive US 101 to milepost 253, about 3 miles east of Port Angeles and about 11 miles from Sequim, and turn uphill on Deer Park road. The first 8 miles are paved, then the way becomes progressively steeper and narrower. At 16 miles go right to the Deer Park Ranger Station and trailhead signed "Obstruction Point Trail," elevation 5233 feet (Hike 84).

The trail descends ¾ mile to a 4900-foot saddle on an abandoned 1930s road (which in that age of exuberant car-touring was planned to go all the way to Obstruction Point!). The trail served as a fireline in 1988 during the Deer Park fire. From the low point the trail is mostly up and often very steep, traversing forests of Green Mountain. It levels off along a 5500-foot ridge top, and pocket meadows full of flowers appear. Forest is left behind as the way ascends a large meadow to a 6000-foot shoulder of Maiden Peak at 3 miles. The views of Port Angeles, Vancouver Island, and Mt. Baker make this a good turnaround for day-trippers.

From the shoulder the way contours tundra close below the twin peaks of 6434-foot Maiden Peak, 4 miles. The crags of Warrior and Constance and the glaciers on Anderson dominate views to the south. Deer Park and the salt water are to the east and Mt. Angeles to the north. Ahead are the naked slopes of Elk Mountain, daunting indeed on a day of blistering sun or roaring winds. The trail drops to Roaring Wind Camp (snowmelt only) and begins the 600-foot ascent of Elk Mountain. At 5¼ miles Mt. Olympus comes in view. At 5½ miles, near the 6600-foot high point of the trail, pass the Badger Mountain trail. In the next 2 miles along the broad, barren slopes of Elk Mountain, the glaciers of Mt. Olympus dominate the horizon. Across Badger Valley can be seen Grand Lake and Moose Lake and a tiny unnamed lake set in green meadows. Steep scree slopes lead down to the road-end at Obstruction Point, 7¾ miles from Deer Park.

The Grand Ridge trail

83

MOUNT ANGELES—
KLAHHANE RIDGE

Round trip: 7 miles
Hiking time: 4 hours (day hike)
High point: 5900 feet
Elevation gain: 1200 feet
Hikable: mid-July through October

Maps: Custom Correct Hurricane Ridge, Green Trails Mount Angeles (No. 135), Port Angeles (No. 103)
Information: Olympic National Park Wilderness Information Center, phone (360) 452-0300

Park Service backcountry use permit required for overnight stay

The simultaneous views of glacier ice and saltwaterways, the unusual geology underfoot (sedimentary strata tilted to the vertical), and the exuberance of flowers—these are reasons enough for Klahhane Ridge to be one of the most popular highland hikes in the Olympics. Thanks to man's meddling, the scene has also become famous (infamous) for mountain goats.

Drive US 101 to the east side of Port Angeles and go left 18 miles on Olympic National Park Highway to Hurricane Ridge Visitor Center. Find the Lake Angeles-Klahhane Ridge trail at the east end of the Big Meadow parking lot, elevation 5225 feet.

Paved path leads east around a green hill to gravel path, which in ½ mile yields to ordinary mountain trail winding 2 miles along Sunrise Ridge, on the crest and around knolls. Just before starting across the south side of Mt. Angeles, pass a boot-beaten path leading toward the summit, the climbers' route. At 2½ miles sniff contemptuously as you pass Switchback Trail. (This shortcut climbs a steep ½ mile from the highway, saving the "bother" of

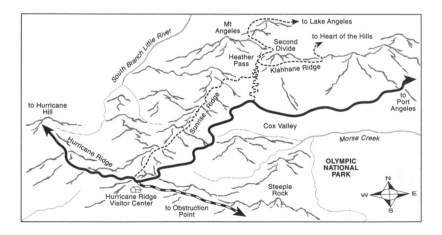

Mount Olympus and Mount Carrie from Klahhane Ridge

hiking 2 of the best alpine miles of the trip.) Continue on, zigzagging 900 feet up to Klahhane Ridge, 5900 feet, 3½ miles, and a junction with the Lake Angeles trail. (By arranging transportation, you can descend this trail 1½ miles to Lake Angeles, 4196 feet, and proceed to the trailhead near Heart of the Hills Campground, 10 miles from Hurricane Ridge Visitor Center—a superb one-way, downhill, meadow-to-forest walk.)

The views from Klahhane are as good as views get: the ice of Mt. Olympus in one direction, in the other the Strait of Juan de Fuca, San Juan Islands, Vancouver Island, and the ice of Mt. Baker.

Now, about those mountain goats. They were less native to the Olympics than bird-eating cats and rabbit-chasing dogs are to your house, for glaciological reasons never having made their way across the Puget Trough from the Cascades. In 1925 the State Department of Game introduced a dozen mountain goats to the northern portion of what in the next decade became a national park, no guns allowed. The bands grew slowly and for years encounters were rare and exciting treats. Then, lacking predators, their population exploded throughout the Olympics. They became camp pests, and, worse than that, a threat to species of endemic plants that live no other place in the world, nor ever will if hooved to death here.

The Park Service has been compelled to take action. The cheapest and most humane remedy would be to hire professional marksmen. This having been vigorously protested, the Park Service helicoptered animals out of the park and trucked them to other mountain ranges where, with no fear of humans, they are sitting ducks for the first guns they meet. Meanwhile, in the Olympics, years must pass before erosion scars are healed.

So much for blithely tampering with nature.

84 | GRAND VALLEY

Round trip: to Moose Lake 9 miles
Hiking time: 6 hours (day hike or backpack)
High point: 6450 feet
Elevation gain: 300 feet in, 1800 feet out
Hikable: July through October

Maps: Custom Correct Gray Wolf—Dosewallips, Green Trails Mount Angeles (No. 135)
Information: Olympic National Park Wilderness Information Center, phone (360) 452-0300

Park Service Wilderness Reservation required for overnight stay

A Grand Valley it surely is, with three lakes and a half-dozen ponds in glacier-scooped bowls, but it would better be called "Kingdom of Marmots." There are meadows to roam and rushing streams and views to admire. However, the abundant wildlife is the outstanding feature: numerous deer and grouse and an unbelievable number of whistlers.

This is an upside-down trip—the trail starts high and descends to the valley; the hard hauling is on the return. Usually open in July, after a winter of heavy snow the road may not open until August; ask the rangers before setting out.

Drive US 101 to the east side of Port Angeles, then turn south and drive 18 miles on Olympic National Park Highway to Hurricane Ridge. Just before the lodge turn left on a narrow and scenic dirt road through parklands along the ridge crest. In 7.9 miles, on the side of Obstruction Point, is the road-end, elevation 6200 feet.

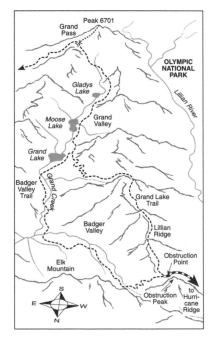

The drive is beautiful and so is the trail south 1 mile along the meadow crest of Lillian Ridge, with views over Elwha River forests to Mt. Olympus, then swinging around rocky slopes of a small peak to a notch in the ridge, 6450 feet, start of a steep drop down slate scree and lush flowers to open forest on the floor of Grand Valley. At 3½ miles, 5000 feet, is a junction. The left fork leads in ½ mile to Grand Lake, 4750 feet, then

Camping in Grand Valley

descends Grand Creek to 4000 feet and climbs through Badger Valley to Obstruction Point, reached in 5 miles from the junction. (The "badgers" actually are marmots; listen for their whistles.) This route is an excellent loop return to the road.

The right fork ascends ½ mile to Moose Lake, 5100 feet, and another ½ mile to little Gladys Lake. Near Moose and Grand Lakes are nice camps, but not *too* near—the allowable minimum distance from lakes or streams is 100 feet.

For more alpine wanderings, continue on the trail to 6300-foot Grand Pass, 6½ miles from Obstruction Point, and scramble westward up Peak 6701 to views of the Bailey Range and Mt. Olympus and Mt. Anderson and more.

If the weather turns bad when it's time to go home, keep in mind that the last mile along Lillian Ridge can be a battle for survival, even in July and August. In such case it may be wise to return via Badger Valley, several miles longer but mostly protected from the killing winds. Moreover, a wood fire is permitted at one site in Badger Valley.

85 | WHISKEY BEND TO LOW DIVIDE

Round trip: to Low Divide 57½ miles
Hiking time: allow 1 week or more
High point: 3602 feet
Elevation gain: about 2500 feet, plus many ups and downs
Hikable: June through October

Maps: Custom Correct Gray Wolf—Dosewallips, Green Trails Tyler Peak (No. 136)
Information: Olympic National Park Wilderness Information Center, phone (360) 452-0300

Park Service backcountry use permit required for overnight stay

Booze is scant but waterfalls and forest scenery are plentiful on the 28-mile Elwha River trail from Whiskey Bend to Low Divide. The valley is very heavily traveled in summer, especially below Elkhorn, but the natural beauty and historical interest more than compensate. Spend a day or weekend on the lower trail—or spend a week hiking the complete trail, loitering at lovely spots, taking sidetrips. Before setting out be sure to read Bob Wood's delightful book, *Across the Olympic Mountains: The Press Expedition, 1889-90.*

Drive US 101 west from Port Angeles 8 miles and turn left on the paved Elwha River road and go 2 miles to the national park boundary. At 2.1 miles from the boundary, just past the Elwha Ranger Station, turn left on Whiskey Bend road and drive 5 miles (sometimes rough and steep) to the road-end parking area, elevation 1150 feet.

The trail is wide and relatively level, the river occasionally glimpsed far below, to Michael's (Cougar Mike's) Cabin at 1½ miles. Here a ½-mile sidetrail descends to the old homestead of Humes Ranch, where elk may sometimes be seen, mainly from late fall to spring.

At 4 miles, 1600 feet, is Lillian Camp beside the Lillian River. Pause for

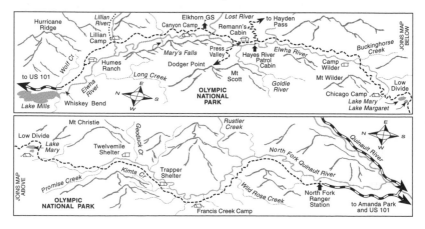

refreshment because the next stretch is the toughest of the trip, climbing 700 feet on the hot, dry Lillian Grade through an old burn, then dropping for the first time to the Elwha River at about 8 miles, 1242 feet.

The trail goes up and down, never near the river very long, to a nice view of Mary's Falls, 8¾ miles. The way climbs again, passing a ¼-mile sidetrip to secluded Canyon Camp, and at 11½ miles, 1400 feet, reaches Elkhorn Guard Station.

The trail crosses an alder bottom where elk or deer may be seen and passes an old summer-home cabin of pre-park days—Remann's Cabin, 13 miles, 1450 feet—and climbs again and drops again into Press Valley. At the upper end of the valley, 16¾ miles, 1685 feet, are Hayes River Camp and Hayes River Patrol Cabin, built in 1969 by 40 volunteer boys (including John Spring, the photographer's son) enrolled in the Student Conservation Program. Here is a junction with the Hayden Pass trail (Hike 77).

At 21 miles, 1900 feet, is Camp Wilder. Easily cross a footlog over Buckinghorse Creek and at 26 miles reach Chicago Camp, 2099 feet, jumping-off point for the first ascent of Mt. Olympus in 1907. The trail now leaves the valley bottom and switchbacks in forest to the meadows of Low Divide, 28¾ miles, 3602 feet, and there connects to the North Fork Quinault River trail.

To complete the classic Press Expedition cross-Olympics route, continue from the pass 18 miles down the valley to the North Fork Quinault River road-end, for a total of 45 miles.

Humes Ranch

86 | APPLETON PASS

Round trip: to pass 14½ miles
Hiking time: 9 hours (day hike or backpack)
High point: 5100 feet
Elevation gain: 3300 feet
Hikable: mid-July through October (or until road is closed)

Maps: Custom Correct Seven Lakes Basin—Hoh, Green Trails Mount Olympus (No. 134)
Information: Olympic National Park Wilderness Information Center, phone (360) 452-0300

Park Service backcountry use permit required for overnight stay

One of the most popular trails in Olympic National Park climbs to green meadows sprinkled with flowers, to views of High Divide and Mt. Carrie, and to possible extensions of the route to near and far places.

Drive US 101 west from Port Angeles about 9 miles and turn left on the Upper Elwha River road, 10.5 miles paved all the way, to the road-end, elevation 1840 feet. Walk an abandoned roadbed 2 miles to Boulder Creek Campground (site of Olympic Hot Springs and its long-abandoned tourist spa), 2060 feet.

The trail sets out from the upper end of the campground, in nice big trees growing from a moss floor. The calypso orchids stage an annual riot hereabouts, usually in early June or so. At a junction in ½ mile, keep straight. The first mile is a breeze with only minor ups and downs. Then the trail crosses the West Fork Boulder Creek and the work begins, climbing past two waterfalls to the South Fork Boulder Creek. An unusual feature of the trail is the superb quality of the bridges and puncheon, which were built by meticulous craftspeople, including Penny Manning, a close relative of one of the co-authors. The path presents no problems but steepness until about 4000 feet, where mud grows deep and lush vegetation crowds in. At 6 miles are snowpatches that may last all summer (ice axes

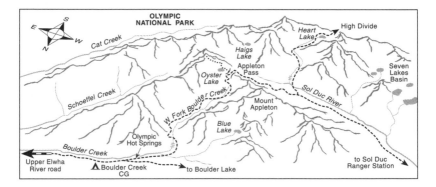

Mount Olympus from Appleton Pass

advised for early-summer hikers). At 7½ miles the trail reaches a 5100-foot high point and descends to 5000-foot Appleton Pass. The first 3 miles of the trail have several small established campsites.

Views at the pass being limited, take an unsigned way trail on the east side of the pass and follow the ridge crest upward, through alpine forest past tiny Oyster Lake, into green meadows, and in 1½ miles to a 5500-foot viewpoint overlooking Cat Creek to glacier-draped Mt. Carrie. Camping (stoves only) is superb along the ridge when there is snowmelt.

From Appleton Pass the trail descends 2¼ miles to the Sol Duc River trail, reached at 6½ miles from Sol Duc Hot Springs (Hike 87).

87 | HIGH DIVIDE—SEVEN LAKES BASIN

Round trip: 19 miles
Hiking time: allow 3 days
High point: 5474 feet
Elevation gain: 4000 feet
Hikable: late July through October

Maps: Custom Correct Seven Lakes
Basin—Hoh, Green Trails Mount Tom
(No. 133), Mount Olympus (No. 134)
Information: Olympic National Park
Wilderness Information Center,
phone (360) 452-0300

Park Service Wilderness Reservation required for overnight stay

Forests of the Sol Duc valley, tarns and gardens of Seven Lakes Basin, meadows of the High Divide, and views across the green gulf of the Hoh River to glaciers of Mt. Olympus and far west to the Pacific Ocean. The fame draws thousands of visitors year after year, the trail so busy and the lakes so crowded that the biowelfare of the area has forced limits on camping in the fragile terrain, the emphasis now on day visits from camps in valley forests. By planning only to *look* at lakes and not camp by them (alternative sites are numerous and reservations not needed) hikers can still enjoy solitude. A loop trip is recommended as a sampler of the riches, but the country is big and beautiful and offers a variety of wanderings short and long.

Drive US 101 west from Lake Crescent (Fairholm) 2 miles to the Sol Duc River road, signed "Sol Duc Hot Springs," and turn left. Keep straight ahead at the hot springs and campground road. At 14.2 miles reach the road-end and trailhead, elevation 2000 feet.

The trail gently ascends splendid old forest 1 mile to the misty and

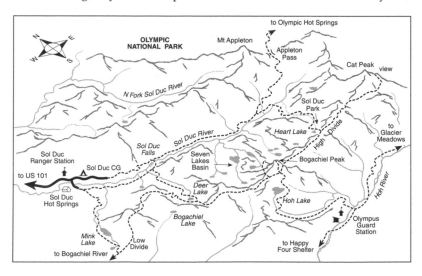

Elk herd on High Divide

mossy gorge of Sol Duc Falls, 1950 feet. Close by is a junction with the Deer Lake trail (see the concluding segment of the clockwise loop described here).

The Sol Duc River trail continues up the valley of gorgeous trees, passes the Appleton Pass trail (Hike 86) at 5 miles, 3000 feet, and soon thereafter crosses the river and climbs steeply to grasslands and silver forest of Sol Duc Park and Heart Lake, 7½ miles, 4800 feet.

Shortly above, at 8½ miles, the way attains the 5100-foot crest of the High Divide, and a junction. The left fork runs the ridge 3 miles to a dead end on the side of Cat Peak, offering close looks at the Bailey and Olympus Ranges.

Turn west on the right fork into a steady ridge-top succession of views far down to trees of the Hoh valley and across to ice of Mt. Olympus. At 10½ miles a sidetrail descends 1½ miles left to 4500-foot Hoh Lake, and from there to the Hoh River (Hike 90). Here, too, a path climbs a bit to the 5474-foot summit of Bogachiel Peak, a former lookout site, and the climax panoramas. Plan to spend a lot of time gazing the full round of the compass.

The route swings along the side of the peak, at 11¾ miles passing the sidetrail to Seven Lakes Basin (often snowbound on the north side until mid-August), and traverses Bogachiel Ridge above the greenery (and often, a band of elk) in Bogachiel Basin. Snowfields linger late on this stretch and may be troublesome or dangerous for inexperienced hikers who try the trip too early in summer.

The trail contours the ridge above the Bogachiel River almost 2 miles, then in subalpine trees drops to Deer Lake at 3500 feet and a junction with the Bogachiel River trail (Hike 89) at 15 miles. Past the lake the trail descends in lush forest to Sol Duc Falls at 18 miles and another mile to the road.

88 | MOUNT MULLER—SNIDER RIDGE

Round trip: to ridge top 6 miles
Hiking time: 4 hours (day hike)
High point: 3250 feet
Elevation gain: 2200 feet

Round trip: to Mount Muller 11 miles
Hiking time: 6 hours (day hike)
High point: 3748 feet
Elevation gain: 3000, return 200 feet

Hikable: May through November
Map: Forest Service handout

Information: Sol Duc Ranger District,
phone (360) 374-6522

Subalpine meadows and great views are seldom enjoyed at an elevation of 3000 feet. By destroying miles of forest in the Sol Duc valley and roaring up slopes of Snider Ridge, the Sol Duc fire of 1925 provided such an amenity, scorching the earth so badly that after almost 75 years meadow flowers brighten the ridge—an interesting lesson in forest ecology.

The Mt. Muller trail is a 12-mile loop. However, for reasons given below, most hikers go and return the same route, described here.

Drive US 101 from Port Angeles toward Forks. Pass Lake Crescent and the Sol Duc Hot Springs road. At some 31 miles from Port Angeles, between mileposts 217 and 216, turn north past a power substation and go 0.3 mile on road No. 3071 to the trailhead, elevation 1000 feet.

From the start take the left fork, following Littleton Creek a bit, soon climbing then leveling for ¼ mile, then tilting up into salal and second-growth.

The Sol Duc valley from Snider Ridge

Huge stumps attest to the old trees killed in 1925. Shortly past the ½-mile marker cross a steep, long-abandoned "mining" road. At 2¾ miles enter Grouse Meadow, first of the many flower displays.

At 3 miles are the ridge crest and Jim's Junction, 3250 feet. The straight-ahead descends ½ mile to a logging road. The left goes 3 miles to Kloshe Nanitch, the right 2½ miles to Mt. Muller. If this is your turnaround, be sure to sidetrip a short ways on the Kloshe Nanitch trail to the top of Grouse Meadow and a grand view of the Sol Duc valley and Mt. Olympus.

For Mt. Muller, take the right along the ridge top ¼ mile to Millsap Meadow (views). Lose 100-plus feet and regain them at ¾ mile (see the Strait of Juan de Fuca). Lose 100 feet to Thomas Gap and gain 400 feet to Jasmine Meadow. At 2½

Tiger lily

miles from Jim's Junction round Mt. Muller; a sidetrail climbs to the top and limited views. For the best, stay on the ridge trail a few feet farther to Panorama Point.

This is the halfway point of the loop. However, the way beyond here is rough and steep for several miles and finishes in 2½-miles within sound if not sight of US 101.

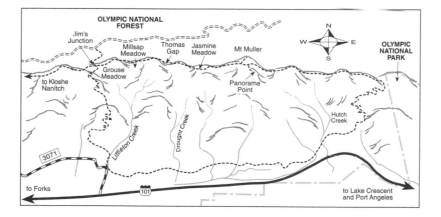

89 | BOGACHIEL RIVER

Round trip: to Bogachiel Shelter 11½ miles
Hiking time: 6 hours (day hike or backpack)
High point: 560 feet
Elevation gain: 260 feet
Hikable: March through November

One-way trip: to High Divide 31 miles
Hiking time: allow 3 to 4 days
High point: 5474 feet
Elevation gain: 4100 feet
Hikable: July through October

Maps: Custom Correct Bogachiel Valley, Green Trails Spruce Mountain (No. 132), Mount Tom (No. 133)

Information: Olympic National Park Wilderness Information Center, phone (360) 452-0300

Park Service backcountry use permit required for overnight stay

The Hoh Rainforest, the Bogachiel Rainforest, or the Queets Rainforest—take your pick. They are alike as three peas in a pod, except only one is famous, has good trails and lots of people. The other two have a degree of solitude, surprising for such beautiful hikes through large old trees, rainforest foliage, and luxuriant mosses. In autumn the vine maple, alder, and bigleaf maple stage a glorious color show. Elk, deer, cougar, bear, and other animals may be seen by quiet and lucky hikers. A late fall or winter visitor in the Bogachiel usually has the forest all to himself, the only footprints on the trail those of elk. The valley offers a superb day trip for virtually any time of the year, or a weekend trip for more extended enjoyment of wilderness greenery and streams, or a magnificent long approach to alpine climaxes of the High Divide.

Drive US 101 to 5 miles south of Forks and directly opposite the entrance to Bogachiel State Park turn left on Undie Road, which passes numerous sideroads and eventually becomes road No. 2932. At 5.5 miles reach a gate and large trailhead parking lot, elevation 350 feet. (In 1997

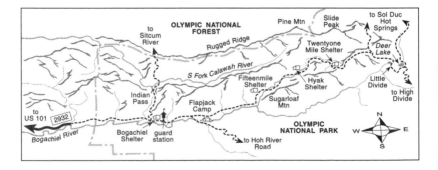

The Bogachiel River (John Spring photo)

the road had serious damage; check before driving.)

The trail descends ¼ mile to intersect and follow an old logging railroad bed 1½ miles to the park boundary and 1½ miles more into the park. Amid second-growth forest (logging done during World War II on the pretext of "national emergency") look for giant stumps with springboard holes in both sides. Then virgin forest begins.

At 5¾ miles from the road, Bogachiel Shelter (emergency use only) and the old guard station, rebuilt by the Student Conservation Program, are a good lunch stop and turnaround for day-hikers.

Near the shelter a branch trail climbs north over 1041-foot Indian Pass and drops to the Calawah River. At about 7¾ miles another sidetrail fords the river and climbs over the ridge south to the Hoh River road.

The valley path continues gently in lovely forest, never far from the river and sometimes beside it, to Flapjack Camp at 8¼ miles. At about 12 miles the river forks. Though the trail follows the North Fork, the narrow but pristine main river valley can be explored on a sidetrip for 6 miles if you don't mind wading creeks and scrambling over high banks and fallen trees.

At 14¾ miles are Fifteenmile Shelter and a bridge crossing the stream. At 15½ miles is Hyak Shelter, where the valley narrows to a slot. At 18¾ miles is Twentyone Mile Shelter, 2214 feet. At around 21 miles the trail abandons gentility, steeply ascends a dry hillside above the North Fork headwaters to 4300-foot Little Divide, 23 miles (a late lingering snowpatch could make the divide risky), drops to Deer Lake at 26½ miles, and climbs in parklands to the meadow crest of the High Divide and Bogachiel Peak at 31 miles. For alternative trails to High Divide, see Hikes 87 and 90.

90 | HOH RIVER—GLACIER MEADOWS

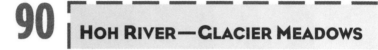

Round trip: to Happy Four Camp 11½ miles
Hiking time: 6 hours (day hike or backpack)
High point: 800 feet
Elevation gain: 225 feet
Hikable: March through November

Round trip: to Glacier Meadows 35 miles
Hiking time: allow 3 days
High point: 4200 feet
Elevation gain: 3700 feet
Hikable: mid-July through October

Maps: Custom Correct Seven Lakes Basin—Hoh, Green Trails Mount Tom (No. 133), Mount Olympus (No. 134)

Information: Olympic National Park Wilderness Information Center, phone (360) 452-0300

Park Service backcountry use permit required for overnight stay

From around the world travelers are drawn to the Hoh River by the fame of the Olympic rainforest. Most of the 100,000 annual visitors are richly satisfied by the self-guiding nature walks at the road-end, but more ambitious hikers can continue for miles on the nearly flat trail through huge trees draped with moss, then climb to alpine meadows and the edge of the Blue Glacier.

Drive US 101 south of Forks to the Hoh River road and turn east 18 miles to the Hoh Ranger Station and Campground, elevation 578 feet. The hike begins on the nature trail starting at the visitor center; before setting out, study the museum displays explaining the geology, climate, flora, and fauna.

The way lies amid superb, large specimens of Douglas fir, western hemlock, Sitka spruce, and western red cedar, groves of bigleaf maple swollen

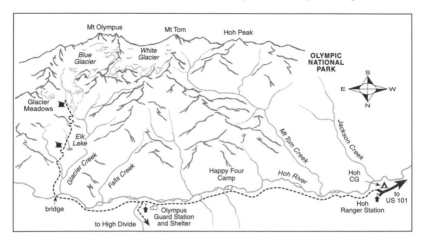

The Blue Glacier

with moss, and shrubs and ferns. Gravel bars and cold rapids of the river are never far away, inviting sidetrips. Here and there are glimpses upward to snows of Mt. Tom and Mt. Carrie. In winter one may often see herds of Roosevelt elk; were it not for their constant grazing and browsing the relatively open forest floor would be a dense jungle.

Any distance can make a full day, what with long, lingering pauses. Happy Four Camp, at 5¾ miles, 800 feet, is a logical turnaround for a day hike and also a good campsite for backpackers.

The trail remains level to the next camp at Olympus Guard Station, 9 miles, 948 feet. At 9¾ miles is a junction with the trail to High Divide (Hike 87). The valley trail then climbs a bit to the bridge over the spectacular canyon of the Hoh at 13¼ miles, 1400 feet, leaves the Hoh valley and climbs more to forest-surrounded Elk Lake, 15 miles, 2500 feet. (No camping within 200 feet of the lake; stove required.)

Now the grade becomes steep, ascending through steadily smaller trees, views across Glacier Creek of snows and cliffs, to Glacier Meadows, 17¼ miles, 4200 feet (stove-camping only). Wander a short way in flowers and parkland to a viewpoint near the foot of the Blue Glacier, where torrents pour down ice-polished slabs to the forest below. Or follow the trail ½ mile to the end of the bouldery crest of a lateral moraine. Admire crevasses and icefalls of the glacier and the summit tower of 7965-foot Mt. Olympus.

91 | THE OTHER HOH RAINFOREST

Round trip: 7 miles
Hiking time: 4 hours (day hike or backpack)
High point: 840 feet
Elevation gain: 115 feet
Hikable: most of the year

Maps: Custom Correct Mount Olympus Climbers Map, Green Trails Mount Tom (No. 133)
Information: Olympic National Park Wilderness Information Center, phone (360) 452-0300

Park Service backcountry use permit required for overnight stay

The world-famous rainforest of the Hoh River has a twin, the rainforest of the South Fork Hoh River. Maybe the moss isn't as thick on the trees and maybe the trail is a bit rougher, but it does have something its famous twin doesn't—a bit of solitude. In fact, compared with the other Hoh, the trail is absolutely lonesome.

Drive US 101 to 0.6 mile south of the Hoh River bridge and turn onto Mainline Road (Department of Natural Resources) signed "Hoh-Clearwater State Forest." At 7 miles turn left on road No. H1000, signed "O.N. Park-S. Fork Hoh Trail 10.5 miles." The roads are not well-signed, so take care at all junctions to stay on No. H1000.

In 7.5 miles (14.5 miles from US 101) keep left, following the sign to "S.F. Hoh Campground." Cross the river on a cement bridge, pass the campground, and switchback up a steep, short stretch. At 10.4 miles the road forks right, straight, and left. Take the right, dropping to the trailhead at the curve of the road, 10.6 miles from Mainline Road, elevation 725 feet.

The trail starts in second-growth spruce forest, at ½ mile entering Olympic National Park. Ups and downs lead to Big Flat, 1½ miles, a large, open glade interspersed with vine maple, alder, and mammoth spruce trees. From here the way goes from glade to glade, sometimes close to the river (numerous campsites) and other times out of sight and sound of the water. At 2½

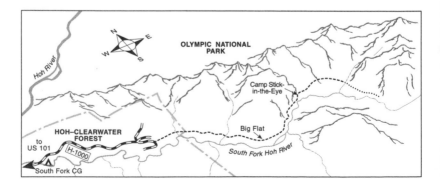

The South Fork Hoh River from trail

miles is Camp Stick-in-the-Eye. At approximately 3½ miles, 840 feet, trail maintenance ceases but the trail continues another mile, often obscured by tall grass.

In the summer the river runs milky, fed as it is by glaciers on the southeast side of Mt. Olympus. The peaks at the head of the valley rise above timberline but are not named on the USGS map.

92 | THE QUEETS

Round trip: to Spruce Bottom 10 miles
Hiking time: 5 hours (day hike)
High point: 800 feet
Elevation gain: 600 feet
Hikable: August through September

Maps: Custom Correct Queets, Green
Trails Kloochman Rock (No. 165)
Information: Olympic National Park
Wilderness Information Center,
phone (360) 452-0300

Park Service backcountry use permits required for overnight stay

The best rainforest (yes, the best!) in the Olympics, old homesteads, elk, and more solitude than companion valleys. The first 5 miles have a few mudholes but overall are as good as any trail in the national park. Why the solitude? Because the Queets River must be forded, not easy any time of year and dangerous except in the low water of late summer. A change of weather can make the river impassable.

Drive US 101 some 17 miles west of Lake Quinault and go right 13.5 miles to the end of the Queets River road, the trailhead, and the ford, elevation 275 feet.

Prepare carefully for the ford. Stout shoes—preferably boots—must be worn to secure placement among the large, slippery boulders. (The neatest trick is to take off boots and socks, don boots only, cross, and on the far side, empty water from the boots and don dry socks, then boots.) A stout pole must be carried to act as a third leg in the swift current. Scout around for a stretch of river that is wide and thus shallower and slower than the narrows; this may vary from year to year.

Once across, walk into the forest a short distance and find the trail, which utilizes a primitive road that was abandoned at least 50 years ago. Go upstream, winding through moss-festooned trees on a "lawn" mowed by elk. In 1½ miles is Andrews Ranch, a large field, and the remains of a barn built in the 1920s and abandoned in the 1940s. Look up at Kloochman Rock, an old lookout site on the park boundary.

In a scant 2 miles, don't miss the ¼-mile sidetrail up Coal Creek to the

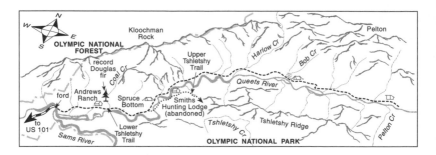

World's largest recorded Douglas fir

world's largest recorded Douglas fir, 17 feet in diameter. The top is missing but even so the height is still an impressive 221 feet.

For the next 2 miles the way passes spectacular moss-covered trees to a junction of the Lower Tshletshy Trail. In another ¾ mile pass Spruce Bottom and a series of campsites, beyond which the trail deteriorates, detouring around fallen giants and slides.

At 5½ miles is a junction with the abandoned Upper Tshletshy Trail. Walk to the river for a view across to Smith's Hunting Lodge, abandoned. The valley trail progressively worsens, though generally is easy to follow. At 11½ miles cross Bob Creek to campsites. If time permits, follow Bob Creek upstream to a series of waterfalls. The trail ends at 800 feet, 16 miles from the road-end, at Pelton Creek Shelter, one of the few not destroyed by nature or park rangers.

93 | SKYLINE TRAIL—NORTH FORK QUINAULT LOOP

Loop trip: 47 miles
Hiking time: allow 4 days minimum
High point: 5200 feet
Elevation gain: 8550 feet overall
Hikable: August through September

Maps: Custom Correct Quinault—
Colonel Bob, USGS Bunch Lake,
Kimta Peak, Mount Christie
Information: Olympic National Park
Wilderness Information Center,
phone (360) 452-0300

Park Service backcountry use permit required for overnight stay

Ascend from moss-covered giants of the rainforest to sky-open meadows, high alpine lakes, and, finally, to ridge-top tundras. Feel the diversity of the national park that extends from the Pacific Ocean to glaciers of Mt. Olympus. However, don't try it until and unless you're ready. Wilderness this deep is not for everyone. Only the canniest routefinders who can read a USGS map and energetic hikers should attempt the Skyline Trail, which, to deliberately deepen the wilderness experience, receives minimal maintenance. Hikers must expect to find trees fallen on the trail and allowed to stay there because that's where nature wants them, and brush that crowds the body and when soaked by rain or fog, mocks the chemist's miracle fabrics, and bogs that suck in boots and go for knees. Discouraging even when visible, on ridges

Skyline Trail

the trail vanishes altogether, marked by occasional cairns which dissolve in the clouds that often roll ceaselessly in from the ocean, days without a break. Miserable hours may be spent probing this way and that for a safe way across a gorge. A cliff may force a long descent, which, of course, leads to long ascent. Now, not the whole loop is like that. Half, at most.

Drive US 101 north from Aberdeen and go off on the South Shore Lake Quinault road 13 miles to an intersection. Turn left, cross the Quinault River, and take an immediate right on the North Fork road 3.5 miles to the road-end, elevation 450 feet.

The first 16 miles are in the ancient forest of the North Fork Quinault River trail, passing numerous campsites, climbing gradually to 3602-foot Low Divide.

The Skyline Trail starts in a meadow on the south side of Low Divide, heads back down the valley ½ mile, then begins the first climb, over a shoulder of Mt. Seattle. The path is rough and narrow but easy to follow in the forest; in the meadows it becomes vanishingly faint. Still, the tread is moderately decent the first 7¾ miles to the scenic campsite at Lake Beauty, 4670 feet. The next 3 miles to Kimta Peak are another story. The traverse that looks so quick and easy on the map is broken by descents to get past cliffs and over creeks, steep climbs up rocky hillsides, long halts to wonder where you are. Don't miss a cairn! Beyond the crossing from drainage of Promise Creek to that of Kimta Creek, the trail, at the edge of an old burn, is rough and tough but simpler to follow.

Skirt Kimta Peak at 5200 feet and feast on the final great view—of the ocean, the Queets River, and the entire Olympic range. Descend to Three Prune Meadows, 3650 feet, the trail now wide and well-graded. Pass a sidetrail down to the North Fork Quinault trail, climb over a 4000-foot ridge, and descend 3 miles past several small ponds to Three Lakes, 3200 feet, 20¾ miles from Low Divide. The next 6½ miles are an easy descent on good trail to the North Fork road. A ¾-mile walk up the road completes the loop.

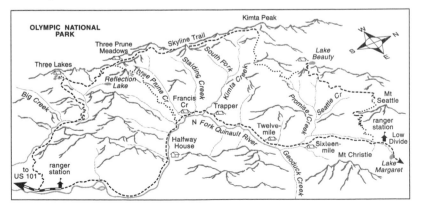

94 | COLONEL BOB

Round trip: north side 14½ miles
Hiking time: allow 2 days
High point: 4492 feet
Elevation gain: 4220 feet

Hikable: July through mid-October
Maps: Custom Correct Quinault—
Colonel Bob, Green Trails Quinault
Lake (No. 197), Grisdale (No.198)

Round trip: south side 8½ miles
Hiking time: 7 hours (day hike or
backpack)
High point: 4492 ft
Elevation gain: 3500 feet

Information: Quinault Ranger Station,
phone (360) 288-2525

Climb to a western outpost of the Olympic Mountains, a former look-out site with views of Olympics nearby and, farther off, volcanoes of the Cascades—St. Helens, Adams, and Rainier. There's water to see, too—look down on sparkling Quinault Lake and out to the Pacific Ocean, particularly spectacular with the sun dunking into it of an evening.

There are two ways, both very steep, to Colonel Bob: The south approach gains 3500 feet; the north climbs 4220 feet and is 3 miles longer.

For the north side drive US 101 to near its crossing of the Quinault River and turn east on the South Shore Lake Quinault road. In 2.5 miles pass the Quinault Ranger Station and at 6 miles spot a sign, "Colonel Bob Trail" (No. 851). Turn onto a narrow road which promptly opens to a large parking lot, elevation 270 feet.

The trail climbs through beautiful rainforest in long, sweeping switchbacks, then sidehills, still going steadily up. At 3 miles is a crossing of Ewells Creek and at 4 miles campsites at Mulkey Shelter, 2550 feet. Now the way switchbacks steeply to a 3250-foot pass and drops a bit, at 5½ miles reaching a junction, 2900 feet, with the trail from the south.

For the south-side approach to this junction, drive US 101 north 25.5

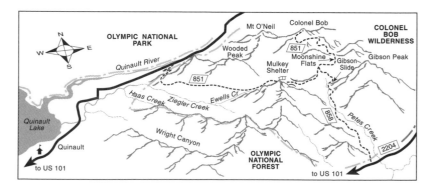

Near the summit of Colonel Bob Mountain

miles from Hoquiam and turn east on road No. 22, signed "Donkey Creek Road, Humptulips Guard Station." At 8.2 miles, where pavement ends, turn left on road No. 2204, signed "Campbell Tree Grove Campground," and proceed 11 miles to a sign, "Petes Creek Trail No. 858," near the crossing of Petes Creek, elevation 1000 feet.

The trail starts on the uphill side of the road and is steadily steep and in places rocky. At 1 mile is a crossing of Petes Creek, underground here most of the year. At 2 miles is a small camp, beyond which is Gibson Slide and then, at 2½ miles, the junction.

About 1 mile beyond, at 6½ miles from the north trailhead and 3⅓ from the south, is Moonshine Flats, featuring all-year water, the most popular camp on the route. At 1¾ miles from the junction, the way emerging from forest into flowers, is the summit, the last few feet to the top blasted from rock.

Few traces of the old lookout cabin remain on the 4492-foot summit. But the views are as glorious as ever. For sunset-watching, camps can be found ¼ mile back, 200 feet below the trail, on a wide, rocky bench covered with snow much of the summer. Bring a stove for cooking; melt snow for water.

95 | ENCHANTED VALLEY

Round trip: 26 miles
Hiking time: allow 2 to 3 days
High point: 1957 feet
Elevation gain: 1300 feet, plus ups and downs
Hikable: March through December

Maps: Custom Correct Enchanted Valley—Skokomish, Green Trails Mount Christie (No. 166), Mount Steel (No. 167)
Information: Olympic National Park Wilderness Information Center, phone (360) 452-0300

Park Service backcountry use permit required for overnight stay

Walk beside the river in open alder and maple forest, and miles through cathedral-like fir forest where future generations of loggers will come to see what their grandfathers meant when they boasted of big trees. The climax is Enchanted Valley, a large alpine cirque ringed by 3000-foot cliffs. The trail has many minor ups and downs and during rainy spells is a muddy mess, but in such country, who can complain?

Drive US 101 to the South Shore Lake Quinault road. Turn easterly, skirting the lake and winding up the valley. Pavement ends at 12 miles. In 13 miles pass the bridge to the North Fork and at 18 miles Graves Creek Campground. Continue on the final narrow road to the trailhead, 18.5 miles from US 101, elevation 646 feet.

The trail immediately crosses Graves Creek on a high log bridge and climbs an abandoned road, passing beneath towering trees that are guaranteed to give a stiff neck looking up, up, up. The cut sections of giants that have fallen across the trail give a graphic measure of their size and age.

At 2½ miles cross Pony Bridge over the Quinault River, admiring the lovely fern-covered canyon. For the next 10 miles go up and down between flat bottoms (alders and maples) and terraces several hundred feet above the

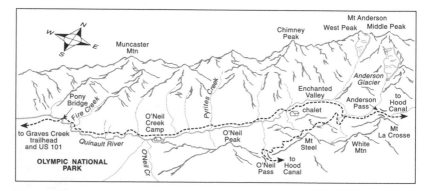

river (groves of tall fir and cedar). With any luck see elk. At 6½ miles pass a junction to O'Neil Creek Camp, ¼ mile off the main track.

All along are tantalizing glimpses of peaks above, but at about 10½ miles the abrupt transition from lowlands into the mountain world of rock and ice is startling. To the left are cliffs of 6911-foot Chimney Peak. To the right is 6400-foot White Mountain. Both are dominated by the twin peaks of Mt. Anderson, divided by a small glacier: The sharp pyramid is 7366-foot West Peak, the highest point; the more massive peak in the middle is 7321 feet.

Coming down to earth, the valley has widened out. The floor of the lower stretch is covered with dense brush but farther up are flower fields. At 13 miles cross the Quinault River, here a small creek. Walk a short bit through meadows to the three-story Enchanted Valley Chalet, 2000 feet, built in 1930 as a commercial hotel and now maintained by the Park Service as a public shelter. The structure often is full (only part of

Pony Bridge

the lower floor is open to camping) so be prepared to camp out. Be sure to carry a stove; cooking facilities are limited in the chalet and wood outside is scarce and probably wet. The full 13 miles needn't be done in a single day; a number of camps lie along the way.

At 2 miles beyond the chalet the trail passes the largest known western hemlock, 8 feet, 8 inches in diameter. From there one can climb Anderson Pass and descend the West Fork Dosewallips River (Hike 76), or go up and over O'Neil Pass, to Hart and Marmot Lakes and Lake La Crosse (Hike 96).

What's the best season for the trip? Well, some winters there is little snow in the lower valley, which thus can be walked in December or March when hardly any other country is open. Early spring is wonderful, birds singing, shrubs and maples exploding new leaves, yellow violet and oxalis blooming, and waterfalls and avalanches tumbling and sliding. So is summer, when alders and maples canopy valley glades in cool green. But autumn is also glorious, bigleaf maples yellowing and the trail lost in a brilliant carpet of fallen leaves. Better try it in all seasons.

96 | LAKE LA CROSSE—O'NEIL PASS

One-way trip: to Lake La Crosse via Quinault River and O'Neil Pass 26¾ miles
Hiking time: allow 5 days minimum, by any route
High point: 4900 feet
Elevation gain: 4000 feet
Hikable: mid-July through September

Maps: Custom Correct Enchanted Valley—Skokomish, Green Trails Mount Christie (No. 166), Mount Steel (No. 167)
Information: Olympic National Park Wilderness Information Center, phone (360) 452-0300

Park Service backcountry use permit required for overnight stay

In the heart of the Olympic wilderness, 25 miles from the nearest road, a group of beautiful alpine lakes sparkles amid a wonderland of heather and huckleberries. Quicker ways of reaching the lakes are mentioned in the last paragraph of this description, but the one described here is the classic approach, via O'Neil Pass, on one of the most spectacular trails in the national park, traversing ridges high above the Enchanted Valley of the Quinault, views magnificent and flower fields too.

Hike the Quinault Valley trail 13 miles to the Enchanted Valley Chalet (Hike 95) and continue up the trail 3½ miles to a junction, 16½ miles from the road, elevation 3300 feet.

Hart Lake and Mount Duckabush

Go right on the O'Neil Pass trail beside a small torrent, heading westward and up, in a few yards passing a small camp. The way alternates between forest and wide-view meadows. At 1 mile are campsites and a crossing of White Creek; a hillside beyond gives the best look at Mt. Anderson. At 1½ miles is a mountain hemlock with a sign saying it is 6 feet, 3 inches in diameter and 136 feet tall—a midget compared with the lowland's western hemlock but huge for this high-elevation species. At 2 miles is an Alaska cedar identified as 7 feet, 6 inches in diameter and 114 feet tall.

The trail climbs to 4500 feet and then contours for miles, mainly in grass and blossoms. Directly across the valley is Chimney Peak, an impressive 6911 feet high. Views are breathtaking down the Quinault River to Lake Quinault and, if you're lucky, the ocean. The trail drops a bit, rounds a shoulder of the ridge, and ascends to O'Neil Pass, 4900 feet, 7½ miles from the river, 25 miles from the road, and close-ups of Mt. Duckabush. Still in meadows, the way descends to Marmot Lake, 8½ miles, 4400 feet. The O'Neil Pass trail ends here in a junction with the Duckabush River trail (Hike 73).

In the higher gardens are Hart Lake and Lake La Crosse. To get there, find the trail at Marmot Lake and switchback upward ¾ mile to a junction. The left fork contours ½ mile to Hart Lake, enclosed on three sides by vertical cliffs. The right fork continues ¾ mile uphill to Lake La Crosse, 4800 feet, perhaps the most splendid alpine lake in the Olympics, with views across the water to massive 6233-foot Mt. Duckabush and more graceful 6300-foot Mt. Steel. An experienced hiker can find more private meadows and lakes.

The camping is stove-only, no wood fires, at Marmot, Hart, and La Crosse Lakes and O'Neil Pass. Best (except for being the most crowded) is the south side of Marmot Lake.

The lakes can be approached in various other ways. For one, hike the Dosewallips trail (Hike 76) and drop over Anderson Pass 1½ miles, losing 1100 feet, to the start of the O'Neil Pass trail. Hike directly to the lakes by way of the Duckabush River trail, 20 miles to Marmot Lake, gaining 4500 feet, including some major ups and downs and one difficult river crossing. Or hike the North Fork Skokomish River trail (Hike 70) 19½ miles to Marmot Lake, gaining 5200 feet, counting ups and downs. The lakes can also be included in imaginative one-way and loop trips.

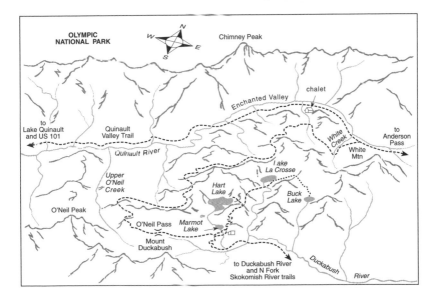

97 | POINT OF THE ARCHES

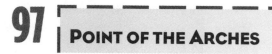

Round trip: to Point of the Arches 7 miles

Hiking time: 4 hours (day hike or backpack)

High point: 150 feet

Hikable: all year

Maps: Custom Correct North Olympic Coast, Green Trails Cape Flattery (No. 98S)

Information: Olympic National Park Wilderness Information Center, phone (360) 452-0300

Park Service backcountry use permit required for overnight stay

The Point of the Arches is the most scenic single segment of the Washington ocean coast, sea stacks, caves, arches, and tidal pools to explore, miles of sand beaches to roam. Once threatened by road-building and subdivision, in 1976 Shi-Shi Beach and the Point were added to the wilderness-ocean section of Olympic National Park.

There are two accesses. The Park Service can officially recommend only the way entirely on public land, the difficult and hazardous route from Cape Alava. Recommended here is the approach from the north, by permission from the Makah Indian Nation, given for payment of a reasonable parking fee.

Drive US 101 west from Port Angeles; between mileposts 242 and 243 go right on SR 112 past Sekiu to Neah Bay, a fishing hamlet mainly inhabited by folks of other-continent ancestry but located within the Makah Indian Nation. At the west side of town go left on a paved road, following signs to "fish hatchery" and "Hoback Beach." At 2.5 miles go left on a dirt road, cross the Waatch River, and at the following intersection stay right, still following fish-hatchery signs. At a left turn in 4.3 miles go straight ahead to a gate signed "Car Vandalism—No Parking." Unload packs here

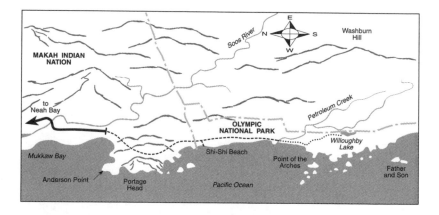

Point of the Arches

and send the car back to the last house for parking.

Beyond the gate the former World War II road over Portage Head, now undrivable, is pleasant walking under a tree canopy. During wet weather be prepared for much mud. In about 1 mile push through the roadway brush for dramatic looks down to the surf. At 2 miles, where the roadway comes to the edge of the bluff for the first unobstructed views of the ocean, are the park boundary and permit box. A trail drops to the north end of Shi-Shi Beach. (If the tide is high, stay on the road, which dwindles to a path and in a mile nearly touches the beach.)

Once on the beach, a short sidetrip north takes you to Portage Head, with its spectacular sea stacks, tidal pools, and whatever is left of a 1950s shipwreck. For Point of the Arches, hike about 2 miles south on the beach, passing a number of good camps (the most reliable source of water in summer is Petroleum Creek). At very low tide the long string of stacks and islands can be explored; the going is rough over sharp and slippery rocks and involves some wading.

Though the beach is the property of all Americans, through a fluke of archaic law the mineral rights are held by a corporation that is demanding access to placer mine the sand. Yes there is gold in the sand—a minute amount. (There is hugely *more* dissolved in the ocean!) The environmental community and the Park Service are determined to protect so absurd a desecration.

98 | CAPE ALAVA—SAND POINT LOOP

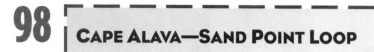

Loop trip: 9½ miles
Hiking time: 6 hours (day hike or backpack)
High point: 170 feet
Elevation gain: about 500 feet
Hikable: all year

Maps: Custom Correct Ozette Beach Loop, Green Trails Ozette (No. 130S)
Information: Olympic National Park Wilderness Information Center, phone (360) 452-0300

Park Service backcountry use permit required for overnight stay

Two trails from Ozette Lake to the ocean, plus the connecting stretch of Olympic National Park wilderness beach, make a magnificent loop hike for one day or several, for winter as well as summer, passing a deserted homestead, site of an Indian village, a fascinating cluster of petroglyphs, and miles of wild surf.

Drive US 101 west from Port Angeles; between mileposts 242 and 243 go right on SR 112 past Sekiu and turn left on the Ozette Lake road to the road-end ranger station, campground, and parking lot where the Ozette River flows from the lake, elevation 36 feet. Both trails begin at the open-air information booth, crossing a bridge over the Ozette and in a few feet splitting. The loop is equally good in either direction.

Camping has a strict quota but good sites are so plentiful there should always be room for all comers. The location of the assigned campsite will determine in which direction one goes. For the counterclockwise loop, take the Cape Alava trail, which goes a short bit on abandoned road and plunges into dense greenery of salal, hemlock, and other shrubs and trees. The path is sometimes flat, sometimes up and down a little, much of the

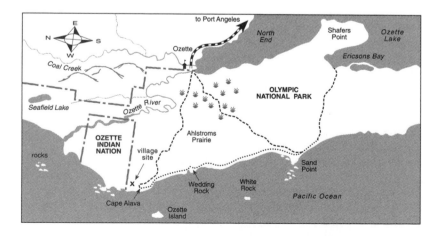

Petroglyphs at Wedding Rock

way on planks—which may puzzle and irritate summertime hikers but not those who do the trip in fall or spring when the bare ground is black muck, or in winter when every depression is feet-deep in water. Walk with caution—the planks can be slippery and memories of the average hiker include a pratfall or two on slippery planks. Lug soles are not recommended; ripple or smooth rubber soles give better traction.

At 2 miles the route magically opens out into a broad bog—Ahlstroms Prairie, partly a onetime lake filled in by natural processes, partly a pasture cleared early in the century by a homesteader, Lars Ahlstrom. Again the trail enters greenery, a mysterious roar can be heard (of what? dragons?), a forested crest is topped—and below are the loud breakers and beyond is the Pacific horizon. The trail quickly drops to the beach of Cape Alava, 3½ miles.

Camping space for scores of people (but often overcrowded in summer by hundreds of people) is available on a grassy wave-cut bench, site of an Indian village occupied for centuries. There are many, many ghosts here; archaeologists have excavated houses buried in a mudslide 500 years ago; other houses, their burials dating back at least 2500 years, are awaiting excavation. Artifacts are on display in the Makah Museum in Neah Bay. For a sidetrip, hike 1½ miles north to the Ozette River and a far look toward Point of the Arches.

The beach south 3 miles to Sand Point is easy walking at anything less than high tide and displays an assortment of sands and rocks and tidal pools; camps and dependable water at several places. A third of the way south, 1 mile, is Wedding Rock, inscribed with easy-to-miss petroglyphs. A dozen or more are scattered over rocks near the line of high tide.

In trees along the beach south of Sand Point are countless good (and in summer, crowded) camping areas. To complete the loop, find the trail in the woods at Sand Point and hike 3 miles to Ozette Lake, again on planks in lush brush and forest.

99 | RIALTO BEACH—CAPE ALAVA— OZETTE LAKE

One-way trip: 23 miles
Hiking time: allow 3 days
High point: 100 feet
Elevation gain: 100 feet
Hikable: all year

Maps: Custom Correct Ozette Beach
Loop, Green Trails Ozette (No. 130S)
Information: Olympic National Park
Wilderness Information Center,
phone (360) 452-0300

Park Service backcountry use permit required for overnight stay

Olympic National Park first became famous for rainforests and glaciers set within a magnificently large area of mountain wilderness. Now, though, it is known far and wide for still another glory—the last long stretch of wilderness ocean beach remaining in the conterminous United States. North and south from the Quillayute River extend miles and miles of coastline that are now almost exactly as they were before Columbus—except that in 1492 (and until fairly recent times) Indians had permanent homes and temporary camps at many places along the coast, now deserted.

Winter and early spring often offer the best hiking weather of the year, but storms can be hazardous. Facing a cold rain with miles of beach to hike is miserable and can lead to hypothermia.

The north section, from Rialto Beach to Cape Alava, is a longer but

Sea stack near Hole-in-the-Wall

easier walk than the south section described in Hike 100. There are no really difficult creek crossings, only one headland that cannot be rounded at low tide, and the way mainly is simple sand and shingle, interrupted by stretches of cobbles and rough boulders.

Be sure to obtain a tide chart beforehand and use it to plan each day's schedule. Much of the route can be traveled at high tide but at the cost of scrambling over driftwood and slippery rocks, plodding wearily through steep, loose cobbles and gravel, and climbing up and down points. Moreover, some headlands cannot be climbed over and the beach at low tide provides the only passage. Be prepared to hike early in the morning or late in the evening, with layovers during the day, if the tides so dictate.

Also beforehand, pick up the Park Service brochure, "Olympic Coastal Strip," which will add immeasurably to your enjoyment by explaining what you see and by helping plan a safe and pleasant trip.

Drive US 101 to 2 miles north of Forks. Turn west on the LaPush road and go 8 miles, then turn right on the Mora Campground-Rialto Beach road and go 5 miles to the parking lot at the beach and head north.

In ½ mile is Ellen Creek, the first permissible campsite. Here and elsewhere the "ocean tea," the creek's water colored by bark tannin dissolved in headwater swamps, is perfectly drinkable when treated as you would any other water in the wilds. At 1½ miles walk through the Hole-in-the-Wall to the first headland, which has several small points, one requiring low tide to get around. At 2½ miles are camps near the Chilean Memorial, which commemorates one of the countless ships wrecked on this rugged coast, and at 3 miles begins the long, rough rounding of Cape Johnson, which has no trail over the top and can be passed at low tide only, as is true of another rough point immediately following. A point at 5 miles must be climbed over on a short trail and one at 6 miles rounded at low tide. At 6½ miles is Cedar Creek (campsites) and immediately beyond is a point that can be rounded at low tide or crossed on a steep, short path.

At the Norwegian Memorial (another shipwreck and more camps), 7½ miles, a rough, abandoned trail leads inland 2½ miles to Allens Bay on Ozette Lake. (There is no trail along the lake, so this is not a shortcut to civilization.) Passing campsites every so often and at 10 miles a low-tide-only point, at 13½ miles the way comes to Yellow Banks; the point at the north end must be rounded at low tide.

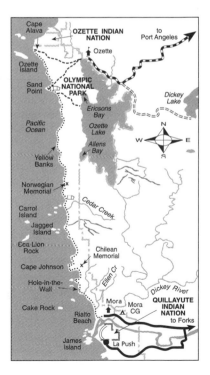

At 15 miles a way trail heads inland 2 miles to Ericsons Bay on Ozette Lake. At Sand Point, 15½ miles, are innumerable campsites in the woods and a trail leading 3 miles to the Ozette Lake road.

Don't stop here. Continue on the wilderness beach 3 miles to Cape Alava, 18½ miles (Hike 98) and finish the trip by following the trail 3½ miles back to Ozette Lake for a total of 23 miles.

100 | THIRD BEACH TO HOH RIVER

One-way trip: 17 miles
Hiking time: allow 3 days
High point: 250 feet
Elevation gain: 250 ft
Hikable: all year

Maps: Custom Correct South Olympic
    Coast, Green Trails La Push (No. 163S)
Information: Olympic National Park
    Wilderness Information Center,
    phone (360) 452-0300

Park Service backcountry use permit required for overnight stay

Wild forest and wild ocean, woods animals and sea birds, tidal pools and wave-carved stacks, the constant thunder of surf, and always the vast, mysterious horizon of the Pacific. This south section of the Olympic National Park wilderness ocean strip is shorter but more complicated than the northern one described in Hike 99, requiring detours inland to cross headlands and creeks and demanding even closer attention to the tide chart.

In stressing minimal impact, the National Park Service says: "No pets, camp on the beach when tides allow, bury human waste in forested areas well back from the beach, streams, trails, and campsites. Dismantle any driftwood shelters or furniture you construct; build campfires in scooped-out depressions in the sand when possible."

Warning: Goodman, Falls, and Mosquito Creeks are high all winter and after periods of heavy rain are virtually unfordable.

Drive US 101 to 2 miles north of Forks. Turn west on the La Push road and go 12 miles to the parking lot at the Third Beach Trail, elevation 240 feet.

Warning: Cars at the Third Beach parking area are occasionally broken into. Do not leave any valuables inside.

Hike the forest trail, descending abruptly to the beach and campsites at 1½ miles. Head south along the sand and in ½ mile look for a prominent marker on a tree above the beach, the start of the trail over Taylor Point, which cannot be rounded at the base. The trail climbs into lovely woods, dropping back to the beach in another 1½ miles beside a small head that can be rounded at a medium tide or climbed over on a steep path.

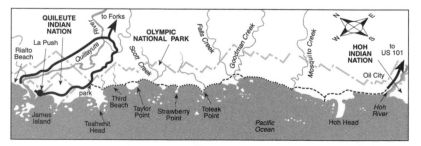

Toleak Point

At 3½ miles is a point that can be rounded at low tide or climbed over by a short trail to reach Scott Creek, with campsites in the woods; another very small point immediately south can be rounded in medium tide or climbed over. At 5 miles is Strawberry Point, low and forested and simple, and at 6½ miles, Toleak Point, ditto. Shortly beyond is Jackson Creek (camps).

At 7 miles a trail ascends a steep bluff and proceeds inland through beautiful forest to crossings of Falls and Goodman Creeks (cliffs rule out a shore passage), returning to the surf at 8¾ miles. The beach is then easy to Mosquito Creek, 11 miles; ford the stream at low tide. Camps here. There now is a choice of routes. On a *minus tide in calm weather* follow the beach, crossing four or five small points; less exciting but more certain, take the overland trail.

At 13½ miles a trail climbs the large promontory of Hoh Head, which cannot be rounded in any tide, and regains the beach at 14½ miles. Going by a campsite or two, at 15 miles the way comes to the last point, a heap of big rocks that must be rounded at low tide. From here a narrow, low-tide-only strip of beach leads to the mouth of the Hoh River, 16 miles. A trail follows the river inland to the Oil City road-end, 17 miles. To find the Oil City road drive US 101 about 0.5 mile north of the Hoh River bridge and go west on the road signed "Cottonwood Recreation Area" 12 miles to the end.

INDEX

ABOUT THE AUTHOR

A well-known outdoor photographer, Ira Spring devotes much of his time to organizations advocating trail and wildlife preservation. He is a co-founder of the Washington Trails Association and was one of twenty-four Americans to receive the Theodore Roosevelt Conservation Award in 1992. Harvey Manning is one of the Pacific Northwest's most influential and outspoken advocates of wilderness preservation. The founder of the Issaquah Alps Trail Club, Manning was instrumental in the fight to preserve the Alpine Lakes area and to establish North Cascades National Park. Both Spring and Manning played rey roles in the passage of the 1984 Washington Wilderness Act.

Over the past thirty years, their guidebooks have introduced legions of hikers, and future environmentalists, to the Northwest wilderness. Spring and Manning have collaborated on over twenty books, including the award-winning *Cool, Clear Water; Wildlife Encounters;* the four-volume *Footsore* series; *Hiking the Great Northwest; Hiking the Mountains to Sound Greenway; 50 Hikes in Mount Rainier National Park; 55 Hikes in Central Washington;* and four titles in the *100 Hikes in*™ series.

THE MOUNTAINEERS, founded in 1906, is a nonprofit outdoor activity and conservation club, whose mission is "to explore, study, preserve, and enjoy the natural beauty of the outdoors. . . ." Based in Seattle, Washington, the club is now the third-largest such organization in the United States, with 15,000 members and five branches throughout Washington State.

The Mountaineers sponsors both classes and year-round outdoor activities in the Pacific Northwest, which include hiking, mountain climbing, ski-touring, snowshoeing, bicycling, camping, kayaking and canoeing, nature study, sailing, and adventure travel. The club's conservation division supports environmental causes through educational activities, sponsoring legislation, and presenting informational programs. All club activities are led by skilled, experienced volunteers, who are dedicated to promoting safe and responsible enjoyment and preservation of the outdoors.

If you would like to participate in these organized outdoor activities or the club's programs, consider a membership in The Mountaineers. For information and an application, write or call The Mountaineers, Club Headquarters, 300 Third Avenue West, Seattle, Washington 98119; (206) 284-6310.

The Mountaineers Books, an active, nonprofit publishing program of the club, produces guidebooks, instructional texts, historical works, natural history guides, and works on environmental conservation. All books produced by The Mountaineers are aimed at fulfilling the club's mission.

Send or call for our catalog of more than 300 outdoor titles:

 The Mountaineers Books
1001 SW Klickitat Way, Suite 201
Seattle, WA 98134
1-800-553-4453
e-mail: mbooks@mountaineers.org
website: www.mountaineers.org

Other titles you may enjoy from The Mountaineers:

100 CLASSIC HIKES IN WASHINGTON, *Ira Spring & Harvey Manning*
A full-color guide to Washington's finest trails by the respected authors of more than thirty Washington guides, written with a conservation ethic and a sense of humor, and featuring the best hikes in the state.

HIKING THE GREAT NORTHWEST: The 55 Great Trails in Washington, Oregon, Idaho, Montana, Wyoming, British Columbia, Canadian Rockies, and Northern California, Third Edition,
Ira Spring, Harvey Manning, & Vicky Spring
The latest edition of this classic hiking guide to the most spectacular trails in the region, featuring new color photos and the personal picks of a trail-tested team of Northwest hiking gurus.

A WATERFALL LOVER'S GUIDE TO THE PACIFIC NORTHWEST: Where to Find Hundreds of Spectacular Waterfalls in Washington, Oregon, and Idaho, Third Edition, *Greg Plumb*
The complete, newly revised guide to Pacific Northwest waterfalls accessible by foot, car, and boat, with fifty new waterfalls described and rated for aesthetic value.

BEST HIKES WITH CHILDREN, IN WESTERN WASHINGTON AND THE CASCADES, Volumn 1, Second Edition, *Joan Burton*
A thoroughly revised edition of the best-selling book in the *Best Hikes with Children*™ series, with approximately twenty new hikes appropriate for families, seniors, and anyone who enjoys an easy dayhike.

AN OUTDOOR FAMILY GUIDE TO WASHINGTON'S NATIONAL PARKS: Mount Rainier, Mount St. Helens, North Cascades, The Olympics, *Vicky Spring & Tom Kirkendall*
A three-season guide to the best selection of outdoor activities in Washington's spectacular national parks, with information on flora and fauna, history, safety, and tips on successful outdoor outings with children.

SEATTLE'S LAKES, BAYS & WATERWAYS: AFOOT & AFLOAT Including the Eastside, *Marge & Ted Mueller*
The newest in the popular *Afoot & Afloat* series, featuring city escapes for boaters and shoreside explorers.

WASHINGTON'S BACKCOUNTRY ACCESS GUIDE: National Parks, National Forests, Wilderness Areas, *Ken Lans*
Completely updated compilation of Washington backcountry information from a variety of sources, highlighting recent regulation changes and featuring the latest access, trail conditions, and permit information.